,

SURFACES

VISUAL RESEARCH FOR ARTISTS, ARCHITECTS, AND DESIGNERS

SURFACES

VISUAL RESEARCH FOR ARTISTS, ARCHITECTS, AND DESIGNERS

JUDY A. JURACEK

W.W. NORTON & COMPANY

NEW YORK • LONDON

Dedicated to Tom Ford

Copyright © 1996 by Judy A. Juracek
All rights reserved
Printed in Hong Kong
First edition

Library of Congress Cataloging-in-Publication Data

Juracek, Judy A.
Surfaces: visual research for artists, architects, and designers / Judy A. Juracek.
p. cm.
"A Norton professional book."
Includes bibliographical references and index.
ISBN 0-393-73007-7
1. Building materials—Surfaces. I. Title.
TA418.7.J87 1996   96-21651
721'.044—dc20   CIP
ISBN 0-393-73007-7

W.W. Norton & Company, Inc., 500 Fifth Avenue, New York NY 10110
http://www.wwnorton.com
W.W. Norton & Company Ltd., 10 Coptic Street, London WC1A 1PU
5 7 9 0 8 6 4

page 1 photo: Cast stainless steel
pages 2–3 photo: Dimension stone veneer backed with protective gauze

The text of this book is composed in Stone Sans
Manufacturing by Colorprint Offset
Book design by Gilda Hannah

CONTENTS

Introduction   8
Research and the Artist   11

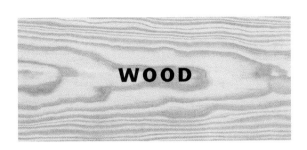

WOOD

General Views   16
Commonly Used Wood   18
Veneer   23
More Wood   25
Interior Woodwork   27
Exterior Woodwork   34
Siding and Shingles   40
Fences   44
Painted and Weathered Wood   46

MARBLE

General Views   90
Commonly Used Marble   92
More Marble   98
Quarried Marble   101
Marble Layouts   102
Architectural Marble   106
Sculpture   116
Worn and Weathered Marble   118

STONE

General Views   52
Commonly Used Stone   54
Types and Finishes   60
Fieldstone   63
Dimension Stone   68
Paving Stone   74
Architectural Stonework   76
Ornamental Stonework   83
Worn and Weathered Stone   86

BRICK

General Views   124
Commonly Used Brick   126
Types and Layouts   132
Mortar   139
Paving Brick   141
Decorative Brickwork   143
Architectural Brickwork   145
Painted Brick   150
Worn and Weathered Brick   152

PLASTER, CONCRETE, AGGREGATES

General Views   158
Commonly Used Materials   160
Exposed Aggregates   163
Plaster and Stucco   164
Concrete   168
Concrete Block   173
Architectural Uses   178
Paving Materials   184
Decorative Uses   187
Worn and Weathered Materials   189

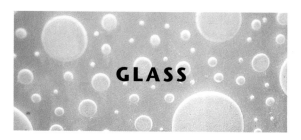

GLASS

General Views   234
Manufactured Glass   235
Specialty Glass   238
Glass Brick   239
Colored and Painted Glass   240
Molded Glass   242
Cut Glass   243
Windows   244
Reflections   248
Broken and Weathered Glass   249
Glass and the Elements   252

METAL

General Views   196
Commonly Used Metal   198
Finishes and Textures   202
Architectural Metalwork   204
Ornamental Metalwork   210
Grates, Plates, and Fences   215
Roofs   217
Lettering   218
Sculpture   220
Painted and Patinated Metal   222
Hardware and Other Objects   224
Worn and Weathered Metal   227

TILE

General Views   254
Glazed Tile   256
Decorative Tile   258
Stone and Marble Tile   260
Sculptured Tile   262
Terra-cotta, Quarry, and Porcelain Tiles   264
Floors and Pavements   265
Mosaics   266
Roof Tile   268
Architectural Terra-cotta   270
Worn and Weathered Tile   274

WORKING PAPERS

Tony Walton, theater and film designer   277

Teri Figliuzzi, resource designer   282

Waclaw Godziemba-Maliszewski, *ébéniste*   284

Dick Ventre, scenic artist   287

Tarek Naga, architect   290

Martin Charlot, muralist   293

Megan Meade, resource librarian   296

Stuart R. Morris, program manager   298

Glossary   302

Annotated Bibliography and Sources   321

Photography Sources   326

Acknowledgments   326

Index   327

About the CD-ROM   336

INTRODUCTION

This collection of photographs began as my private file of photo research for my work as a scenic artist and designer. I took some pictures for specific projects, others as a result of spotting a material in a certain condition or situation that I thought might come in handy on a future job; others were taken simply because I wanted to remember the particular surface. As the collection evolved into this book, I took pictures intentionally for the book. A few of the pictures are the work of other photographers. Because one person has taken or chosen these pictures, *Surfaces* offers a subjective view of the built environment and is not intended to be a complete compilation of the thousands of materials that exist.

The pictures in this book are of two varieties: photographs of materials that are strictly for the purpose of identifying a surface, with the particular usage being of secondary importance, and photographs of materials in different settings. The latter pictures, taken in many locations, are categorized based on how the materials are used architecturally, what the visual effect is of materials applied a certain way or subjected to different surface treatments, and how materials have weathered. The pictures in the sections titled Commonly Used or Manufactured were, for the most part, photographed in a studio. Because the quality of light striking a surface dramatically affects the color, and the architectural applications of the material usually command attention, these studio pictures, taken in a reasonably color-neutral lighting situation with the focus on the material, offer a more objective view.

I consulted people who work in industries that use the materials and representatives of industry associations about the visual and technical aspects of the materials. They suggested where to find representative examples, made samples available to me to photograph, and helped me to identify the pictures. The intent of these identifications is not only to particularize, but to provide the basis of a vocabulary so artists and designers can communicate with the technicians who make the designers' visions into realities.

Terminology and definitions change not only from country to country, but from region to region within a given country, so in the captions I have attempted to use general (USA) industry terms to refer to materials and processes. Because some finishes and processes are unique to one or a few companies, proprietary terms and materials are unavoidable. It is not always possible to make an absolutely positive identification from a photograph, so in some cases the captions state what the material appears to be based on general physical attributes and usage. For example, brass is usually more yellow than bronze, but anyone who works with the material knows that the difference can be so subtle that only a metallurgical analysis or the construction records of the installation will reveal the true material with certainty.

The specific use of a material often is the clue to its identity. When I asked a technical advisor at the National Terrazzo Association about the content of the metal divider strips used between aggregate panels, he replied that the gold-colored strips were half-hard brass; he asked why I was interested in the specific composition because the important thing was that the metal used for terrazzo dividers be hard enough to wear well, but soft enough to allow the divider to be ground down at the same rate as the aggregate and the matrix to form a smooth surface. If the material used for the divider strip is too hard, it will form a ridge when the terrazzo is ground and polished during the final steps of installation. Brass is defined as "a yellow, green, or brown alloy in which the chief constituents are copper and zinc," and different brasses are categorized based on percentage of copper, zinc, and other constituents. All of this is useful information, but the technical advisor was right: the content was not as important as how the metal had to perform. It strikes me that this example of what determines the choice of a specific divider for terrazzo is representative of how building materials in general are chosen. Various colors and qualities are developed in a design and guide the visual selections, and those choices are reviewed based on the physical requirements. The question always is: What is the material that will provide the desired look and fulfill the practical demands of the situation?

The following photographs of architectural surfaces are organized into sections based on the materials, each of which has specific characteristics that often do not apply to all of the groups. For example, we speak of stone, plaster, and metal finishes; this is not an appropriate subcategory for other sections. Latin names are traditionally used in the wood industry, and bonding patterns apply only to stone, brick, concrete block, and tile. The terms used in the captions are listed in the glossary, and are relevant terms you might encounter in dealing with the materials. For complete and authoritative information on the technical aspects of specific materials, however, seek the expert advice of the publications and organizations listed at the back of the book.

NOTES ON THE MATERIALS

Wood. In the section titled Commonly Used Woods, both the common and the Latin names are given because the same variety of wood may be known by several common names. Although general characteristics within the species are consistent, natural factors affect each tree; the color changes as a result of applied stains and dyes and aging; how the wood is cut determines the look of the grain.

Stone. The attributes of many stones are distinct enough that general categories (limestone, granite, sandstone, slate, etc.) are usually clear—if the stone is not excessively weathered or covered with stucco, mortar, or some other material. The surface treatment, the use, and the pattern in which the units have been joined determine the description of stone as much as the specific names. These descriptions also vary from region to region, have changed through the years, and are sometimes proprietary. For example, one style of bond is called *mosaic* by some stonemasons and *cobweb* by others. In the section titled Commonly Used Stone, several granites are listed, and these are identified by their commercial names, which are fairly standard. Other stone in this section is identified by general category. Travertine is a stone that can be classified as marble, depending on whether or not it can be polished. In this book it is classified as stone unless it was specifically identified as "travertine marble."

Marble. Of course marble should appear in the section on stone, since it is classified first as a stone and then as marble, and is viewed this way by the construction industry. Marble is defined as "A category of dimensional stone that includes a variety of compositional and textural types of metamorphic rock composed largely of calcite or dolomite. All stone in this category must be capable of taking a polish." Because it has a visual quality generally different from other stones, however, I have placed it in a separate section. In Commonly Used Marble, listings are identified as to their commercial names and country of origin, which is standard nomenclature in the industry.

Brick. Although a major characteristic of brick is its color, this is one feature you will seldom find mentioned in the captions. Brick is usually manufactured from clay and other materials close to the factory, so color is a function of geography, and industry descriptions generally refer to size, manufacturing process, shape (if other than rectangular), and the style of bond. But "brick red" will vary from place to place.

Plaster, Stucco, and Aggregates. The broadest in scope of all the sections is the collection of building materials that are products of dry materials which, when mixed with liquid, set to form a hard surface. Besides plaster and stucco, these include asphalt, concrete, agglomerates, and terrazzo. This category contains some of the earliest manufactured building materials, and is part of the construction history of almost every culture. As a result, styles, techniques, and terminology are old and location-specific, and terms may vary with local craftsmen and contractors.

Metal. Because so many of the metals used for building are alloys, it is a complex material to identify, and one specific metal can seldom be identified as firmly as one would a type of wood or stone. Applications and manufacturing processes so determine the look of the surface that most of the identifications focus on the use, finish, or circumstances that caused the material to look the way it does, rather than on the name of the specific metal.

Tile and Glass. The tile and glass sections have a narrower range than the other surfaces collected here, but they have been important decorative, finishing, and to a lesser degree, structural materials from early on in the history of building. Because it is usually a decorative surface element, architectural terra-cotta has been included in the section on tile, although it could just as easily have been grouped with brick.

Every artist and designer deals with the relationship of form and function. We turn ideas, words, concepts, requests into some visual form. The media in which we work may be anything from plaster, wood, or steel to a web site or videotape. Whether we are designing a building or an industrial product or a dramatic production, we all need to find a design that solves the specific problems of the job. There is no one process or answer, but all of us have in common the need for some sort of research to find a form that suits the function.

Research is as vital to us as it is to the historian, scientist, lawyer or novelist. The libraries and laboratories we frequent may differ from theirs, but the categories of investigation fall into groups they would recognize—primary research that we see, touch or experience ourselves, and secondary research that comes to us filtered by another person's observations and reported in sources such as books, illustrations, photographs, written descriptions. We want to see what's happening in the petri dish, and we want to gather other views of the event.

Thus, a costume designer working on the designs for a play or film set in the nineteenth century might start by using the costume collection in a museum in order to see and perhaps touch garments of the period. This direct experience reveals the boned structure of the bodice and tells how the undergarments and shoes dictated the owner's posture and movement. The quality of the fabric and the construction details impart information about the social position of the person who wore the garment. Other primary sources might be copies of period dressmakers' patterns or a fabric sample book from a nineteenth-century dry goods company. Secondary research sources might include costume history books, paintings, descriptive writings of the time, collections of period illustrations, or even recordings of music written in the period.

To see research in another light, an architect restoring a very old structure might look at buildings of the same period, measure them, and study how hand-hewn timbers were joined before the advent of power tools—primary source research. The volumes of published measured drawings used by builders of that period detailing room dimensions, profiles of molding, and door sizes are also primary research. But when that same architect refers to photographs or old engravings, the source is secondary, because what is seen has been determined by the photographer or engraver and the information is not purely objective, as were the measured drawings.

The line between primary and secondary research sometimes blurs. An illustrator working on a historical scene of working-class people in their home might use genre paintings or illustrations done in that period for information on wall treatments, table accessories, furniture, clothing, and even the physical features of the people. Strictly speaking, this is secondary research, since the material is filtered through the eyes of the painter. Total accuracy would require finding a museum with a collection of the necessary items. However, the work of period artists offers another sort of information that is also important: the style of brushwork or drawing conveys an attitude from those historical times that gives a view of the period unavailable from collections of household items. Think of the difference between a Renaissance sepia drawing of a wagon and an Art Deco poster of a train. Both will give fairly complete, although stylized, visual information about vehicles of those times, but in looking at the artists' renditions, we are also looking at a vehicle through the eyes of someone who lived in that period, and a whole subtext is opened to us.

Design ideas come from every conceivable source. Artists develop a keen eye and visual memory for the world around them, and everything from sociologists' statistics and Neilsen ratings to hardware stores and teenage fashions is a potential solution to a problem. To stay current, magazine subscriptions are often a necessity, and special topical publications are available on every imaginable subject. It is not uncommon for architecture and design firms to subscribe to forty-five different magazines, and for the staff librarian to keep indexed files of applicable photographs and articles. Sometimes the selection of subscriptions is surprising. Design and building-trade magazines are predictable subscriptions, but the American firm that designs office spaces for Japanese-based companies will probably also subscribe to some general life-style periodicals from Japan.

Many artists keep extensive files of material clipped from magazines, photo books and other sources, and then organize these "clip" or picture files into appropriate categories. An interior designer will compile sections on residential interiors, windows, general historical periods, kitchen styles. An illustrator's files might hold photocopies of sixteenth-century etchings of peasant farmers, a

CD-ROM of space age clip art, and postcards from the 1950s. The camera is an important tool in building picture files. A photo collection might include travel shots, interestingly aged walls, or close-ups of exotic birds found at the local zoo—it all depends on the needs of the artist. And there is an interesting fringe benefit of taking research photographs: you remember the material in a different, more complete way.

Designers using easily damaged research or large-format art books photograph the sources and keep the photos in their clip files. That way, delicate prints and cumbersome books do not have to be carted around to production meetings or to the copy center. The camera is also a convenient way to record presentations, past projects, and materials used in the execution of projects. For example, many architects find it useful to keep photographic files of how various materials used on specific sites changed with time and weather conditions. This information becomes invaluable to future choices about materials.

Personal files are also a way of storing items other than pictures. They provide a place for fabric samples, paint chips, trade catalogs, and information published in magazines that is so recent that it has not yet found its way into the more permanently bound forms of books or source directories. In these files, you not only have research that is unavailable at the bookstore, but material that is readily accessible when you need to pull a presentation together quickly, or find source material for a rendering that must be finished the next day. You will also find that as you develop the habit of accumulating and organizing information, you will notice visual details, materials, and topics that might otherwise have passed you by.

Photo books, magazines, catalogs, or picture files are usually the first stops when looking for visual research. Libraries are an obvious resource, and the artist and designer who has command of this territory has a valuable skill. Beside the collection of publications, many libraries have picture collections, and telephone research services can save an enormous amount of time when you are looking for a specific book or even the address of a distant manufacturer who carries a special paint. The research sections of major libraries house directories of art galleries, product distributors, international telephone books, and titles of articles in specific periodicals. Many libraries are now linked by computer, so a trip to the closest one can provide access to other facilities within a system and sometimes to those a continent away. University libraries are of particular interest, because their collections may be more specialized.

The research facilities of universities are another source of information. For example, the metallurgy section in an engineering school may be the best place to find out about specific patinas. Finding the appropriate academic institution or collection for your query has been made easier by the Internet, but topical journals and industry periodicals are still a primary source for locating the specialty you need.

Museums offer a wealth of diverse and specific information. In addition to the permanent and temporary exhibits, they often house research collections which are accessible upon request. Some museums are dedicated to research, and it is possible to find catalog collections of everything from door hardware and wallpaper to fifteenth-century stonemasons' tools. Nature illustrators, for example, use natural history museums to study the specimens of birds they are portraying, using sketches and photographs of the species from different angles and viewing collections of film footage depicting the bird in flight and in its habitat. Museums offer educational and information services, and the curators and other staff members are usually very helpful in providing insights into styles and details, or suggesting other sources that might aid your search. Museum publications include books of reproductions, exhibition catalogs, periodicals, and monographs on specific collections, which are excellent sources for photographs of things like decorative arts and costume accessories. Major museums have mail-order catalogs of their publications. Museum directories found in the reference sections of most libraries give summaries of

collections and locations of museums that may interest you.

Another excellent institutional source is trade associations. If you are looking for examples of a specific type of marble, for instance, you might refer to books and catalogs and make the rounds of showrooms of local marble distributors. But if you still cannot find what you want, draw on the services of the Marble Institute of America or the Italian Trade Commission—Marble Division. Such trade organizations regularly publish and update written data and photographs detailing materials, applications, installation processes, product availability, and sources. Many have technical and educational consultants readily available. Topical organizations such as landmark societies or groups interested in specific materials often have publications, bibliographies, or other services. One example is the line of historically accurate paint colors developed for the English National Trust houses—fifty-seven colors chosen by three generations of paint experts at the National Trust and commercially manufactured. A list of associations relevant to the subjects in this book appears in the Annotated Bibliography and Sources section at the back of the book.

It is a short jump from files of photos and clippings to collections of actual materials. Some designers and artists own boxes full of materials that may be useful in the future, or things that just strike their fancy. These "toy boxes" or "goodie bags" of odds and ends serve as a source of inspiration. It is interesting how often designers' styles are reflected by things kept in their workplace.

Designers who deal not only with concepts and illustrations but also specify what material will enable the ideas to become a reality keep more than pictorial information in their files: lists of suppliers and contractors, product brochures, trade magazine articles, copies of current codes, technical periodicals, and data sheets from industry organizations. These designers (interior design and architecture firms, toy designers, graphic arts studios, and theatrical designers) will also have some sort of materials library. In larger companies such collections may fill several rooms and be organized by material: paint and carpet samples, textile swatches, ceramic tile, stone, marble, and metal samples. As new products are introduced and others phased out, each category of samples will be maintained and updated by the staff librarians, who may also be charged with locating materials and suppliers.

Although it helps, you do not need to have direct access to an extensive professional library of materials and manufacturers' sample books to explore materials and products. Besides information from trade magazines and industry associations, you will find product and manufacturers' directories at the library. *Sweet's Catalogs,* a major American resource, is organized alphabetically by material. It provides information about structural, finishing, and decorating products and their manufacturers; industry associations; building code requirements; and technical support data sources for the building and construction industry. *Thomas Register,* a regularly updated registry of American manufacturers from most industries, lists alphabetically by product. Both directories also index the manufacturers' names with address and telephone number.

You can go directly to manufacturers to solve specific technical problems; even if your situation does not yield them a large order, their research and development departments can be very helpful in suggesting materials or different ways to use existing products, and are often excited to hear about artistic uses for their products. Paint, adhesive, and photoprocessing companies represent only the tip of the iceberg of manufacturers who readily give product information and samples.

Some companies even form established working relationships with artists—for example, an architectural metal fabricator who also executes the work of metal sculptors, offering them a wide selection of surface treatments and technical input. Comments and suggestions by the people who make the materials and execute the plans can greatly enhance the work of the artist.

It is easy to understand that architects and interior designers need detailed product information, but other artists and designers take materials and technologies developed for seemingly unrelated industrial applications and give those products new lives. Theater scenery is held together with "space-age" Velcro, and the techniques of artists who produce specialty glass have been transformed by the ceramic materials designed for the space shuttle. Theme park rides are not only conceptually based on *Star Wars,* but use the technology developed for flight-training simulators in engineering the rides. The world of movie special effects is a synthesis of computers, physics, and traditional filmmaking.

Why research? The need to find information required by a particular project is what motivates most of us to research a topic. But one of the fringe benefits of the search is that it tunes the eye to observing and retaining a wide spectrum of the world around us, which is vital to most of us in art-related fields. Later in this book are conversations with a range of professionals who use visual research, who discuss how they find and use sources. The specifics vary greatly, but what is common to all is an enthusiasm for the hunt for information, and the observation that the process of discovery is a necessary part of their art.

WOOD

PHOTO: GUY GURNEY

W-1   Doorway detail

W-2   Pressure-treated piling

W-3   Gilt wood carved detail

W-4   Plywood construction barrier

W-5   Cedar clapboard with tar-paper shingle

W-6   Weathered painted oak

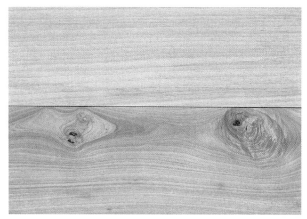

W-7   Anigre (*Aningeria* spp.)

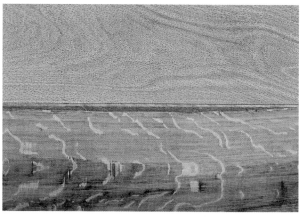

W-8   Red oak (*Quercus rubra* spp.) (top); English brown oak (*Quercus petraea*) (bottom)

W-9   Poplar or American tulipwood (*Liriodendron tulipifera*)

W-10   Yellow birch (*Betula alleghaniensis*)

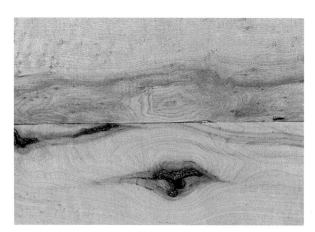

W-11   Bird's-eye hard sugar maple (*Acer saccharum*)

W-12   Hard sugar maple (*Acer saccharum*)

W-13   Eastern white knotty pine (*Pinus strobus*)

W-14   Wormy chestnut (top); American chestnut (bottom) (both are *Castanea dentata*)

W-15   Ash (*Fraxinus americana*)

W-16   Butternut (*Juglans cinerea*)

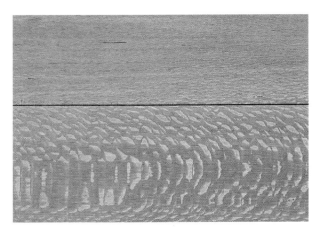

W-17   Lacewood (*Cardwellia sublimis*)

W-18   American black cherry (*Prunus serotina*)

W-19   Shedua or amazaque (*Guibourtia ehie*)

W-20   Teak (*Tectona grandis*)

W-21   Honduran rosewood (*Dalbergia stevensonii*)

W-22   Cocobolo (*Dalbergia retusa*)

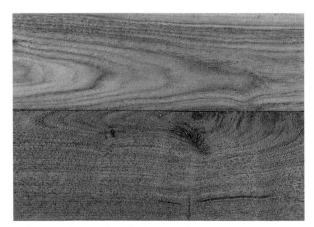

W-23   American walnut (*Juglans nigra*)

W-24   Honduran mahogany—quilted (*Swietenia macrophylla*)

W-25   Sugar pine (*Pinus lambertiana*)

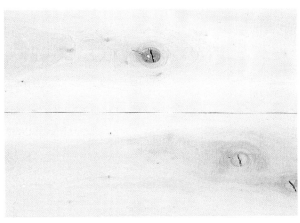

W-26   Holly (*Ilex opaca*)

W-27   Gonçalo alves (*Astronium fraxinifolium*)

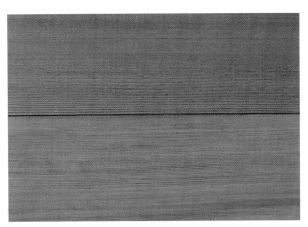

W-28   Sequoia or redwood (*Sequoia sempervirens*)

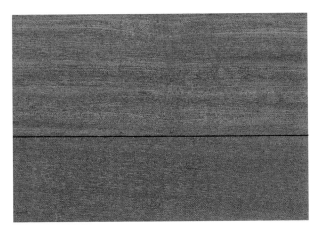

W-29   Purpleheart or amaranth (*Peltogyne* spp.)

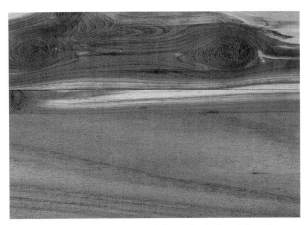

W-30   Red cedar (*Juniperus virginiana*) (top); Spanish cedar (*Cedrela odorata*) (bottom)

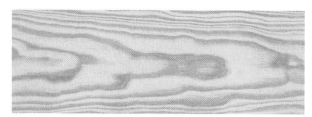

W-31   Southern yellow pine (*Pinus elliottii*)

W-32   American beech (*Fagus grandifolia*)

W-33   Sitka spruce (*Picea sitchensis*)

W-34   Cypress (*Taxodium distichum*)

W-35   Padauk or vermilion (*Pterocarpus macrocarpus*)

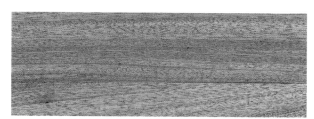

W-36   Red lauan (*Shorea negrosensis*)

W-37   Bubinga (*Guibourtia demeusii*)

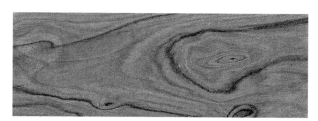

W-38   Paldao (*Dracontomelum dao*)

W-39   Zebrawood or zebrano (*Microberlinia brazzavillensis*)

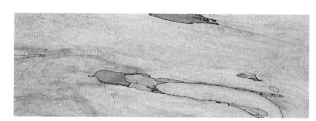

W-40   Spalted maple (*Acer saccharum*)

W-41   Wenge (*Milletia laurentii*)

W-42   East Indian ebony (*Diospyros* spp.)

VENEER

PHOTOS ON PAGES 23-24: BACON VENEER

W-43   American white oak, quarter-cut, flake figure, two-leaf, book-matched

W-44   European olive ash, plain-sliced (flat cut), olive character, two-leaf, book-matched

W-45   American chestnut, plain-sliced, "wormy" character, two-leaf, book-matched

W-46   American black walnut, plain-sliced, crossfire figure, two-leaf, book-matched

WOOD

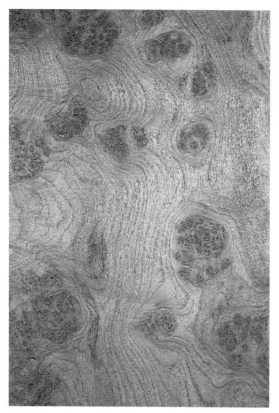

W-47 American white oak, rotary-cut, cluster burl character, single leaf

W-48 Kewazinga or bubinga, rotary-cut, swirly grain, two-leaf, book-matched

W-49 American black walnut, rotary-cut, stump figure, four-leaf, book- and flip-matched

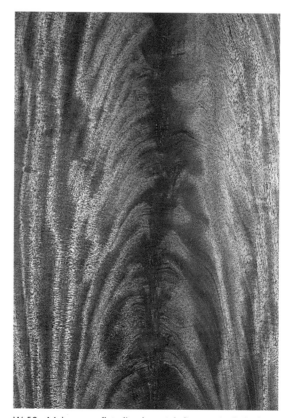

W-50 Mahogany, flat-sliced, crotch figure, single leaf

W-51   Weathered oak

W-52   Cedar decking

W-53   Fir lattice

W-54   Cedar tongue-and-groove board siding

W-55   Pressure-treated pine with marks from processing

W-56   Bird's-eye maple (outer); maple (inner); stained maple molding

W-57 Walnut and gold-leaf door panel

W-58 Gilt wood wall panel detail

W-59 Gilt wood and painted wood door detail

W-60 Carpathian elm burl or English oak burl and boxwood inlay

W-61 Bird's-eye maple with mahogany and ebonized hardwood inlay

W-62 Walnut burl with mahogany trim (top panel); boxwood carving on mahogany, rift-sawn white oak frame (center)

W-63 Walnut door panel

W-64   Figured mahogany door panel

W-65   Rosewood marquetry panel

W-66   Mahogany and boxwood inlay

W-67   Walnut burl with mahogany panels; white oak frame and carved detail

W-68 Wormy wood in frame

W-69 Walnut burl (outside); figured walnut, light oak molding (center)

W-70 Oak panel with cathedral grain

W-71 Oak panel with quarter-sawn figure, gilt border

W-72   Tight-grained unidentified wood

W-73   Tight-grained unidentified wood

W-74   Cherry door frame and cap

W-75   Rosewood and rubberwood in diamond parquet pattern

W-76   Walnut and quartered red oak in border design

W-77   Teak with rosewood border in Mt. Vernon–pattern parquet

W-78   Red oak board floor

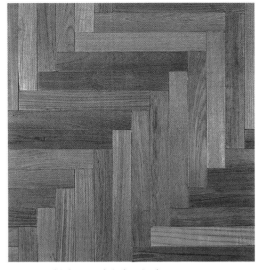

W-79   Multiple woods in herringbone parquet pattern

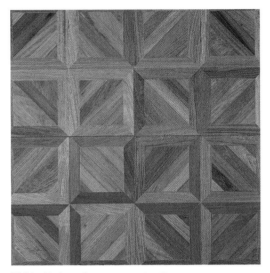

W-80   Teak starburst parquet pattern

W-81   Asian rosewood in finger parquet pattern

W-82   Teak in starburst pattern

W-83   Lauan in Haddon Hall parquet pattern

W-84   Oak panel door

W-85   Oak panel door

W-86   Pine panel door

W-87   Mahogany panel door

W-88   Single-bead diagonal boarding

W-89   Half-timber, wood peg construction

W-90   Wood window sill and shutter in adobe structure

W-91   Split barn door, wood peg construction

W-92   Quarter-sawn oak door

PHOTO: DUANE LANGENWALTER

W-93   Laminated arch with wood beams

W-94   A variety of joints in country door

W-95   Oak-paneled door

W-96   Half-timber, wood peg construction

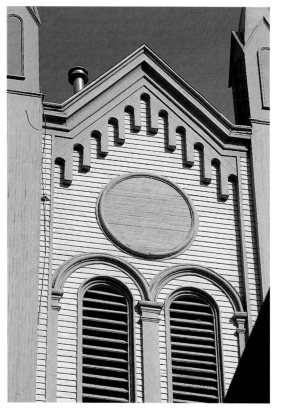

W-97 Clapboard construction

W-98 Knotty cedar in reverse board-and-batten siding

W-99 Modern exposed timber and stucco

W-100 Painted barn

W-101 Modern pine log cabin construction

W-102   Rough-hewn, wood peg joint

W-103   Plywood construction-site door

W-104   Pine shutters and clapboard

W-105   Shaped cedar shakes

W-106   Painted wood shingles

W-107   Cedar-shake siding

W-108   Cedar diagonal tongue-and-groove board siding

W-109   Clapboard siding

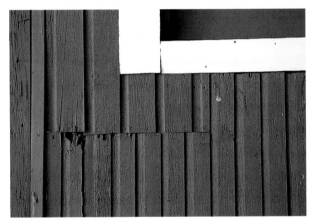

W-110   Board-and-gap or channel siding

W-111   Cedar ship-lap siding

W-112   Cedar diagonal ship-lap siding

W-113   Cedar butt-joined rough-sawn siding on cylindrical surface

PHOTO: GUY GURNEY

W-114   Woven split bamboo

W-115   Pressure-treated butt-joined lumber

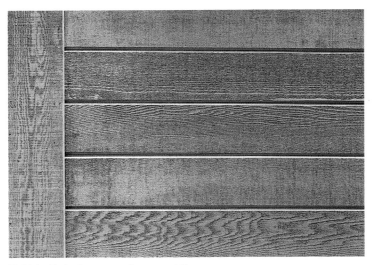

W-116   Cedar tongue-and-groove siding

W-117   Elm waney-edged siding

W-118   Decorative cedar-shake siding

W-119   Weathered picket fence

W-120   Woven garden fence

W-121 Garden fence

W-122   Picket fence

W-123   Split-rail gate

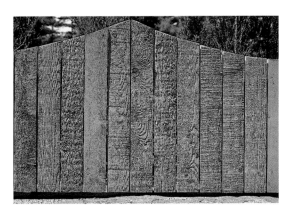

W-124   Rough-cut butt-joined board fence

W-125   Stockade-style fence

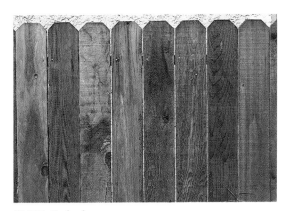

W-126   Cedar fence

W-127   White wash over red paint

W-128   Boardwalk planks weatherproofed with creosote

W-129   Wood with rot

W-130   Clapboard siding and peeling paint

W-131   Freshly painted clapboard

W-132   Oxidizing paint

W-133   Layers of old paint

W-134   Oak

W-135   Exterior enamel pulling away from soggy miter joint

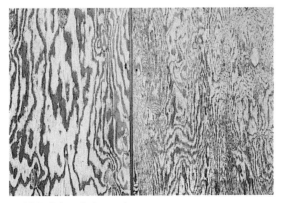

W-136   Painted plywood

W-137   Old door with multiple joints

W-138   Weathered ship's hull with ship-lap joints

W-139   Board-and-gap-joined boards

W-140   Patina

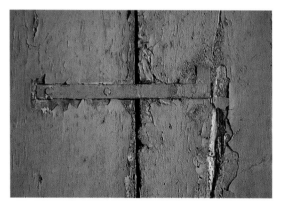

W-141   Very old paint

W-142   Barn-red and white paint

W-143   Recently painted porch

W-144   Boardwalk sign detail

W-145   Diagonal board panel

W-146   Weathered door

W-147   Oxidizing paint

W-148   Single-bead board siding

W-149   Weathered louvered shutter

STONE

S-1 Wall of marble, granite, and volcanic stone surrounded by brick

S-2 Split finished granite

PHOTO: DUANE LANGENWALTER

S-3 Dimension stone forming corners of coursed rubble wall

STONE

S-4   Fieldstone set in stucco over brick

S-5   Coursed fieldstone surrounding dimensioned granite

S-6   Limestone surrounded by slate

S-7   Old dimension-stone facade with concrete block

S-8   Carved facade under stucco

STONE

53

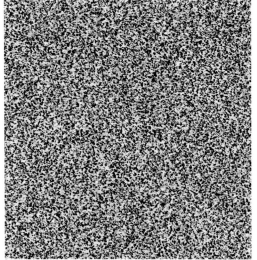

S-9   Pinot Noir granite

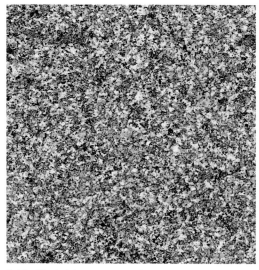

S-10   Verde Meragozza granite

S-11   Verde Lavras granite

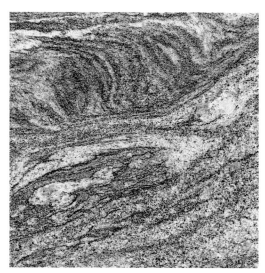

S-12   Kinawa granite

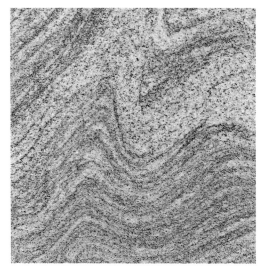

S-13   Silverado granite

S-14   Artificial stone

S-15   Rosa Porino granite

S-16   Ruby Red granite

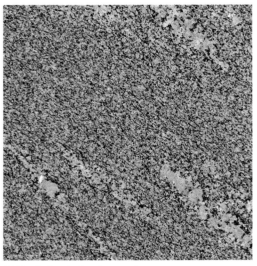

S-17   California Sunrise granite

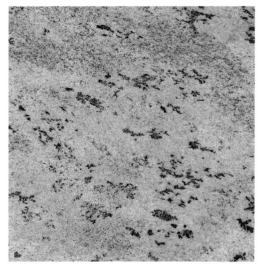

S-18   Eucalyptus granite

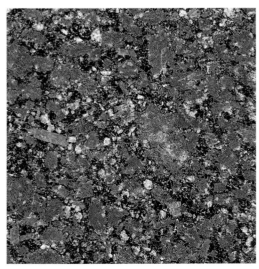

S-19   Santiago Red granite

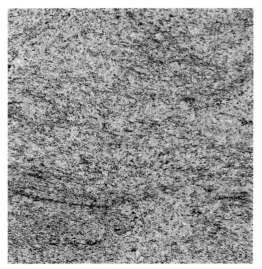

S-20   Juperano Tigeretto granite

S-21 Blue Pearl granite

S-22 Azul Aran granite

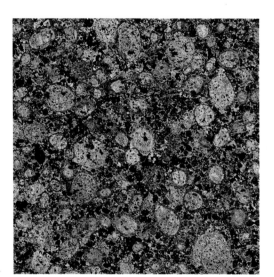

S-23 Baltic Brown granite

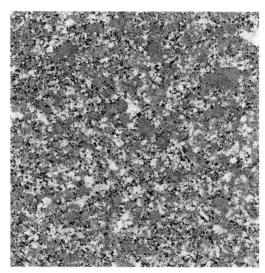

S-24 Ghiandoe granite

S-25 Peperino stone

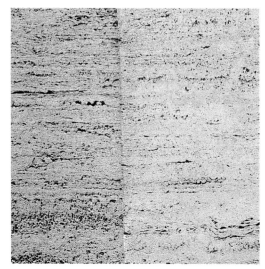

S-26 Travertine

S-27 Slate

S-28 Slate

S-29 Slate

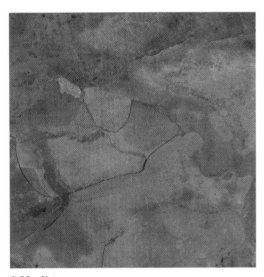

S-30 Slate

S-31 Slate

S-32 Onyx

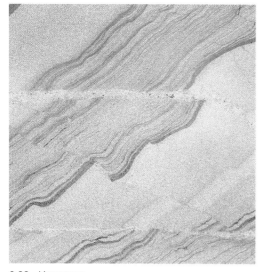

S-33   Limestone

S-34   Limestone

S-35   Limestone

S-36   Limestone

S-37   Limestone

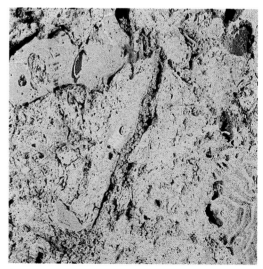

S-38   Fossil stone or shell stone

S-39   Sandstone (with sawn finish)

S-40   Sandstone (same stone as S-39, with natural cleft finish)

S-41   Sandstone

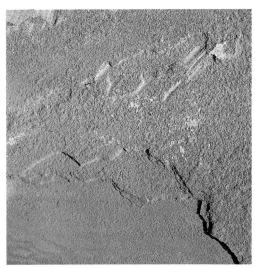

S-42   Bluestone

S-43   Quartzite

S-44   White quartzite

S-45 Granite with bush-hammered finish (top and bottom), shot-sawn finish (center)

S-46 North Dakota granite, polished (top), flamed finish (bottom)

S-47 Limestone with hand-tooled finish

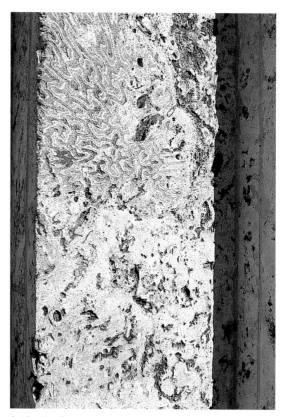

S-48 Fossil stone or key stone with sawn finish

S-49   Slate with natural cleft finish

S-50   Limestone with shot-sawn finish

S-51   Granite with partially honed split finish

STONE

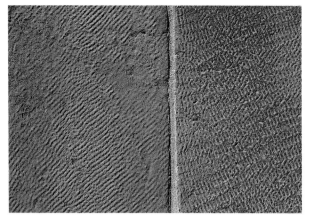

S-52   Brownstone with bush-hammered finish

S-53   Sandstone with rusticated finish

S-54   Sandstone with hand-tooled finish

S-55   Brownstone with bush-hammered finish

S-56   Sandstone with picked finish

S-57   Coursed granite fieldstone

S-58   Coursed fieldstone and roughly shaped stone

S-59   Sandstone in mosaic or cobweb pattern

S-60   Volcanic rock and stone in mosaic or cobweb pattern

S-61   Sandstone in mosaic or cobweb pattern

S-62   Mixed stone in mosaic or cobweb pattern

S-63 Granite fieldstone or cobble set in concrete

S-64 Roughly shaped fieldstone in dry wall

S-65 Shell stone or fossil rock in uncoursed rubble

S-66   Black granite, granite, sandstone used in uncoursed rubble

S-67   Uncoursed rubble fieldstone

S-68   Uncoursed rubble; some split-faced

S-69   Fieldstone with dimension brownstone corner

S-70   Granite fieldstone and cobble used as coursed rubble

S-71   Split-faced beach pebbles

S-72   Random rubble

S-73   Uncoursed rubble; some split-faced

S-74   Uncoursed rubble

S-75   Natural-cleft slate used on a roof

S-76   Sandstone in coursed ashlar bond

S-77   Granite set in coursed random ashlar pattern

S-78   Rusticated limestone

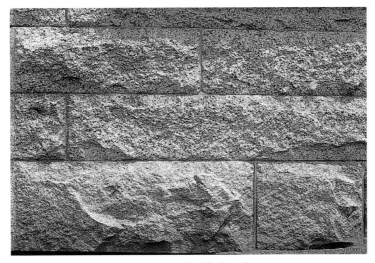

S-79　Rusticated granite set in coursed ashlar bond

S-80　Quartzite set in random ashlar pattern

S-81　Split-faced, rusticated granite set in random ashlar pattern

S-82 Sandstone with sand finish in coursed ashlar pattern

S-83 Roughly squared sandstone (repaired with stucco) in random ashlar pattern with black mortar

S-84 Sandstone and quartzite set in coursed ashlar

S-85 Sandstone set in coursed ashlar pattern

S-86 Split-faced, roughly squared sandstone set in broken-bond ashlar pattern

S-87 Rusticated brownstone quoins with rusticated sandstone set in ashlar pattern

S-88 Roughly squared brownstone with sawn finish set in random ashlar pattern

S-89 Sawn sandstone set in coursed ashlar pattern

S-90 Brownstone set in random ashlar pattern

S-91 Limestone with demi-bullnose or pillow-cut arris set in coursed ashlar pattern

STONE

S-92   Slate with cleft edge used as roof tiles

S-93   Coursed roughly squared rubble bordered by dimension stones

S-94   Split-faced roughly squared granite in coursed rubble

S-95   Slate with cleft edge used as decorative panel

S-96   Granite with flamed finish

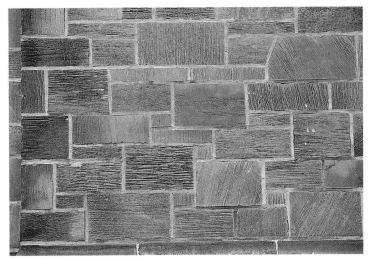

S-97   Stone with shot-sawn or plucked finish set in random ashlar pattern

S-98   Painted granite paving stone

S-99   Granite pavers partially covered with concrete

S-100   Granite cobblestones

S-101   Granite cobblestones set in basket-weave pattern

S-102   Travertine and other stone with picked finish

S-103 Travertine laid in running bond

S-104 Flagstone patio

S-105 Variety of river stones or beach pebbles

S-106 Granite paving stone in pattern

S-107 River stones or beach pebbles in mortar in garden walk

S-108 Travertine flagstone in red mortar

S-109   Lapis-lazuli inlaid column

S-110   Polished granite molding with rusticated surfaces

S-111   Granite with rough-sawn and sandblasted finish

S-112   Granite turned column with sawn finish

S-113   Carved limestone doorway with alternating hand-tooled and honed blocks

S-114   Sandstone capital surrounded by travertine

S-115   Travertine capital with brick above and granite column

S-116 Carved sandstone capital with hand-tooled lower blocks

S-117 Honed, rusticated, and carved limestone

S-118 Limestone carved capitals with tooled columns

S-119 Tooled, carved, and honed sandstone

S-120 Carved and honed limestone

S-121   Fieldstone and rusticated brownstone

S-122   Volcanic stone and sandstone set in coursed broken-ashlar pattern

S-123   Rusticated sandstone

STONE

S-124 Carved limestone with bush-hammered wall blocks

S-125 Travertine on volcanic stone base

S-126 Granite pedestal with polished finish

S-127   Carved limestone

S-128   Rusticated and honed stone

S-129   Polished granite window detail

S-130   Limestone blocks with tooled border around rusticated face

S-131   Carved limestone border and sawn blocks

S-132   Turned granite

S-133   Turned, honed limestone

S-134   Hand-tooled limestone

S-135   Turned limestone

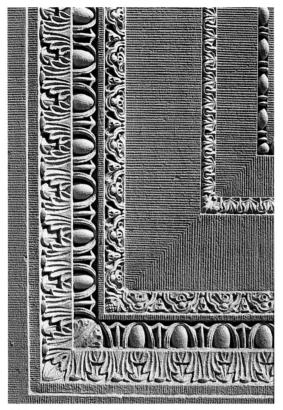

S-136 Painted stone with hand-tooled detail

S-137 Polished and chiseled granite

S-138 Polished granite with V-grooved letters

S-139 Granite with polished and chiseled finishes

S-140 Limestone building address

S-141 Rusticated border on granite tombstone

S-142   Granite arch with sawn finish and carved detail

S-143   Carved sandstone (top) and limestone

S-144   Carved limestone

S-145   Brownstone with alternating sawn and split (or pitched) finishes

S-146   Sandstone window arches

S-147   Travertine carving

W-148   Sandstone ornament

S 149   Detail of carved capital

S-150   Limestone on a colored stucco wall

S-151   Possibly limestone column

S-152   Roughly squared brownstone, severely weathered

S-153   Turned and tooled limestone, severely weathered

S-154   Recent limestone repair

S-155   Neglected columns and bases

S-156   Limestone with picked finish over fieldstone

S-157   Granite with a honed finish

S-158   Sandstone with hand-tooled finish (top and right) with roughly squared blocks in ashlar pattern

MARBLE

MA-1   Ancient Roman marble colonnade

MA-2   Weathered carved marble

MA-3   Ancient Roman marble column

MA-4   Possibly Luna marble

MARBLE

MA-5   Modern marble tile floor

MA-6   Section of fluted marble column

MA-7   Fior di Pesco Classico (left); brecciated marble (right)

MARBLE

MA-8   European White, Turkey

MA-9   Cremo Delicato, Italy

MA-10   Calacatta, Italy

MA-11   Dove White, Greece

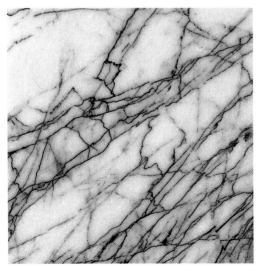

MA-12   Lilac Classic, Turkey

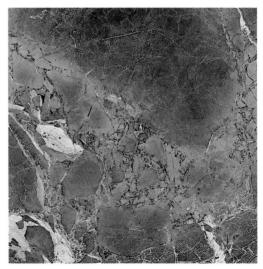

MA-13   Paradiso, Italy

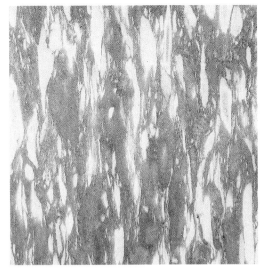

MA-14   Norwegian Rose, Norway

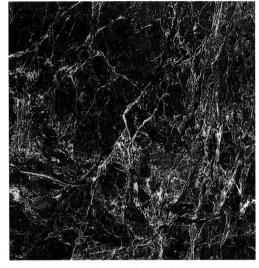

MA-15   Vermont Verde Antique, USA

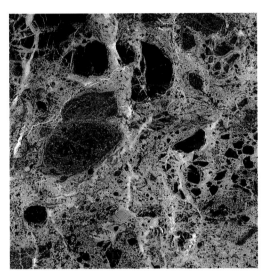

MA-16   Averia Green, Greece

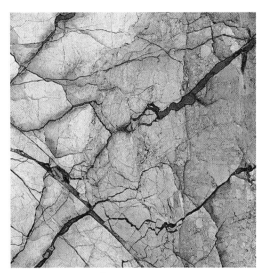

MA-17   Rosa Morada, Mexico

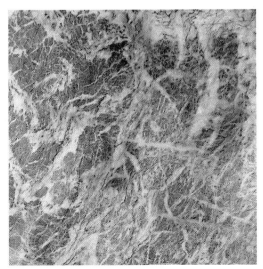

MA-18   Jaspe, Mexico

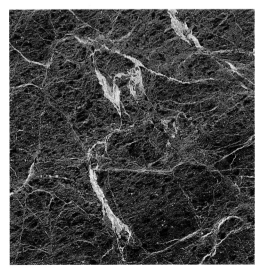

MA-19   Taiwan Green Dark, Taiwan

MARBLE

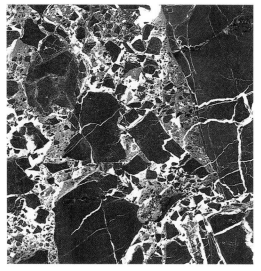

MA-20   Elazig Cherry, Turkey

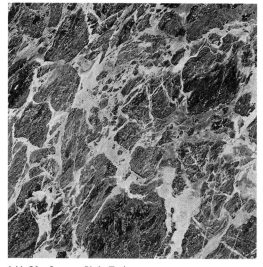

MA-21   Supren Pink, Turkey

MA-22   Grigio Carnico, Italy

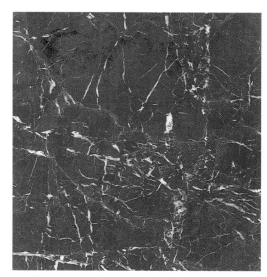

MA-23   Rosso Sicilia, Italy

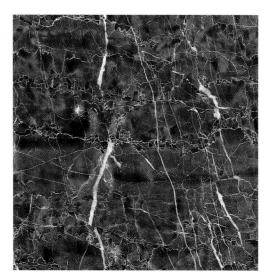

MA-24   Mystique, China

MA-25   Antique Green, Turkey

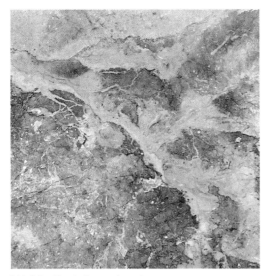

MA-26   Classic Pecan, Jamaica

MA-27   Rojo Coralito, Spain

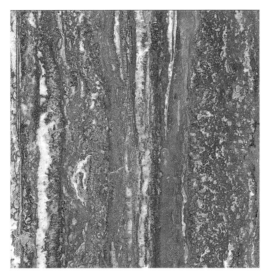

MA-28   Red Travertine, Pakistan

MA-29   Silver Travertine, Italy

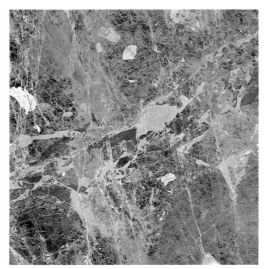

MA-30   Paradiso, Italy

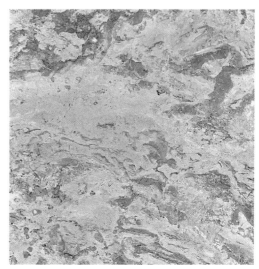

MA-31   Breccia Tavira, Portugal

MARBLE

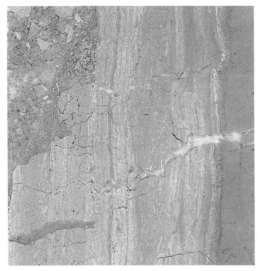

MA-32   Tigre, Greece

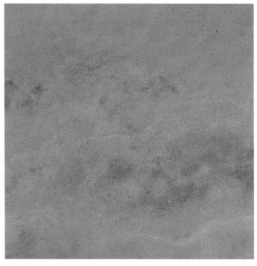

MA-33   Paradise Blue, Brazil

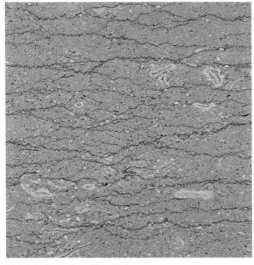

MA-34   Perlatino Blue, Italy

MA-35   Ming Green, China

MA-36   Pink Agento, Greece

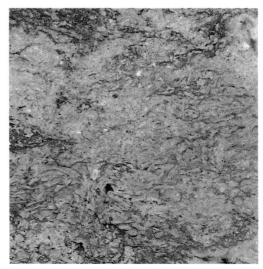

MA-37   Verde Rosa, Mexico

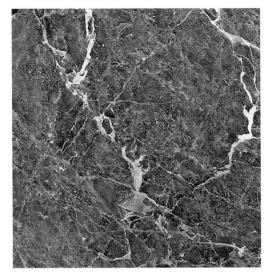

MA-38   Salome, Turkey

MA-39   Salome, Turkey

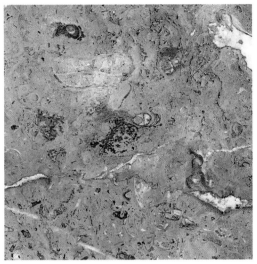

MA-40   Gris Fossil, Mexico

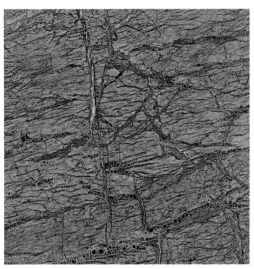

MA-41   Emerald Green, India

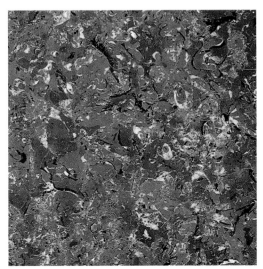

MA-42   Fantasia, Mexico

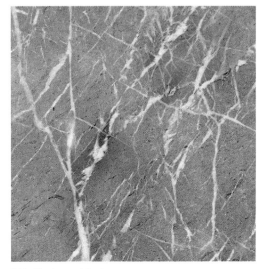

MA-43   Jaspe, Mexico

MARBLE

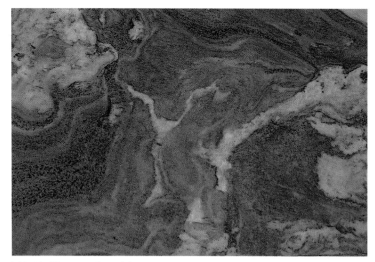

MA-44   Vermont Crystal Stratus

MA-45   Possibly Fabricatti

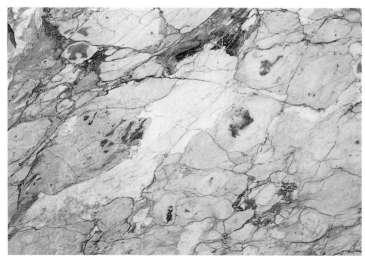

MA-46   A variety of brecciated marble

MA-47   Veneer marble

MA-48   Possibly Verde Antique

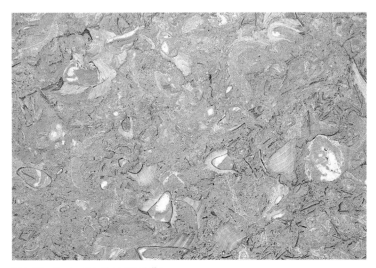

MA-49   Rouge Royal or Danielle

MA-50   Old variety of Supren

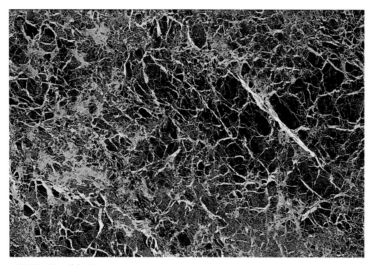

MA-51   Possibly Portoro

MA-52   Travertine, probably Desert Gold

MA-53   Canadian Sunset

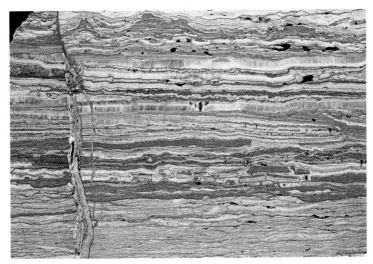

MA-54   Travertine marble

MA-55   Weathered Botticino

MA-56   Varieties of marble set in colored mortar

MA-57   Travertine blocks with serpentine bands

MA-58   Striped Brocadillo blocks, random matched

MA-59   Numidian marble panels and molding, loosely end matched

MA-60   Spanish Coralito random-matched veneer (top), Verde Alpi (bottom)

MA-61   Vermont Danby varieties: Royal, Montclaire, Duro Danby

MA-62   Siena marble veneer, loosely end matched

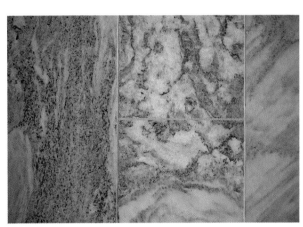

MA-63   Vermont Crystal Stratus, book-matched center joining

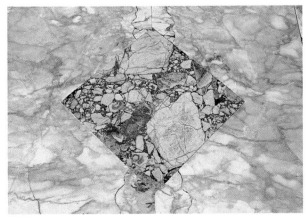

MA-64   Brecciated marbles in floor design

MA-65   Unknown marble, loosely book matched

MA-66   Unknown, Calacatta band, Rosso Levanto in floor design (left to right)

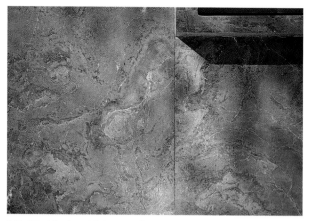

MA-67   Mexican Violet exterior veneer

MA-68   Vermont Danby Imperial, random matched

MA-69   Emperado Dark or Marron Braun in random-matched wall veneer

MA-70   Split-faced ashlar Vermont Danby in ashlar pattern

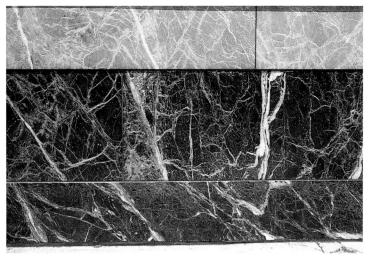

MA-71   Unknown, Verde Aosta, possibly Verde Antique (top to bottom)

MA-72   Rose Alhambra (top), Siena (bottom)

MA-73   Fior di Pesco Carnico (left); possibly Rojo Alicante (right)

MA-74   Carved molding

MA-75   Mexican Violet rope molding

MA-76   Unknown marble floor tiles with incised design

MA-77   Siena marble carved staircase detail

MA-78   Giallo Siena marble background for carved detail

MA-79   Carved fireplace detail

MA-80   Marble pedestal

MA-81   Skyros Greek marble pedestal

MA-82   Vermont Verde Antique

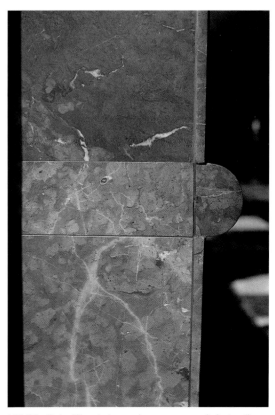

MA-83   Rojo Alicante in modern veneer and chair rail
(side view)

MA-84   Fior di Pesco Classico column

MA-85   Brecciated marble column

MA-86   Brecciated marble column

MA-87   African or Italian marble column

MA-88   Rouge Griotté fireplace

MA-89   Campagna marble with gilt bronze detail

MA-90   Giallo Siena marble base molding

MA-91   Numidian marble fireplace and pilasters with gilt bronze detail

MA-92   Campagna marble wall panel detail

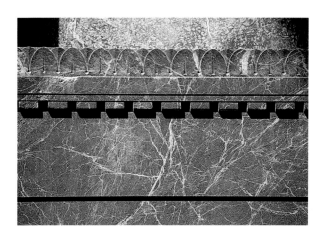

MA-93   Probably Emperado marble molding with dentil and carved detail

MA-94   Polished travertine capital

MA-95   Weathered white marble with serpentine banding

MA-96   White marble column with travertine capital and surround

MA-97   Carved marble capital and molding

MA-98   Serpentine ground with white and rose marble inlay and white rope molding

MA-99   White marble with patina

MA-100   White marble with dentil molding, rose marble and serpentine inlay

MA-101   Carved marble arch

MA-102   Carved detail

MA-103   Solid ancient Roman column surrounded by travertine

MA-104   Marble pilaster with tooled finish

MA-105   Tuckahoe marble capital and facade

MA 106   Carrara marble doorway detail

MA-107   Marble doorway detail

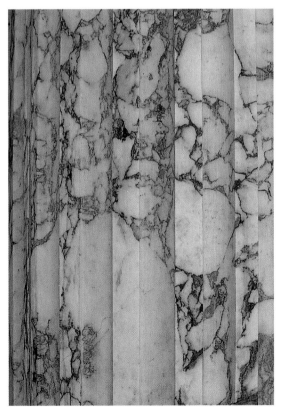

MA-108   Variety of Cremo marble fluted column

MA-109   White and rose marble and serpentine facade

MA-110   Travertine marble cornice

MA-111   Spiral column

MA-112   Spiral column

MA-113   Weathered marble

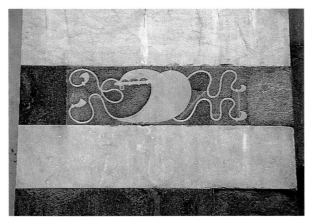

MA-114   White marble inlay in serpentine

MA-115   Marble facade

MA-116   Ancient carved cornice detail

MA-117   Inlay floor detail

MA-118   Breccia Pernice and white marble fountain

MA-119   Hand-tooled finish, probably Alabama white marble

MA-120   Chiseled letters

MA-121   Sculptural surface finishes

MA-122   Weathered carving

MA-123   Carving with light sand finish

MA-124   Carving with honed finish

MA-125   White, serpentine, and rose

MA-126   Tooled finished layer, worn

MA-127   Mossy surface

MA-128 Partially cleaned marble scroll trim

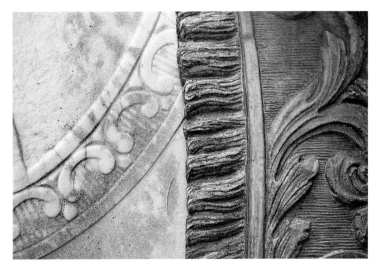

MA-129 Metal bleeding on marble

MA-130 Iron-discolored fountain

MA-131   Weathered ancient capital

MA-132   Weathered ancient frieze

MA-133   Roman ruins

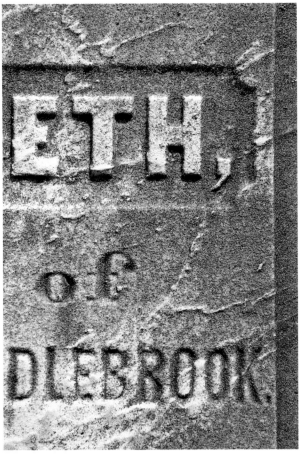

MA-134   Marble tombstone

MA-135   Weathered brecciated marble

MA-136   Cracked veneer

MA-137   Floor design with stress cracks

MA-138   Fior di Pesco on an exterior wall

MA-139   Worn marble floor

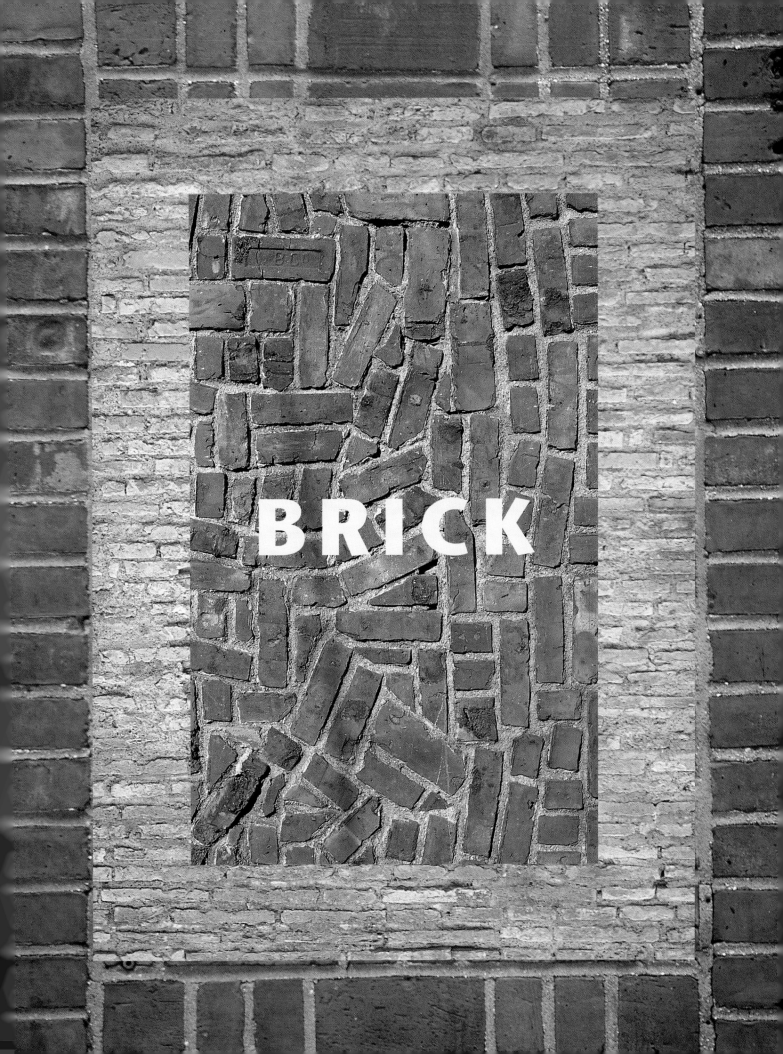

B-1   Dry-pressed or molded, possibly Flemish bond

B-2   Facing brick in Flemish bond over building brick in running bond.

B-3   Dry-pressed brick in Flemish bond.

B-4 Ancient hand-molded Roman brick, ⅓ running bond

B-5 Brick in running bond with header rows, whitewashed

B-6 Modular brick in varied bonds

B-7   Handmade, Flemish bond

B-8   Modular, wood-molded, sand finish, full-flashed with cross sets

B-9   Modular, extruded, unflashed, wire-cut, velour texture

B-10   Modular, wood-molded, sand finish, full-flashed with cross sets

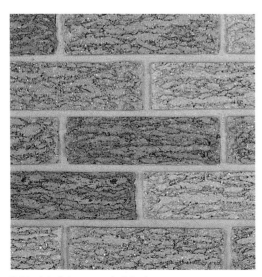

B-11   Modular, extruded, bark texture

B-12   Modular, extruded, sand finish, tumbled

B-13   Modular, extruded, wire-cut

B-14   Modular, extruded, textured, painted

B-15   Modular, extruded, wire-cut

B-16   Modular, extruded, smooth texture

B-17   Modular, extruded, wire-cut, full-flashed, velour texture

B-18   Modular, molded, sand-struck

B-19 Modular, molded, simulated water-struck, full-flashed

B-20 Modular, molded

B-21 Modular, hand-molded, water-struck

B-22 Standard and econo, extruded, sand finish, ashlar bond

B-23 Modular, paving brick, extruded, wire-cut, basket-weave

B-24 Modular, paving brick, molded

B-25   Modular utility, extruded, wire-cut, ironspot

B-26   Modular econo, extruded, wire-cut, ironspot

B-27   Modular, extruded, textured

B-28   Modular, extruded, wire-cut, matte texture

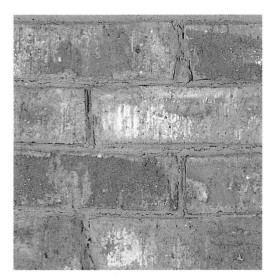

B-29   Modular, extruded, simulated tumbled

B-30   Modular, extruded, wire-cut, velour texture

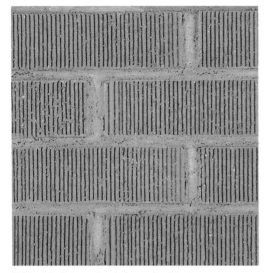

B-31   Modular, extruded, combed texture

B-32   Modular, extruded, sand finish

B-33   Modular, extruded, sandblasted finish

B-34   Modular, extruded, textured

B-35   Modular, extruded, smooth finish, applied ironspot

B-36   Modular, extruded, sand finish, antique

B-37   Modular, extruded, sand finish, antique

B-38   Modular, extruded, wire-cut, painted, new-used

B-39   Modular, extruded, wire-cut

B-40   Utility, extruded, sand finish, stack bond

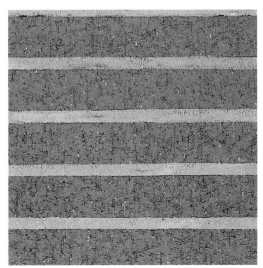

B-41   Modular Roman, extruded, wire-cut, stack bond

B-42   Modular Norman, extruded, wire-cut, ironspot, stack bond

BRICK

131

B-43   Modular, extruded

B-44   8x8, extruded, wire-cut, ironspot

B-45   8x8, extruded, wire-cut (top); modular, extruded, wire-cut texture (bottom)

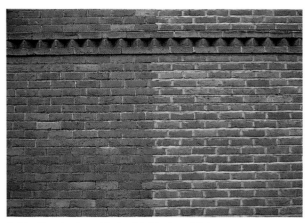

B-46   Standard, molded, with black and light gray mortars

B-47   Common, molded, custom bond, with swell bellies

B-48   Standard, molded

B-49   Modular, extruded, wire-cut texture, ⅓ running bond

B-50   Modular, extruded, bark texture

B-51   Modular, extruded, bark texture, Flemish bond

B-52   Standard, extruded, wire-cut texture, running bond with rowlock course

B-53   Modular, extruded, sandblast-cleaned

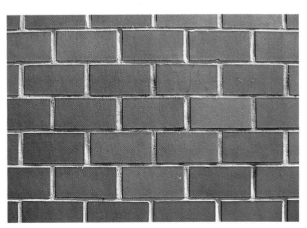

B-54   Econo, extruded, smooth texture

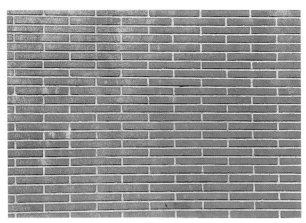

B-55   Modular, Roman, extruded, wire-cut, with slight efflorescence

B-56   Handmade, molded, sand-struck, Flemish bond

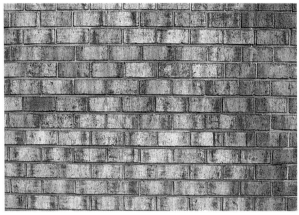

B-57   Closure, extruded, sand finish

B-58   Roman

B-59   Modular, extruded, wire-cut texture, sand finish, running bond (left), stack bond (right)

B-60   Probably modular, molded, sloppy running bond, with occasional header course

B-61 Modular, extruded, glazed with black speckle

B-62 Extruded, rolled texture, stack bond

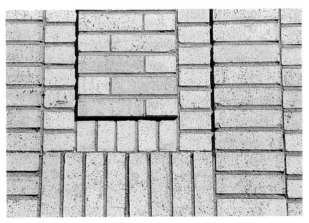

B-63 Extruded, smooth finish, ironspot, stack bond, rowlock and soldier courses around running bond

B-64 Handmade, molded, sand-struck, blue ("glazed") header brick, garden-wall bond

B-65 Modular, extruded, smooth finish, ironspot, English bond

B-66 Modular, extruded, combed, flashed, soldier course with sixth course common bond

B-67　Modular, extruded, sandblast-cleaned; center band: Roman, extruded, ⅓ running bond

B-68　Modular, extruded, wire-cut texture with ironspot

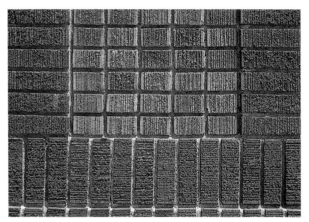

B-69　Modular, extruded, combed, stack header bond bordered by stack bond and lower soldier course

B-70　Old-used, possibly common, dry-pressed or extruded, running bond with headers

B-71　Molded, sand finish (left); common brick, hand-molded, water-struck, English bond (right)

B-72　Common, molded, mixed header and stretcher bond

B-73   Modular, molded, sand finish, running bond with one header course or sixth course common bond

B-74   Engineer, molded or extruded, sand finish

B-75   Adobe

B-76   Molded, old common, varied bond

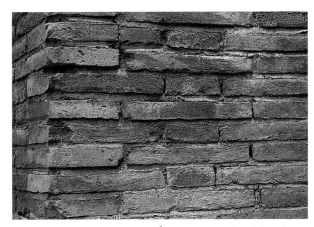

B-77   Ancient Roman, molded, ¼ running bond with headers

B-78   White ceramic glazed brick or tile, stack bond (left), modular, extruded, combed, Flemish bond (right)

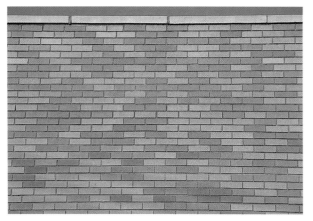

B-79   Modular, extruded, smooth (die-skin) finish

B-80   Econo, extruded, wire-cut

B-81   Modular, extruded, flashed, wire-cut texture

B-82   Modular, extruded, bark texture, common bond with sixth row header

B-83   Modular, extruded, smooth texture, ironspot, flashed, common bond

B-84   Modular, extruded, wire-cut and smooth texture, Flemish bond

B-85 Pink mortar, heavy sand content, flush joint, repaired with gray common screened mortar

B-86 Gray/tan mortar, common sand, probably flat or concave joint originally

B-87 Adobe mud mortar, flush joint

B-88 Gray common mortar, concave or V joint (left); dark gray, concave joint (right)

B-89 Mortar with heavy sand content

B-90 Flush or concave mortar joint

B-91   Tan mortar, heavy sand and pebble content, untooled joint

B-92   Untooled or extruded mortar for interior wall, not intended to be seen

B-93   Light gray mortar, concave joint, with efflorescence

B-94   Molded brick on edge in herringbone pattern

B-95   Molded brick on edge in herringbone pattern

B-96   4x8 paver, extruded, die-skin finish, diagonal bond with a sailor course border

B-97   Molded, basket-weave pattern

B-98   Roman, laid on edge, yet to be filled with sand

B-99   Roman brick set on edge with cobbles and travertine

B-100   Extruded, wire-cut, vitrified, running bond

B-101   Handmade Roman pavers

B-102   Modular, extruded, herringbone pattern, sawtooth edge

B-103   Dry-pressed brick column, arches, and trim

B-104   Molded brick capital

B-105   Molded brick in special patterned bond

B-106   Old molded, upper portion dentil-work headers, lower border sawtooth pattern

B-107 Modular, extruded, combed texture, running bond with herringbone inset and rowlocks forming circle

B-108 Probably molded, red brick diaper pattern in (probably) common-bond wall

B-109 Modular, extruded, or dry-pressed, smooth texture; bottom trim dog-tooth pattern, architectural terra-cotta cornice with soldier bricks above

B-110 Modular, extruded, smooth texture, ironspot, custom pattern

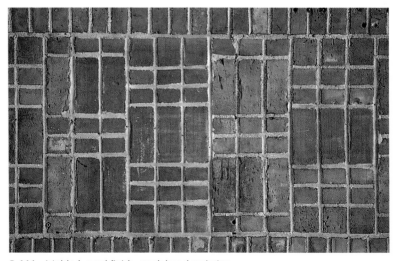

B-111 Molded, sand finish, stack bond variation

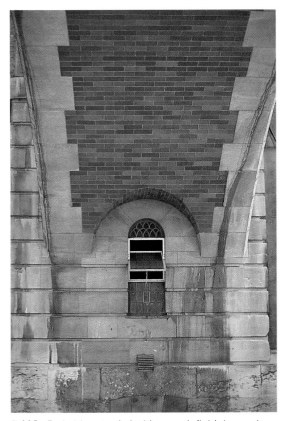

B-112 Probably extruded with smooth finish in running bond

B-113 Modular, probably extruded; running bond (left); Flemish bond with shaped corner (right)

B-114 Nonmodular, old Roman arch

B-115 Modular, extruded, smooth finish, running bond with curved corners

B-116 Modular, extruded, wire-cut, segmental Roman arch (left), running bond (right)

B-117 Modular, extruded, wire-cut, running bond, segmental Roman arch, cove molding, stack bond under arch

B-118 Possibly modular, molded, sand finish, bonded radial arch, common bond with sixth-course Flemish headers

B-119   Modern Italian brickwork with brick fill between larger (possibly tile) units

B-120   Handmade molded, running bond, radial arch variation

B-121   Hand-molded, water-struck, stack and running bond

B-122   Roman, extruded, possibly sandblasted, running bond, bonded jack arch

B-123   Modular, molded, sand finish, Flemish bond, water-table rowlock

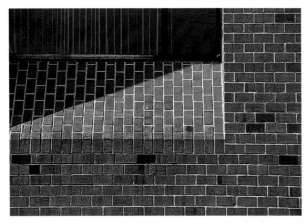

B-124   Closure, extruded, sand finish, running bond; sill vertical running bond

B-125   Modular, extruded, running bond, with projecting rowlock sill

B-126   Modular, extruded, ironspot, running bond, soldier course common bond

B-127   Modular, extruded, smooth, running bond, gothic arch with concrete keystone

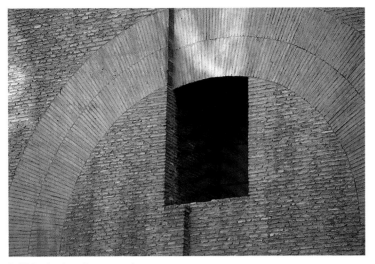

B-128   Ancient Roman arch

B-129   Ancient Roman, ⅓ running bond, semicircular arch

B-130   Modular Roman, ⅓ running bond variation with architectural terra-cotta bands

B-131   Modular, extruded, and raked mortar joint, with flat exterior paint

B-132   Common brick, running bond, with oil-based exterior sign paint

B-133   Modular, extruded, wire-cut, smooth texture, flush mortar joint painted with oil-based exterior paint and spray enamel

B-134   Modular, extruded, wire-cut, common bond, painted with spray enamel

B-135   Extruded, wire-cut, common bond, painted

B-136   Common brick, common bond, painted

B-137   Common brick, common bond, full-flashed, with oil-based exterior sign paint

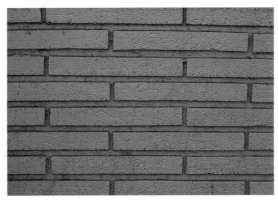

B-138   Roman, running bond, raked mortar joint, flat exterior paint

B-139   Modular, extruded, smooth, raked mortar joint, with flat exterior paint

B-140   Used brick, running bond, painted

BRICK

151

B-141   Modular, extruded, smooth surface, with mortar weathering

B-142   Old Roman, $\frac{1}{4}$ running bond, with efflorescence

B-143   Common, pink mortar with extruded joints under facing brick

B-144   Common, hand-molded, sand-struck, with weathering mortar

B-145   Common, possibly molded, white mortar with medium aggregate; spalling caused by weathering

B-146   Adobe, running bond, mud mortar

B-147 Modular, extruded, smooth surface, running bond; deteriorating flush mortar joints

B-148 Ancient hand-molded, possibly water-struck, multiple bonds, heavy aggregate mortar

B-149 Possibly molded, Flemish bond with moss

B-150 Old hand-molded, multiple bonds

B-151 Hand-molded, water-struck, Flemish bond, sand-screened mortar

B-152 Modular, extruded, painted; spalling brick

B-153   Molded, common bond, spalling brick

B-154   Hand-molded, water-struck, primarily running bond, weathering mortar

B-155   Roman screen wall, in state of general deterioration

B-156   Molded, water-struck, Flemish bond, normal weathering

B-157　Ancient Roman bricks used as rubble concrete

B-158　Roman wall, a portion demolished

B-159　Modular, extruded, applied exterior paint

B-160　Ancient Roman, exposed wall; spalling brick

B-161 Graffiti on Norman, running bond

B-162 Common, with peeling waterproofing

B-163 Molded paving brick, herringbone pattern

P-1   Painted plaster

P-2   Colored stucco finish coat over brick and stone

P-3   Colored stucco

P-4   Cast concrete with weathered paint

PLASTER, CONCRETE, AGGREGATES

P-5 Painted stucco

P-6 Natural and tinted concrete block with concave mortar joints

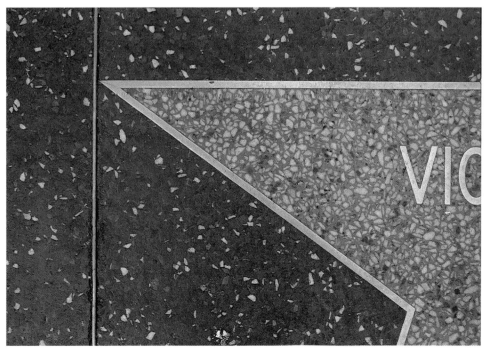

P-7 Terrazzo with half-hard brass dividers

PLASTER, CONCRETE, AGGREGATES

P-8   Stipple-textured stucco

P-9   Painted plaster, with brown coat visible

P-10   Textured stucco with following finishes (from left to right): fine sand skip trowel, sand float finish, directional skip trowel

P-11   Stucco with combed texture and knocked down finish

P-12   Mud plaster over adobe bricks

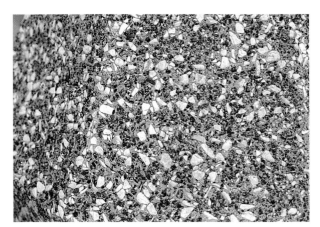

P-13   Exposed aggregate floor

PLASTER, CONCRETE, AGGREGATES

P-14 Tinted concrete block: split face, coarse aggregate, medium aggregate (left to right)

P-15 Fine aggregate concrete with combed texture

P-16 Cast exposed coarse aggregate concrete with split fluted texture

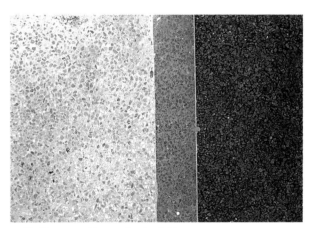

P-17 Terrazzo with metal strip dividers

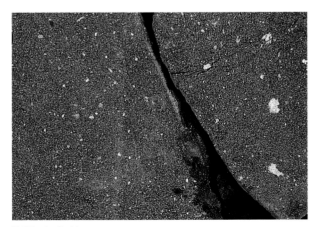

P-18 Asphaltic concrete

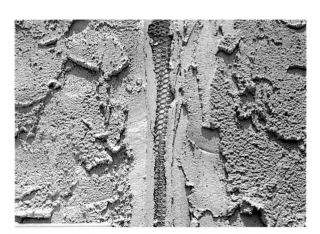

P-19 Heavy textured cement over expanded metal lath

PLASTER, CONCRETE, AGGREGATES

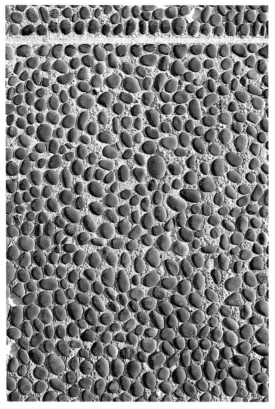

P-20   Exposed pebble aggregate concrete

P-21   Precast and colored concrete paving units

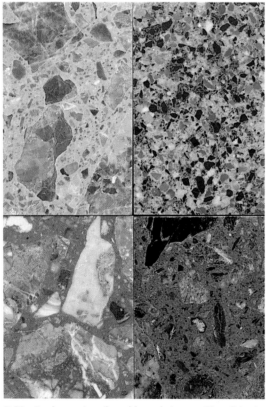

P-22   Agglomerates of marble and stones with polished surface

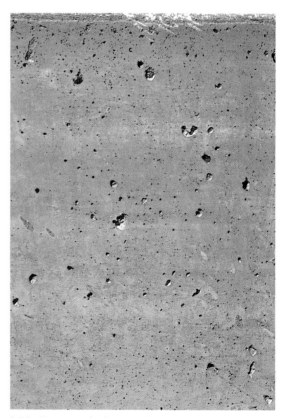

P-23   Honeycombed cast-in-place concrete

PLASTER, CONCRETE, AGGREGATES

P-24　Medium-size exposed marble and/or stone aggregate

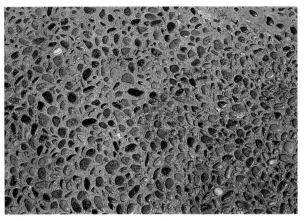

P-25　Beach pebble aggregate in tinted concrete

P-26　Marble or quartz chips in fine aggregate concrete

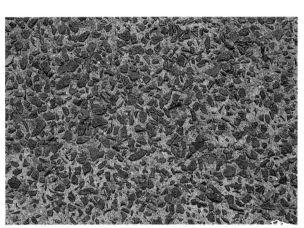

P-27　Process or trap rock in fine aggregate concrete

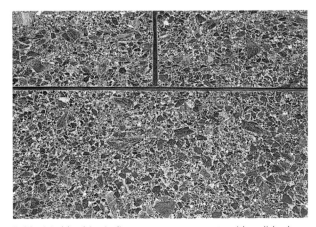

P-28　Marble chips in fine aggregate concrete with polished finish

P-29　Pea gravel in fine aggregate concrete

PLASTER, CONCRETE, AGGREGATES

P-30   Painted stucco with spray or dash texture and knocked down finish

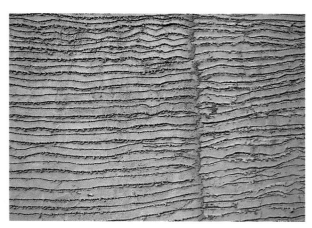

P-31   Stucco scratch coat

P-32   Pigmented textured stucco with a trowel-sweep finish

P-33   Painted stucco with skip-trowel finish

P-34   Painted stucco with random troweled texture

P-35   Whitewashed plaster over adobe brick

P-36　Coarse aggregate colored stucco

P-37　Painted sprayed textured stucco with knocked down finish

P-38　Painted textured stucco with floated sand finish

P-39　Painted sprayed textured stucco

P-40   Painted textured stucco with scallop or dab finish

P-41   Painted plaster

P-42   Painted smooth-finish stucco

P-43   Painted smooth-finish stucco

P-44   Painted plaster

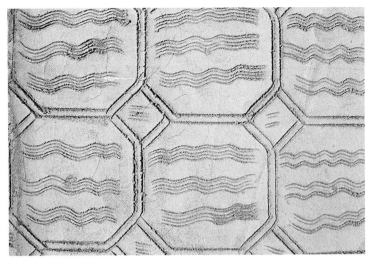

P-45   Troweled-smooth stucco with scored pattern

P-46   Painted stucco with patterned directional skip-trowel finish

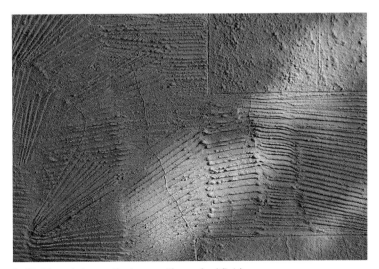

P-47   Troweled smooth stucco with combed finish

P-48   Precast fine aggregate concrete

P-49   Precast fine aggregate concrete, mortar joint

P-50   Precast fine aggregate concrete, grooved texture

P-51   Fine aggregate concrete over steel grate

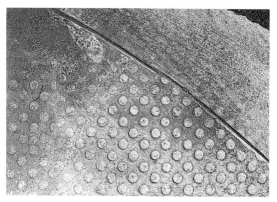

P-52   Poured concrete impressed pattern, broom-textured band

P-53 Cast-in-place concrete

P-54 Precast coarse aggregate with tile inlay

P-55 Painted coarse aggregate concrete

P-56 Precast concrete under stucco coat

P-57 Deteriorated coarse aggregate concrete

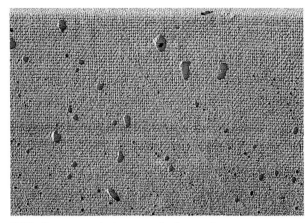

P-58　Fine aggregate honeycombed concrete

P-59　Tinted, textured concrete sidewalk

P-60　Fine aggregate concrete sidewalk, brushed finish with tooled finish border

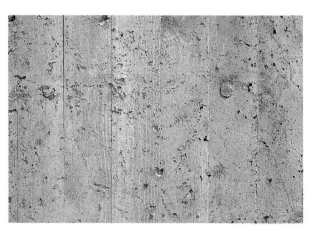

P-61　Cast concrete, wood texture

P-62　Cast honeycombed concrete

P-63　Cast concrete, plywood texture

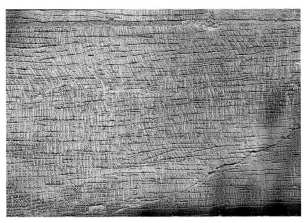

P-64   Precast concrete

P-65   Poured concrete walk with swirl broom or floated swirl finish

P-66   Poured concrete walk with broom finish

P-67   Cast concrete

P-68   Rough-cast anchoring concrete

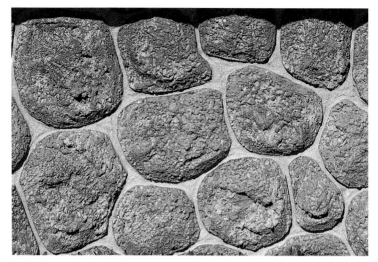

P-69 Precast concrete "stone" units set in mortar

P-70 Precast concrete artificial stones

P-71 Stamped concrete paving

P-72   Split-faced concrete block

P-73   Split-faced retaining wall block

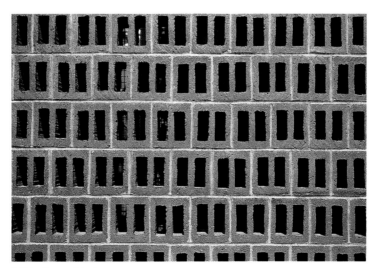

P-74   Screen block

PLASTER, CONCRETE, AGGREGATES

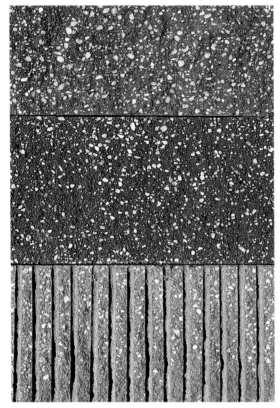

P-75 Tinted medium aggregate concrete block: split-faced with shaped edge, split-faced, ribbed texture (top to bottom)

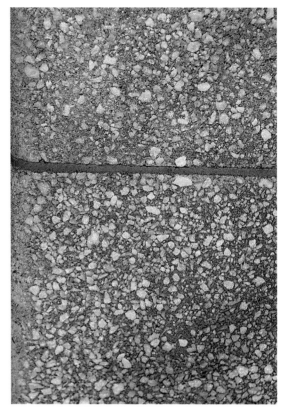

P-76 Coarse aggregate block, fine texture dark mortar

P-77 Split-faced colored block, running bond

P-78 Paving block, pink mortar, flush joint

P-79 Pea gravel textured block, stack bond, raked joint

PLASTER, CONCRETE, AGGREGATES

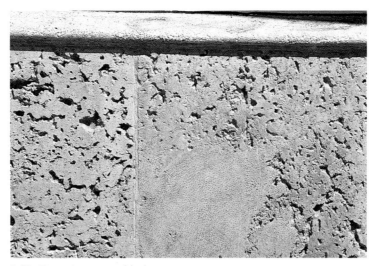

P-80   Travertine texture block

P-81   Colored, fluted block

P-82   Tinted block, running bond, raked joint

PLASTER, CONCRETE, AGGREGATES

P-83 Natural block, running bond, concave joint

P-84 Custom block, custom bond

P-85 Structural block wall, running bond, flush joint

P-86 Precast rustic face, coarse aggregate block

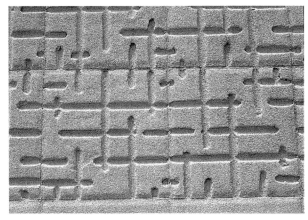

P-87   Decorative block, stack bond

P-88   Split-faced manufactured stone, running bond

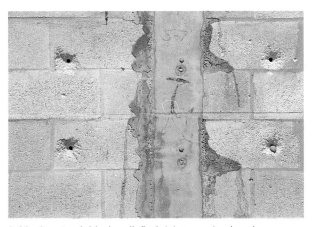

P-89   Structural, block wall, flush joint, running bond

P-90   Split-faced colored block, concave joint, running bond

P-91   Structural, block wall, running bond

P-92 Tinted cement stucco troweled over weathered brownstone

P-93 Painted stucco over brick (top); textured stucco with floated finish (bottom)

P-94 Painted smooth stucco over adobe brick

P-95 Whitewashed smooth stucco over brick

P-96 Manufactured stone

P-97 Painted smooth stucco over scratch coat, expanded metal lath, and brick

P-98   Cast concrete

P-99   Varieties of stucco over brick

P-100   Painted stucco between exposed timber framing

PHOTO: GUY GURNEY

P-101   Cast concrete

P-102   Tinted cement stucco over brownstone

PLASTER, CONCRETE, AGGREGATES

P-103   Troweled-smooth stucco, grooved to resemble stonework

P-104   Varieties of stucco textures and finishes

P-105   Cast coarse aggregate concrete

P-106   Textured stucco over weathered stone

PLASTER, CONCRETE, AGGREGATES

P-107   Probably tinted concrete quoins and natural stone masonry

P-108   Scored stucco over brick or stone

P-109   Stucco

P-110   Precast fine aggregate concrete

PLASTER, CONCRETE, AGGREGATES

P-111   Painted precast concrete

P-112   Patterned pebble dash

P-113   Painted troweled textured stucco

P-114   Incised coarse aggregate stucco

P-115   Painted and colored stucco

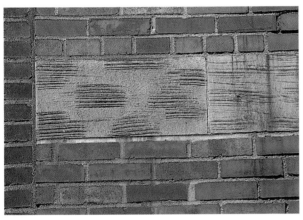

P-116   Brick wall with combed stucco inserts

P-117   Varieties of stucco

P-118   Smooth stucco over brick with scratch coat visible

P-119   Precast concrete

PLASTER, CONCRETE, AGGREGATES

P-120   Terrazzo

P-121   Poured concrete with broom texture, smooth border, expansion joint

P-122   Poured concrete with brushed texture, incised breaks with brick

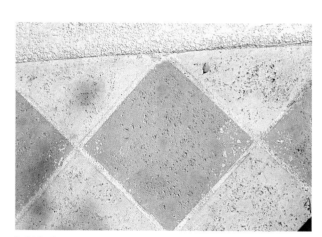

P-123   Precast concrete pavers

P-124   Painted asphalt

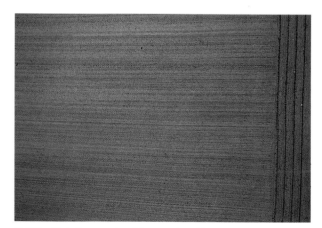

P-125   Tinted concrete with scored and broom textures

PLASTER, CONCRETE, AGGREGATES

P-126   Precast concrete pavers

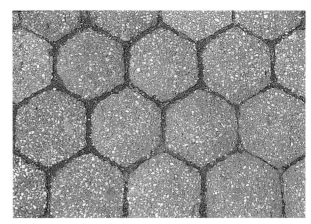

P-127   Shaped asphaltic concrete

P-128   Precast concrete pavers

P-129   Precast concrete pavers

P-130   Painted asphaltic concrete

P-131   Precast concrete pavers

PLASTER, CONCRETE, AGGREGATES

P-132   Terrazzo

P-133   Terrazzo

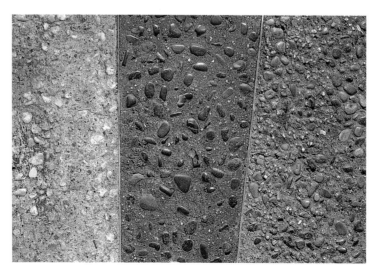

P-134   Rustic terrazzo

PLASTER, CONCRETE, AGGREGATES

P-135   Precast concrete

P-136   Stucco with incised pattern

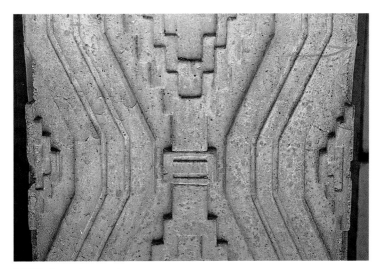

P-137   Precast concrete

PLASTER, CONCRETE, AGGREGATES

P-138   Precast concrete

P-139   Precast concrete

P-140   Precast concrete

P-141   Molded-in-place detail on textured stucco

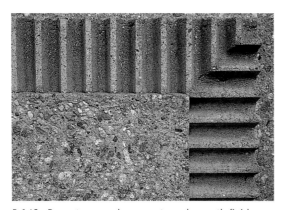

P-142   Precast exposed aggregate and smooth-finish concrete

P-143   Painted custom concrete detail

PLASTER, CONCRETE, AGGREGATES

P-144   Precast concrete

P-145   Mud plaster over adobe brick

P-146   Stucco with scratch coat and expanded metal
lath exposed

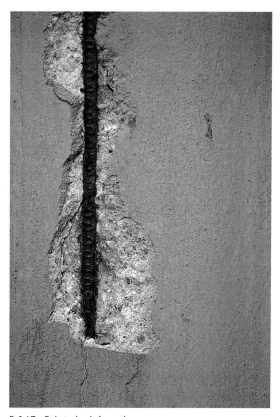

P-147   Painted reinforced concrete

PLASTER, CONCRETE, AGGREGATES

P-148   Painted and colored smooth stucco

P-149   Colored smooth stucco

P-150   Stucco over brick

PLASTER, CONCRETE, AGGREGATES

P-151   Painted and colored smooth stucco

P-152   Smooth stucco with natural patina

P-153   Painted cast concrete

P-154   Colored stucco over brick

P-155   Painted and colored smooth stucco

PLASTER, CONCRETE, AGGREGATES

P-156   Deteriorating smooth stucco

P-157   Smooth plaster over brick

P-158   Exposed reinforcing rod in concrete retaining wall

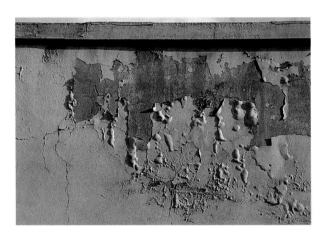

P-159   Blistering paint on concrete wall

P-160   Multiple coats of colored and tinted stucco

PLASTER, CONCRETE, AGGREGATES

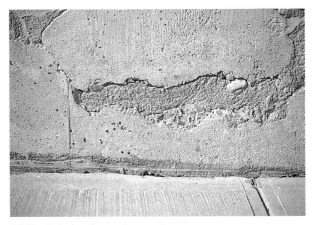

P-161   Deteriorating cast concrete

P-162   Smooth stucco over brick

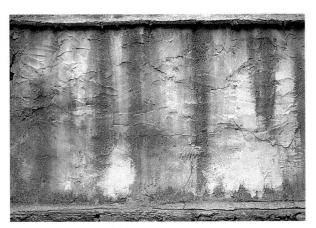

P-163   Stucco over adobe

P-164   Concrete block with metallic bleed

P-165   Deteriorating cast concrete

PLASTER, CONCRETE, AGGREGATES

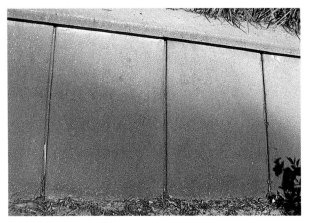

P-166   Concrete and rust

P-167   Whitewashed stucco

P-168   Colored stucco with mildew and mold

P-169   Painted plaster

P-170   Exposed reinforced concrete and concrete detail

P-171   Exposed interior plaster wall with lime putty trowel finish over structural brick wall

PLASTER, CONCRETE, AGGREGATES

METAL

ME-1   Patinated cast bronze

ME-2   Metal leaf over plaster relief

ME-3   Aluminum conduit

ME-4   Bronze door knocker

METAL

ME-5   Painted steel beam with cast fastener

ME-6   Cast iron machine parts

ME-7   Cast bronze architectural detail

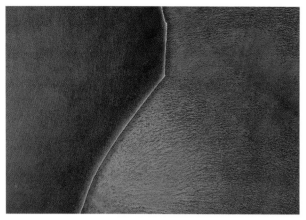

ME-8   Patinated silicon bronze (left), weathering steel not fully developed (right)

ME-9   Bronze with random etched surface

ME-10   Polished pewter

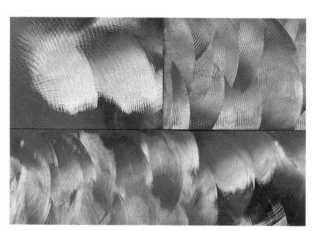

ME-11   Brass, copper, and stainless steel with hand-brushed finishes

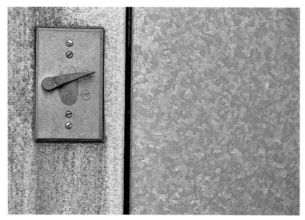

ME-12   Zinc galvanized steel

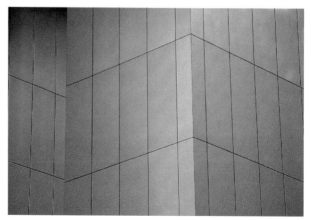

ME-13   Anodized aluminum

ME- 14   Brake-formed Muntz metal

ME-15   Lead muntins

ME-16   Bronze, natural patina

ME-17   Cast aluminum or zinc

ME-18   Nickel-silver plated bronze or cast stainless steel

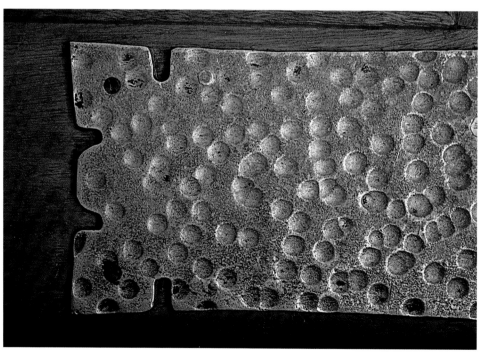

ME-19   Forged iron

ME-20   Brake-formed stainless steel mirror and satin finishes

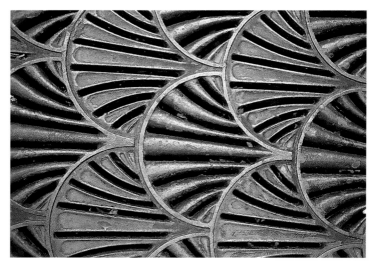

ME-21   Cast iron

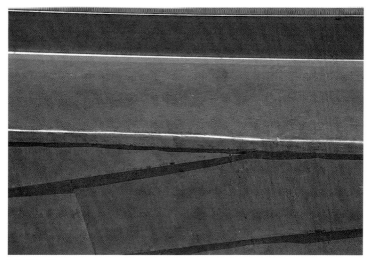

ME-22   Copper

ME-23 Clear-coated aluminum with hand-brushed directional finish

ME-24 Anodized aluminum quilted or diamond pattern

ME-25 Bronze (left), fluted, brushed-finish stainless steel (right)

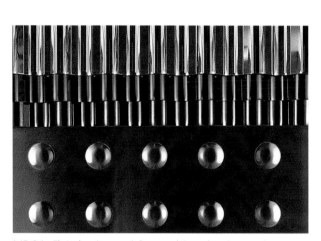

ME-26 Fluted, mirror stainless steel (top three), proprietary surface (bottom)

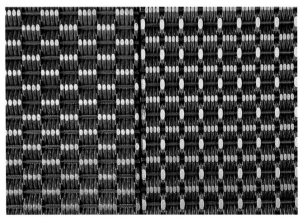

ME-27 Stainless steel and woven brass architectural mesh

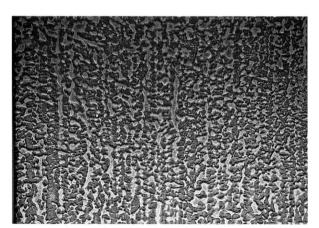

ME-28 Metal and Formica laminate

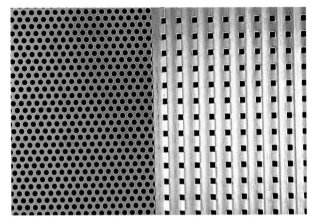

ME-29   Aluminum with satin finish, perforated and fluted

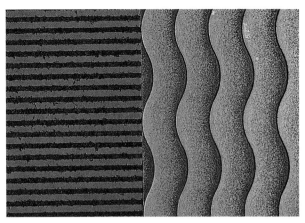

ME-30   Metal and Formica laminate

ME-31   Hand-brushed nondirectional stainless steel proprietary finish

ME-32   Bronze with hand-brushed finish, fluted stainless with mirror finish, fluted stainless with satin finish (left to right)

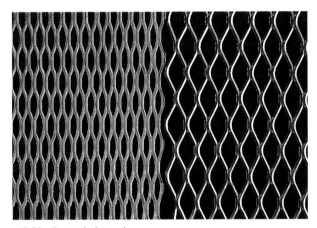

ME-33   Expanded metal

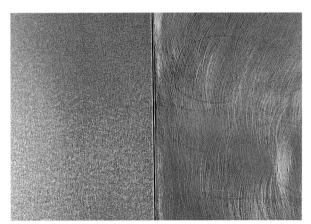

ME-34   Stainless steel nondirectional finish (left), hand-brushed satin finish (right)

ME-35   Muntz metal and satin-finish stainless steel entryway

ME-36   Two different bronzes in a door panel

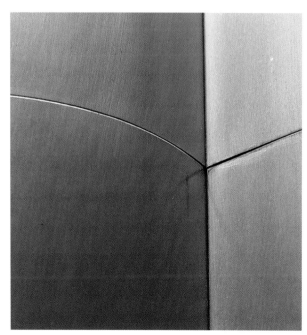

ME-37   Muntz metal facade

ME-38   Stainless steel muntins

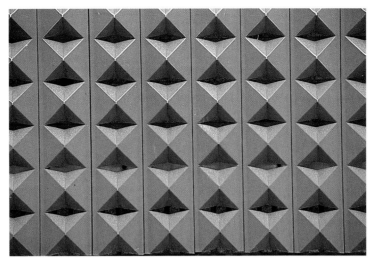

ME-39   Anodized aluminum facade

ME-40   Aluminum facade

ME-41   Bronze with mechanical-finish facade detail

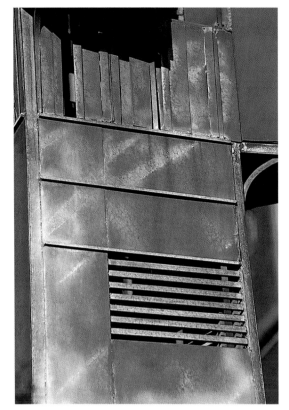

ME-42   Stainless steel sculpture

ME-43   Bronze over stainless steel window detail

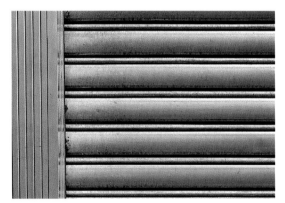

ME-44   Galvanized steel security door

ME-45   Bronze over stainless steel facade

ME-46   Muntz metal exterior molding

ME-47   Stainless steel canopy

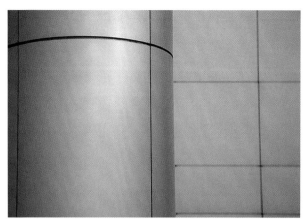

ME-48   Aluminum

ME-49   Mirror-finish stainless steel facade

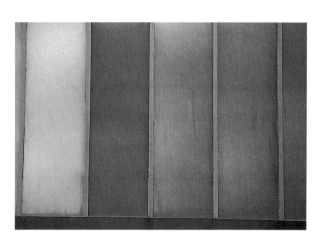

ME-50   Anodized aluminum facade

ME-51   Column with metallic finish

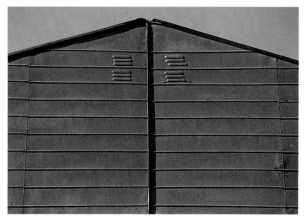

ME-52   Rusted steel siding

ME-53   Copper bay window, natural patina

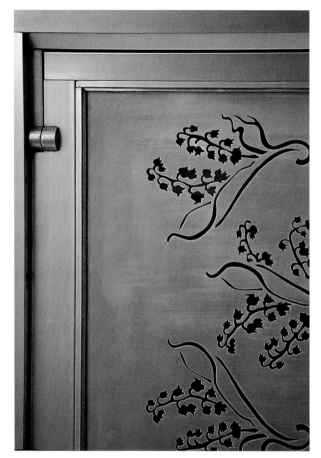

ME-54   Stainless steel door, perforated design

ME-55   Cast iron facade

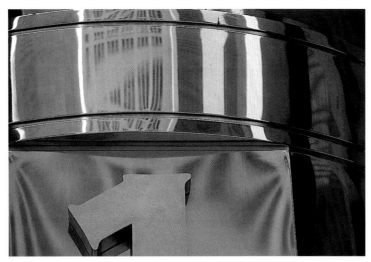

ME-56   Brass decorative entryway

PHOTO: COPPER DEVELOPMENT ASSOCIATION

ME-57   Newly installed copper dome (no patina)

ME-58   Satin-finish stainless steel doorway

ME-59   Cast bronze, natural patina

ME-60   Cast bronze with painted (possibly copper) background

ME-61   Cast iron

ME-62   Cast iron with incised detail

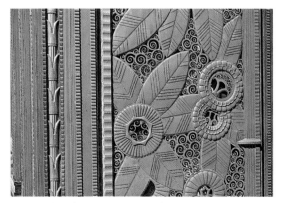

ME-63   Cast bronze

ME-64   Cast iron

ME-65   Painted cast iron

ME-66   Cast bronze, natural patina on statuary finish

ME-67   Cast bronze, statuary finish

METAL

ME-68 Bronze with protective sealant to prevent patination

ME-69 Cast bronze with natural patina

ME-70 Well-maintained bronze

ME-71 Cast bronze with gilt details

ME-72   "Bonderized" bronze (proprietary)

ME-73   Well-maintained bronze detail on statuary finish

ME-74   Cast bronze, natural patina

ME-75   Punched and fabricated bronze

ME-76   Cast bronze, natural patina

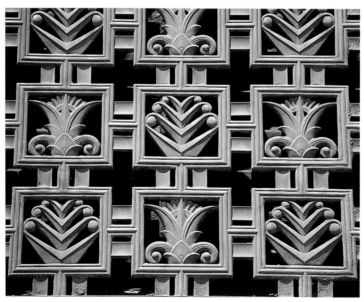

ME-77   Cast bronze, statuary finish

METAL

ME-78   Cast and welded steel

ME-79   Wrought iron

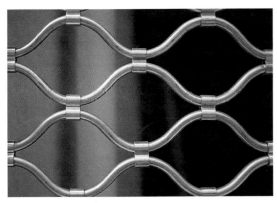

ME-80   Stainless steel

ME-81   Bronze with waxed protective coating

ME-82   Painted cast iron

ME-83   Galvanized steel chain link

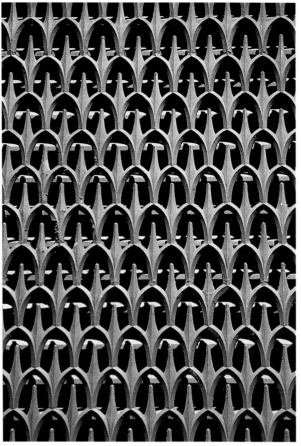

ME-84   Cast iron

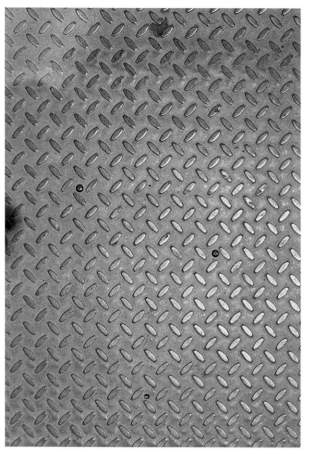

ME-85   Steel street plate

ME-86   Cast iron

ME-87   Cast iron

ME-88   Anodized aluminum with gold-colored weatherproofing

ME-89   Copper bent-sheet roofing

ME-90   Old and new copper roofing units

ME-91   Brass

ME-92   Cast bronze, natural patina

ME-93   Bronze with protective coating

ME-94   Bronze, probably sand cast, statuary finish

ME-95   Cast bronze, natural patina

ME-96   Cleaned bronze

ME-97   Welded steel

ME-98   Brass

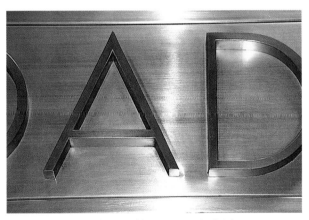

ME-99   Buffed stainless steel letters on satin finish

ME-100   Bronze letters on satin-finish stainless steel

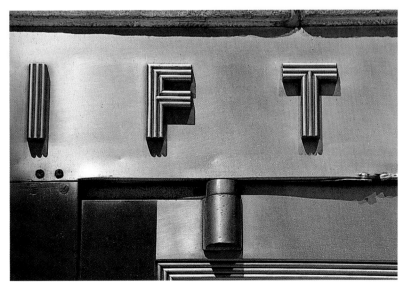

ME-101   Cast aluminum letters on satin-finish stainless steel

ME-102   Cast stainless steel

ME-103   Classic statuary bronze

ME-104   Patinated bronze

ME-105   Aluminum

METAL

ME-106   Bronze, natural patina

PHOTO: GUY GURNEY

ME-107   Bronze, natural patina

ME-108   Lacquered bronze

ME-109   Bronze, natural patina

PHOTO: COPPER DEVELOPMENT ASSOCIATION

ME-110   New copper

METAL

ME-111 Exterior enamel and spray paint on steel

ME-112 Exterior enamel on steel

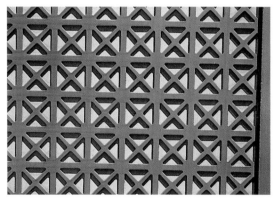

ME-113 Baked enamel on punched sheet aluminum or steel

ME-114 Cast iron rusting through exterior enamel

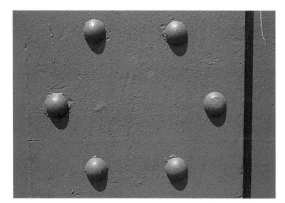

ME-115 Exterior enamel on structural steel

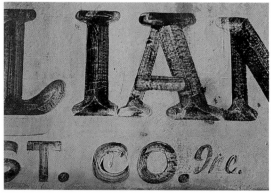

ME-116 Oil enamel over exterior enamel

ME-117   Bronze before application of chemical patina

ME-118   Bronze after application of chemical patina

ME-119   Statuary bronze finish

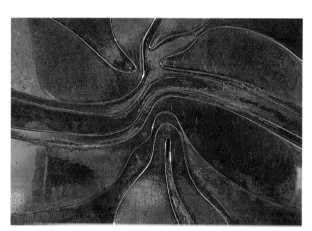

ME-120   Muntz metal appliqué with chemical patina

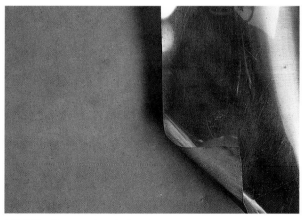

ME-121   Copper, chemical patina

ME-122   Bronze, natural patina

ME-123   Cast bronze building plate

ME-124   Cast-iron doorknocker

ME-125   Spun bronze and stainless steel clock

ME-126   Cast bronze handles and horizontal members, stainless verticals

ME-127   Multiple bronzes in door handle

ME-128   Welded galvanized steel

METAL

ME-129   Copper drainpipe

ME-130   Cast and assembled bronze

ME-131   Cast iron

ME-132   Cast and polished bronze

PHOTO: GUY GURNEY

ME-133   Cast bronze, natural patina

ME-134   Cast and assembled brass

ME-135   Wrought iron, steel, and gilded bronze

ME-136   Unpainted steel

ME-137   Painted cast iron

ME-138   Formed tin

ME-139   Bronze-cleaning in progress

ME-140   Bronze, natural patina

ME-141   Cut and assembled iron

ME-142   Marine enamel over steel

ME-143   Metallic paint over steel

ME-144   Painted wrought iron

ME-145   Cast iron

ME-146   Forged or cast iron

ME-147   Exterior enamel over steel

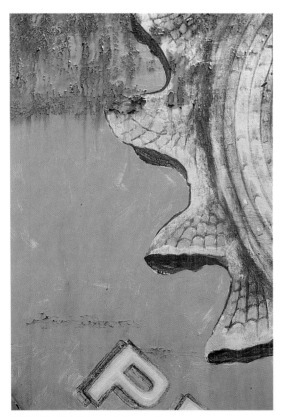

ME-148   Oxidizing paint over steel

ME-149   Rust on galvanized steel

ME-150   Rusted metal plate

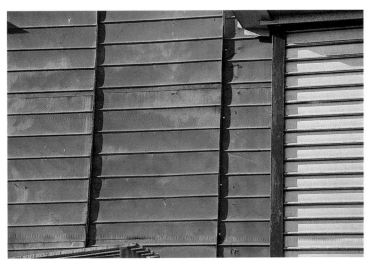

ME-151   Rusted steel siding

ME-152   Inlaid copper sheet in boat's hull, natural patina

ME-153   Rusted steel

ME-154   Exterior enamel over cast iron

ME-155   Rust penetrating zinc coating of galvanized steel

ME-156   Weathered anodized aluminum

ME-157   Corrugated steel

ME-158   Rust on tower

GLASS

G-1   Reflection in building windows

G-2   Baccarat crystal prisms on a chandelier

G-3   Cyanite window glass

G-4   Leaded window panes

G-5   Colored glass in window

G-6   Textured window glass

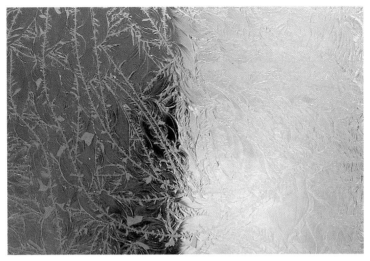

G-7   Chip glass

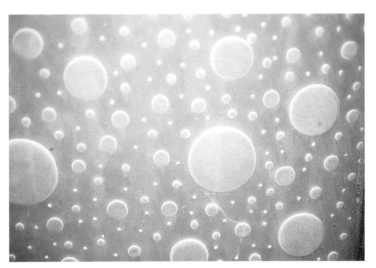

G-8   Frosted pattern

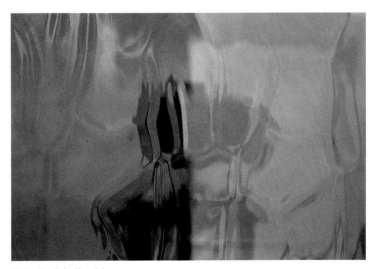

G-9   English-Flemish

G-10   Burlap

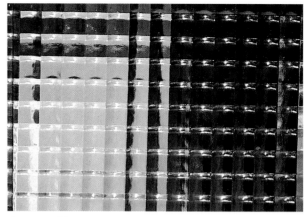

G-11   Doublex

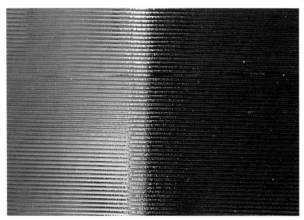

G-12   Ribbed

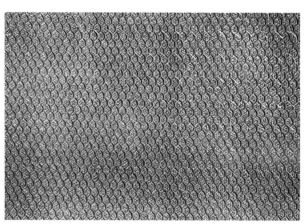

G-13   Wire with hammered texture

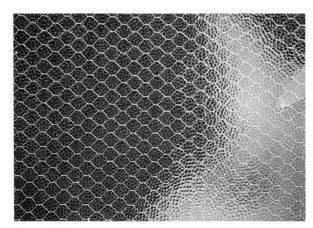

G-14   Chicken wire or rough wire

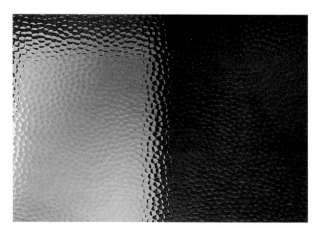

G-15   Hammered

G-16   Frosted antique

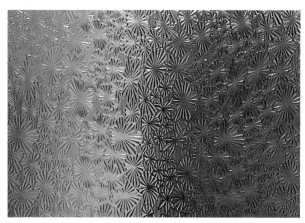

G-17   Florentine

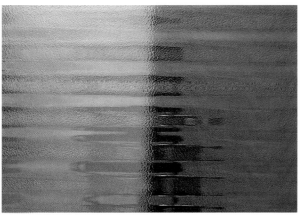

G-18   Flutex

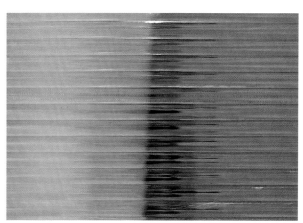

G-19   Puralite

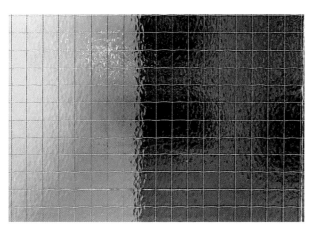

G-20   Rough wire

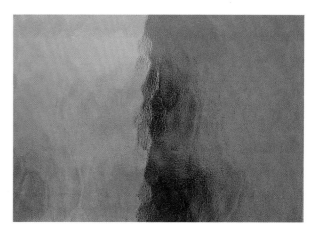

G-21   Smooth rough

G-22   Molded

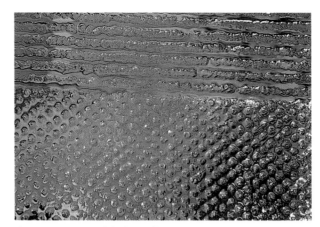

G-23   Impression, kiln-formed

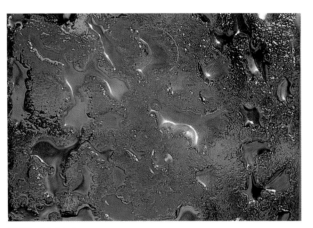

G-24   Molded

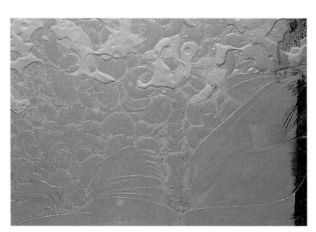

G-25   Glue chip

PHOTO: PETER ZSIBA

G-26   Impression, kiln-formed with applied gold leaf and grout

G-27   Glass brick in window wall

G-28   Glass brick in exterior entryway

G-29   Glass brick in basement window

G-30   Glass brick window with white grout

G-31   Patterned and clear glass brick in window

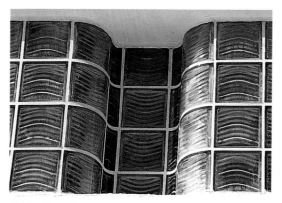

G-32   Shaped corners in glass brick window

G-33   Colored glass in leaded window

G-34   Colored and uncolored textured glass

G-35   Colored draped glass

G-36   Colored glass in leaded window

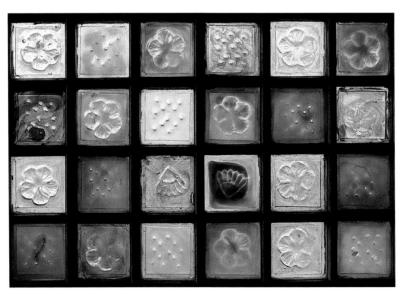

G-37   Opalescent glass tile

G-38 Stained and painted glass

G-39 Stained and painted glass

G-40 Stained and painted glass

G-41 Opalescent and stained glass

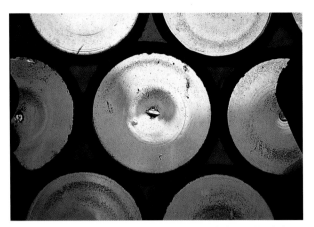

G-42   Clear and tinted roundels with stained glass in leaded window

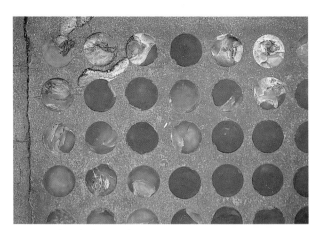

G-43   Colored glass in glass concrete

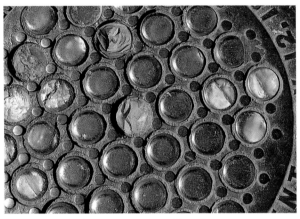

G-44   Colored glass set in cast iron sidewalk grate

G-45   Tinted rondels set in window with mortar

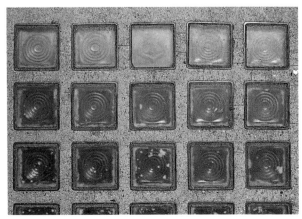

G-46   Glass concrete in metal grate

G-47   Molded glass window

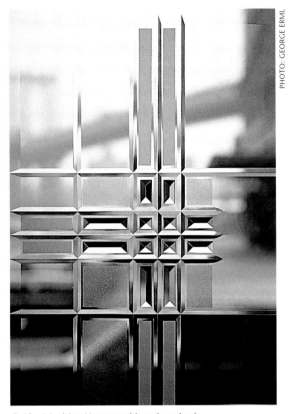

G-48 Machine V-grooved bevel, etched

G-49 Brilliant-cut gold glass illuminated ceiling

G-50 Beveled facets set in leaded window

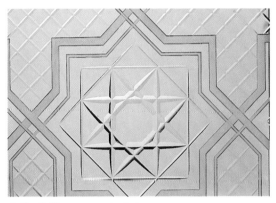

G-51 Brilliant-cut, etched glass

G-52 Crystal and glass mirror crest

G-53 Beveled door glass

G-54   Variety of glass panes in leaded muntins

G-55   Window glass in wood muntins

G-56   Antique glass in lead or zinc muntins

G-57   Variety of glass panes in wood muntins

G-58   Tinted antique glass in metal muntins

G-59   Tinted opalescent glass

G-60   Clear and stained glass in leaded muntins

G-61   Antique glass in leaded muntins

G-62   Modern fanlight

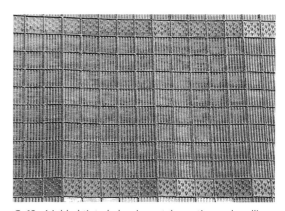

G-63   Molded tinted glass in metal muntins and mullions

G-64   Antique glass in metal muntins

G-65   Leaded beveled glass

G-66   Factory windows

G-67   Antique glass in wood muntins

G-68   Tinted mirror skyscraper windows

G-69   Leaded glass detail

G-70   Tinted glass

G-71   Painted factory windows

G-72   Glass building facade

G-73   Window reflections

G-74   Stainless steel and glass reflections

G-75   Reflections

G-76   Ballroom ceiling reflections in mirrored overdoor

G-77   Broken window

G-78   Wire glass behind wrought-iron-door grill

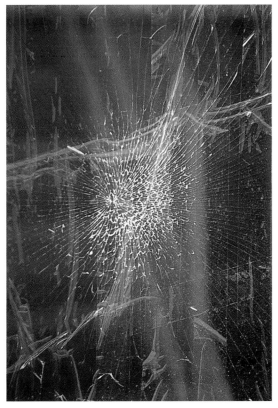

G-79   Shattered safety glass

G-80   Cyanite window glass

G-81   Glass brick

G-82   Replacement glass behind broken pane

G-83   Chicken wire glass

G-84   Partially painted windows

G-85   Broken pane

G-86 Glass brick window repaired with concrete

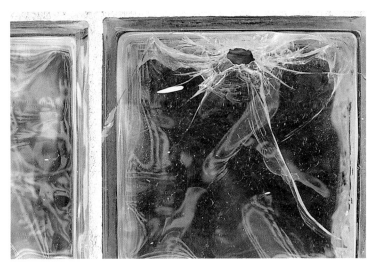

G-87 Hole in glass brick

G-88 Broken safety glass

G-89   Frost crystals

G-90   Condensation

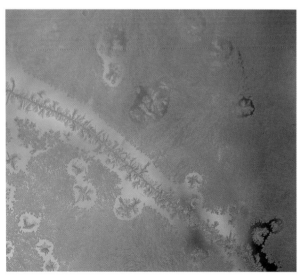

G-91   Frost crystals

G-92   Frost crystals

TILE

T-1 Terra-cotta tile roof

T-2 Paving tile

T-3 Glazed and sculptured tile

TILE

254

T-4   Mosaic tile

T-5   Guastavino ceiling tiles

T-6   Stone or marble tiles in mosaic

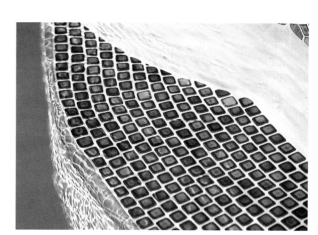

T-7   Glazed mosaic tiles

T-8   Glazed exterior tile

TILE

255

T-9　Glazed tile in mosaic floor

T-10　Glazed ceramic wall tile with sculptured molding

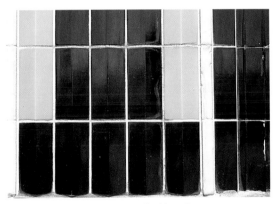

T-11　Glazed exterior tile, stacked bond

T-12　Glazed exterior tile

T-13　Glazed exterior tile

T-14　Glazed ceramic wall tile with sculptured bullnose molding

T-15   Glazed ceramic floor tile (faience tile)

T-16   Glazed ceramic wall tile

T-17   Glazed ceramic wall tile

T-18   Glazed ceramic wall tile

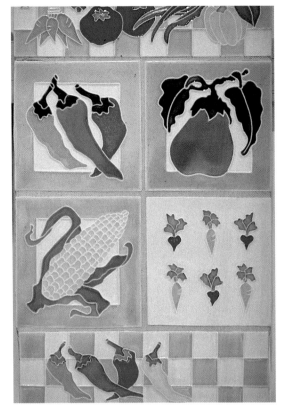

T-19   Cuenca decorated tile

T-20   Majolica painted tile

T-21   Majolica painted tile

T-22   Hand-painted tiles with glazed border, weathered

T-23   Hand-painted clay tile, weathered

T-24   Stenciled tile

T-25   Hand-cut and painted tile

T-26   Hand-painted tile

T-27   Hand-painted tile

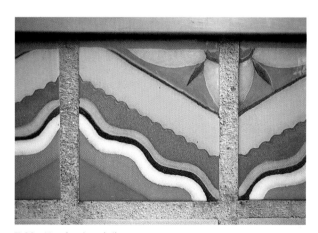

T-28   Hand-painted tile

T-29   Tumbled marble

T-30   Marble floor tile

T-31   Marble floor tile

T-32   Limestone and black stone tiles

T-33   Marble in mosaic

T-34   Marble in mosaic

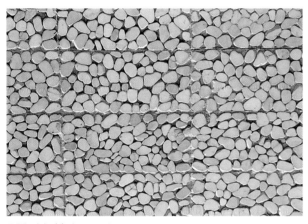

T-35   Marble in mosaic

T-36   Tumbled marble and travertine stone tile

T-37   Tumbled marble

T-38   Marble tile

T-39 Glazed interior borders

T-40 Embossed pattern tiles, glazed wall tile, sculptured molding tiles

T-41 Hand-painted tile with glazed sculptured borders

T-42   Glazed sculptured exterior tile

T-43   Glazed sculptured tile

T-44   Encaustic relief

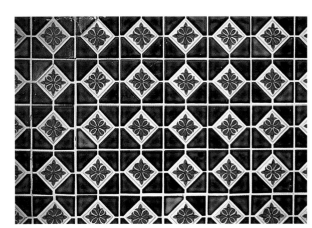

T-45   Embossed tiles

T-46   Glazed sculptured exterior tile

T-47   Terra-cotta with glazed details

T-48   Terra-cotta in pebble aggregate concrete

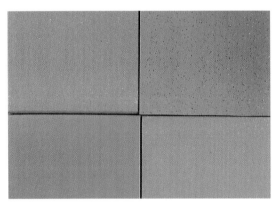

T-49   Quarry tile

T-50   Quarry tile

T-51   Porcelain tile

T-52   Handmade glazed natural clay tiles

T-53   Terra-cotta and stone or marble tile

T-54   Mexican paving tile

T-55   Terra-cotta with tumbled marble border

T-56   Paving tile

T-57   Terra-cotta set in mortar

T-58   Stone and marble mosaic floor

T-59   Mosaic, stone, and glass tiles

T-60   Handmade glazed tile in floor mosaic

T-61   Stone and marble mosaic floor

T-62   Marble and glazed ceramic tiles in wall mosaic

T-63   Glass mosaic tile in wall mosaic

T-64   Ceramic mosaic tile in exterior ceiling mosaic

T-65   Handmade glazed tile in floor mosaic

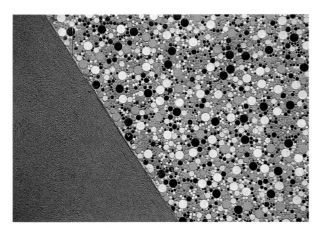

T-66   Ceramic mosaic tile in wall mosaic

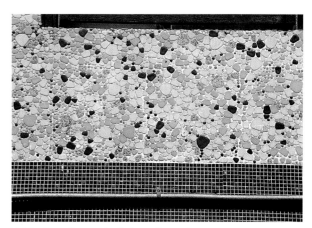

T-67   Ceramic mosaic tile in wall mosaic

T-68   Flat terra-cotta roof tiles

T-69   Modern roof tiles

T-70   Glazed terra-cotta tiles

T-71   Weathered terra-cotta tiles

T-72   New terra-cotta tiles

T-73   Flat and shaped terra-cotta tiles

PHOTO: DUANE LANGENWALTER

T-74   Roof tiles

T-75   Shaped terra-cotta roof tiles

TILE

T-76 Glazed terra-cotta

T-77 Natural clay terra-cotta figure and arch molding detail

T-78 Weathered architectural terra-cotta

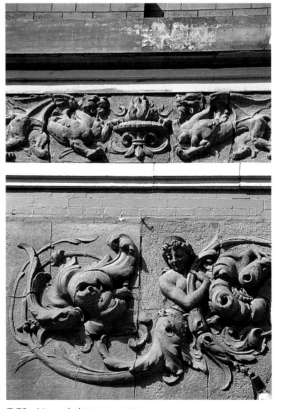

T-79 Natural clay terra-cotta

T-80   Natural terra-cotta and brick window treatment

T-81   Speckled glazed terra-cotta

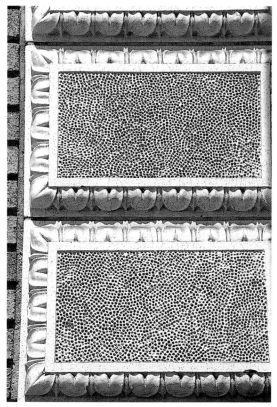

T-82   Glazed terra-cotta in stone motif on building
facade

T-83   Spattered glaze on building detail

T-84   Matte glazed terra-cotta

T-85   Glazed terra-cotta entry motif

T-86   Matte glazed terra-cotta

T-87   Natural clay terra-cotta cornice

T-88   Spattered glaze on building detail

T-89   Matte glazed terra-cotta band

T-90 Terra-cotta capital on weathered pilaster

T-91 Terra-cotta figure with sprayed spatter glaze

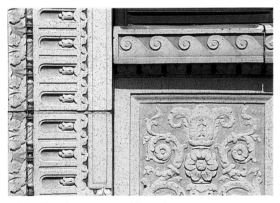

T-92 Glazed terra-cotta with crazing

T-93 Terra-cotta imitation stone

T-94 Glazed terra-cotta figured cornice and archway decoration

T-95 Terra-cotta building top with sprayed spatter glaze

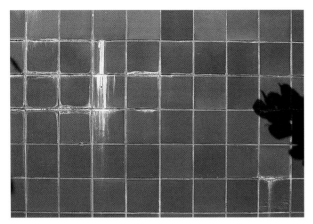

T-96   Glazed tile on exterior, with efflorescence

T-97   Glazed tile on exterior

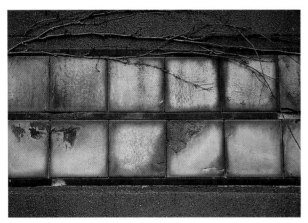

T-98   Glazed tile on exterior

T-99   Glazed tile with metal lath and scratch coat

T-100   Mosaic tile

T-101   Weathered architectural terra-cotta

T-102   Sandblasted terra-cotta egg-and-dart cornice

T-103   Architectural terra-cotta with crazing

TILE

275

T-104   Weathered terra-cotta tile floor

T-105   Painted natural clay glazed tile

T-106   Chipped architectural terra-cotta column base

T-107   Weathered architectural terra-cotta

T-108   Broken natural clay terra-cotta

T-109   Natural terra-cotta

The following interviews are intended to give insight into the various research demands of professionals working in the visual arts. The artist who is suddenly struck by inspiration and proceeds to create great art is a rare phenomenon, and various fields demand different training and preparation. These conversations with eight design professionals explore their information needs, some of the types of research they use, the many approaches to finding that information, and how

WORKING PAPERS

research affects their work. While everyone interviewed here works in venues that have some connnection to the photographs in this book, the intent is not to discuss how they would use this particular visual research, but rather to see how these individuals go about the business of finding the answers to problems that confront them as they design, whether the result be building or interior space, mural, fine woodwork, or scenery for film and theater.

INTERVIEW WITH TONY WALTON
THEATER AND FILM DESIGNER

Tony Walton has designed sets and costumes for over a hundred productions in theater, opera, ballet, film, and television. His designs for theatrical productions, including *Guys and Dolls, The House of Blue Leaves, A Funny Thing Happened on the Way to the Forum, Grand Hotel,* and *Sophisticated Ladies,* have been seen on stages from Broadway and Lincoln Center to London and the many stops of international tours. He has served as production and costume designer for such films as *Murder on the Orient Express, Prince of the City, Farenheit 451, Regarding Henry,* and *Death of a Salesman.* Mr. Walton also designs Broadway posters and has illustrated seven books.

Q What are your responsibilities as a theater and film designer?

A Designing for film and designing for the theater are very different. In theater you are, in a sense, selecting the image as a kind of visual funnel through which the audience perceives this special event. In movies that is not the case at all. You are making the environment available for the director and cinematographer to select what image will be perceived by the audience.

A film production designer is essentially responsible for the appearance of everything in the film except for the way it will be lighted or the way the selection of the images is made, although you may be involved in those selections. You give to the director and the cine-

matographer a visual alphabet for the film—everything from the flavor of the environment to hair styles and shoes. You provide the raw material from which the director and cinematographer can draw their images.

That can be tough, because often there is quite a difference between what you may imagine as you are putting it all together and what eventually transpires. Sometimes it can be frustrating; sometimes it can be exhilarating. There have been cases, particularly with Bob Fosse, Mike Nichols, and Giuseppe Rotunno, Fellini's cinematographer, where they have taken something that was perhaps only marginally interesting from my end and made it magnificently more visually exciting through what they did with it.

Q What is the advantage of designing both sets and clothes?

A You have more control over the overall appearance of the piece. It is possible to make wonderful marriages with costume designers, lighting designers, cinematographers, whatever, but it is often potluck—unless of course you have a relationship that has been going for a while and have developed a solid common language.

Q When you design a play or film, how do you determine the physical requirements of the set—where the doors are located, and so forth?

A You meet with the director as early as possible so that you have a sense of what he or she plans to use.

Some directors are wonderful about doing their homework. Sidney Lumet, for example, is extraordinary. By the time he is in rehearsal, he really knows what he is going to do, so if you are building the setting, you can map out pretty exactly what he will need. On the other hand, there are moments when, as a result of something fresh that comes from the actors, there suddenly is a need for an element you haven't provided for. That can be rough if you don't have the alternative of swapping walls around or some other very fast solution.

For example, while Sidney was filming *The Book of Daniel* (designed by Philip Rosenberg), he suddenly needed to see a gravestone in close-up. It had to belong to a specific character with a specific name and date and all that, so he couldn't use just any gravestone. It had to be improvised on the spot by the scenic artist at enormous speed while the crew was standing and waiting. Those situations, regardless of how well you prepare, result in hair-raising moments.

Q Is that situation particular to film, or do you also encounter it in the theater?

A In theater, what you do is not going to be recorded for posterity at that moment. You will probably have the chance to address the problem later. But other problems arise. In a new musical, for example, when a change has been made to the book and the set does not accommodate that new approach—that can be very awkward. Something has to be radically altered or even thrown out.

Q Where do you get your first ideas for a production?

A Again, it depends on what it is. Almost every production has such a different point of departure that it could be anything. A director may have a strong idea with some strong imagery in mind—a painting or something like that. But an idea could come from a blob on a coffee saucer—from anywhere.

Q Can you give any examples?

A One of my strangest was for the stage production of *Six Degrees of Separation,* which was written very like a movie script—high speed, going from scene to scene, with about thirty-five different locations. At the first meeting, the director, Jerry Zaks, and the playwright, John Guare, felt we probably couldn't do it in the Mitzi Newhouse Theater at Lincoln Center, because it needed to be in a proscenium theater where we could do whirlwind changes from scene to scene with traditional stage techniques.

Coincidentally, it followed not long after my working on *Grand Hotel,* which had evolved through workshop rehearsals in which the actors sort of sat around the stage area and waited to be called on for their numbers. That idea worked its way into the eventual production style of *Grand Hotel* with beat-up banquettes built around the columns where the cast lounged or lurked when they were not actually performing on stage.

As I was flailing for something for *Six Degrees,* that idea came back. I realized that I didn't really know what was crucial scenically, but I did know that it was important that the actors be immediately available so that the production could flow seamlessly. From that came the idea of the actors sitting in the front row of the audience, so they could just step into the action. I tried to interest Jerry Zaks and John Guare in this, but they were initially alarmed by the idea. Then, about two weeks later in a middle-of-the-night call, Jerry said, "I've got it. I've got it. I suddenly see I can have the policeman stand up in his seat and say, 'Do you want to press charges?' and then sit right down again." He then took the idea and really ran with it, being Jerry Zaks.

From there we figured out how little we could work with physically on stage, given that point of departure. We were a bit nervous because in a couple of previous instances plays we had done there (in the Newhouse) had moved to the Beaumont Theater, which is not hospitable to the kind of sparse and simple look that works in the Newhouse. I came up with the idea of the high, upper level entrances that had to do with the imagination, or dreams, or phone calls, or information coming from long distance. I did this chiefly because the Beaumont audience would be obliged to physically move their heads about and get actively involved in the energy of the production. When *Six Degrees* did move to the less intimate Beaumont, we slightly enlarged the furniture and scenic elements, and we tipped the stage floor so that the relationship between the stage and the audience remained nearly the same as it had been in the Newhouse, where actors don't feel that they are far away from any member of the audience.

The Beaumont is actually the reverse of the Newhouse. The angle of the orchestra seating is very slight. And then there is the second tier. So we kept angling the stage until it came close to the angle that existed between the Newhouse stage and the audience. But we still kept saying, "Oh God. How are we going to establish all these different environments?" Then we decided that the text would just announce where the actors were when necessary. (That convention became a stylistic signature for the play.)

Q Several years ago you designed the film version of *A Glass Menagerie.* Would you describe transporting that play to a film version?

A If one were approaching it as a stage production, one would dig much more for the poetic flavor of the writing and the story, and try to evoke that by making a framework in which the poetic style would live most vibrantly on the stage. In a film you have to make things more stylistically believable, as it is harder to call on the audience's imagination. So we had to start from a basis of heightened reality rather than from the visual equivalent of poetry. Not long before *A Glass Menagerie,* I had worked on the television film of *Death of a Salesman.* Arthur Miller was very concerned that it shouldn't be another screenplay version of the play but the original text. He pointed out a complicated situation in the text. Much of what appears to be flashbacks in the original film version were actually things really happening simultaneously in Willy Loman's mind while he was going through his breakdown.

The challenge of solving that problem for *Salesman* overlapped *A Glass Menagerie* where, although we had to deal with a strong level of reality, we had to walk a tightrope between film and a photographed play. Paul Newman (the director) had starred in films of plays by Tennessee Williams, and knew that Tennessee was disappointed that many of the plays had been changed to make them more "movie-like." He was determined to film a version that was faithful to Tennessee's text.

Q That production was primarily shot on a sound stage in New York. What sources did you use in designing the scenery?

A First of all, I got a past assistant, Ed Pisoni, now a production designer, who was from St. Louis (where the play is set), to photograph the kind of building we thought might have been the home of Tennessee and his mother and sister. We also studied a short story that Tennessee had written earlier, which he had then developed into the play. This had some very helpful specific descriptions. We were trying to start with the reality of where he had lived and what it was like. And then enhance the romantic aura of his memory and add to that the savage and cold reality of the actual story from which the romanticized memory had evolved.

We found a building on the fringes of Harlem that had something in common with our visual research from St. Louis. Then, for the interior sets, we tried to choose the textural characteristics from the St. Louis interior research we had—all the period tin molding and

so on. That is when Dick Ventre (the scenic artist) started trying to reproduce some of those textures—flaking paint and all. I had a strong feeling that we had to heighten the reality of the wallpaper, the tin moldings, and so on, from their conventional form into this feeling of something romantically recalled. So we started experimenting on the wallpaper with color glazes. Dick and his gang did samples that were taken to a point just before you could say it wasn't real, but at the same time you couldn't quite say it was painted. I had given the scenic artists reproductions of paintings with areas of color circled, and they used those as their guide.

Q How do you explain an idea like this to a director? Do they generally understand this painterly language when they want to know how the set will look when it is finished?

A Not necessarily. Though of course, it is a great help if we have some trust established. At times they really need to see examples of what you are talking about. In *Glass Menagerie* it was very helpful to have those four-foot-square scenic samples that were done early on, so that Paul Newman and Michael Ballhaus, the cinematographer, could see them and know exactly what it was going to look like.

Q How do you deal with making the sets, props, and set dressings in a studio as believable as a location in a movie?

A It used to be that the major studios would have extraordinary scenic and prop shops, and they all cooperated, so between them you could find anything from Scottish castle fixtures and furnishings to ultramodern furniture. But that is almost gone. Now, when I deal with a set decorator, I try to get out with them and explore what is available. If there's not time for that, it is very important for them to bring in samples, photographs, whatever.

Q What sort of instructions do you give a set decorator?

A Some verbal description. But not exclusively. In the case of *A Glass Menagerie,* we imagined that the family had found a great deal of their furnishings in the Sears, Roebuck catalog. We selected their things from the appropriate period catalog and sent the shoppers out hunting with that research. In *Death of a Salesman* much valuable all-American information was available in the paintings of Norman Rockwell. The furnishings in his paintings are so meticulously chosen and specific to the period that you always know exactly where you are. In some cases we had pieces of furniture duplicated from those illustrations.

Q How do you make a location and the studio-shot portions of a film become one movie?

A You generally work back and forth. You try to know in advance of the studio construction what you will be using as locations, and then photograph those things as completely as possible. And, if possible, bring chunks of the actual location into the studio so you have something real to match. In *Regarding Henry,* because we were filming some locations in New York and all the studio shots—the bulk of the film—in California, a rough assembly of the film was done while we were shooting. In one case, script adjustments resulted in part of the New York location film being unusable. It was too expensive to return to New York, and we didn't even have time to send someone back to the location to get pictures. So we had to recreate in a California studio another view of a huge New York location that had been filmed, but not from the newly needed angle. From the footage we had, we guessed how the moldings, walls, marble, etc. would continue in that vast interior. That scene is a shot-by-shot combination of location and studio. In the end, it may have been the best way to do the scene—we had more control than we did in the actual location. But you never really feel secure about what will happen during the shooting or when editing begins.

Q Do you keep files of samples of materials you have used in past designs?

A Only if they are not easily accessible. A lot of stuff gets discontinued, so it's frustrating to keep swatches of it. I photograph those things—fabrics, prints, theatrical materials. I take an enormous number of research photos not just directly related to the field, but paintings, textures, and so on, and I put them together in folders and eventually refer to them. For example, when I did Paramount's *Christmas Carol,* I referred often to those research folders on period London. The pictures could be bank interiors, plastered walls, mailboxes, street lamps, street exteriors, whatever. Sometimes they are photographs of photographs or paintings I have come across in the course of researching. It is easier to look through this snapshot file than hauling around the originals, which may be in coffee-table books. I put folders into categories, and assemble specific folders for individual productions. I try to include whatever is relevant in these with the drawings and paint elevations, so that

the builders and painters executing the scenery know the visual sources.

Q When a production goes into a film or theater shop, what information do you give the carpenters and painters?

A The two (theater and film shops) are pretty much the same. Copious drafting of everything, and sepia prints of the drafting, so additional copies can be made. On the paint elevations, which are the scaled paintings I provide, I usually make copious notes and refer to the specific drafting sheet, so the scenic artist can find out the construction details, if necessary. Along with that is as much source material as I can come up with.

Q Do you approach a period design differently than you do a contemporary design?

A No, I don't think so. You do tend to be more on guard with a contemporary design than with a period one, particularly if you are involved with costumes. Because absolutely everybody is convinced they know exactly what it should look like. There is always something in the (actor's or director's) wardrobe which is "perfect" for the character. But the impulses are the same. You want to project yourself into whatever world is required, whether it is a period or contemporary one, whether the palette is romantic or highly restrained.

Q Is costume design different for film and theater?

A In film, costume design is almost always about close-ups and interesting details—buttons and buttonholes, and things that are on the upper body. If you happen to see a full-length figure, the chances of seeing much of the shoes is pretty remote. But the shoes are very important in how the actors walk and stand. In the theater, it's about the entire silhouette, which can define character immediately. The costumer provides a visual signpost of the character. You have much more control over that in theater than you do in film, due to the choppy way the costume is usually revealed in a movie. Ideally, you help the actors find their way into the part. One of the most extraordinary moments for a designer is when the actor has the first fitting for his or her costume. You both then see if you have jointly arrived at the same character. Sometimes it can be very explosive. Your job is to give the actors physical encouragement for the role. To have the color, the fit, the movement, the fabric be appropriate. To provide places to put their keys or whatever, things like that. For example, I costumed Albert Finney in a film role for *Murder on the Ori-*

ent Express that required padding, make-up, slicked back hair, etc., to transform him into a very different character than the attractive young man he was playing at night on the London stage. I gave him a ring made from a bullet casing. He would knead the ring to remind himself that his character had a limp from a bullet wound. The right cuff links are something the audience may never be aware of, but it does help the actors, especially if they happen to be engraved with the character's initials.

Q When you did the revival of *Anything Goes* in New York, you designed something very different from the original production. How did that happen?

A Part of that was serendipity. Because Lincoln Center ran a repertory season and was not geared to long runs, there was a very low budget. When we started, I knew that whenever possible I had to take advantage of whatever already existed from other shows that I had worked on that season at the Beaumont. For *The Front Page,* I actually incorporated some things into the design that I knew would be useful for *Anything Goes.* In designing the lobby of *The Front Page* criminal court, I introduced a spectacular double staircase. I realized this would be perfect for the liner SS *American* in *Anything Goes.* It also provided *The Front Page* with a huge, cold lobby element that contrasted wonderfully with the warmth of the tobacco-stained press room adjacent to it. At the time Cole Porter was slightly out of vogue, so we passionately hoped that with *Anything Goes* we could create a sort of Valentine to his work that wouldn't have a musty nostalgic feel about it. Serve it up as a sort of cocktail. And I think having to do that show under those circumstances—on a thrust stage and not a conventional proscenium—made it more interesting. We got many compliments for the sound. It was strictly dumb luck, based on the need to find a place for the band. I put them on the upper deck because I wanted to get my money's worth out of that damn deck. It just happened that when I decided to put the continuation of the smokestack running vertically behind them, it worked as a perfect reflector for sound in that theater.

Q How did scene changes in that show affect your design?

A You find out what works for the director. In this case we did not want to see things coming in from outside the boat, and the set had to revolve so that the cabin units could become different interior and exterior places. To accomplish this, the bandstand couldn't have any supporting legs, so in fact we supported the bandstand wholly by the ship's rigging. The limitations really did force the character of the piece.

Q What is in your library?

A Everything. I am an obsessive collector of books. I can't get near a bookstore without coming out with an armful. Part of the fun of this work is the research, and it is wonderful to have so much of it at your fingertips. Your enthusiasm can frequently lead you rapidly on to something else. I have a lot of secondhand books with illustrations that might someday be an inspiration. I also have the same sort of problem with music stores. Music is probably as valuable, sometimes more so, than visual imagery, as an insight into the nature of something. Sometimes, when you are working on a musical, it is not just the music of that specific piece that you need available but, if possible, other pieces from that composer or period to help suck you into that world.

Q Aside from the gathering of necessary information, what is the importance of research to your work?

A For me it is as much musical as it is visual. Music is a way of sensually getting into the appropriate environment or mood for whatever the piece is. It is very hard to imagine imposing an idea on material, because I can only find my way into something through the things that seem to be evocative of it—the special character of the era, the colors, or whatever. I face this early on. I find it really hard and unsatisfying to come up with something based only on an idea, and not on a mood or the glimmering of an image. I need to know who will wear this outfit and why, where they are going, and what is particular about their time. It is essential to get completely in touch with the special nature of the piece. You try to assimilate the piece the best you can, so that it kind of creeps through you, and you try to make yourself be what the playwright or composer would be if he could be his own designer.

INTERVIEW WITH TERI FIGLIUZZI
DESIGN ASSOCIATE, KOHN PEDERSEN FOX ASSOCIATES PC

Teri Figliuzzi specializes in the design, selection, and specification of furniture and finishes. Her area of responsibility covers the development of floor patterns and wall and furniture treatments, and the design of textiles, carpets, and other items. Among her major projects have been a 50,000-square-foot residence and the Rockefeller Foundation offices in New York City, the Tokyo Europoert Hotel, and the United Overseas Bank Corporate Headquarters in Singapore. Her work has taken her to Greece, Italy, and England to select stone, to China to purchase art and antiques, and to Hong Kong to design custom carpets.

Q Would you describe the work you do?

A We are an international corporate interior architectural firm. One thing that is unique about our firm is that we have a special group of designers who concentrate on furniture and finishes. When I came to the firm eleven years ago, they hired me to concentrate on finishes. Most of the architects and designers draw on paper and build models when they design a three-dimensional space; I come up with the concepts for the color schemes, the materials used, and the patterning and surface treatments. Beyond the initial concept, there is a lot of follow-through—selecting actual materials, wherever they may be found, and finding the technical information we need. We work in teams here, so I am part of a group consisting of a design partner, project architect, project manager, and a varying number of architects and designers, depending on the size of the project. When we begin work in a space, it usually comes as a core without walls, except the window wall, and we design the ceilings, floors, partitions—everything.

Q Tell me a bit more about this team.

A There is a designer, sometimes several, who design the interior space. They give us a blocking diagram or partition plan of the proposed space with indications of possible styles and materials for the partitions, floors, etc., and I come in as the finishes and furniture specialist and contribute my ideas. We throw ideas back and forth and eventually evolve a design concept.

Q How do you present these concepts to the client?

A We produce drawings, bring in sample materials, sometimes do an elaborate concept collage which is almost a work of art itself. Usually we present our ideas by doing a loose arrangement of inspirational found objects, fabrics, a piece of carpet, or a picture from *Vogue* or some magazine—anything we can find that gives us and them the feeling of the skin of the project. We might go through three of these arrangements before the client decides which color combination is the one we should develop. As a design team, we want the client to get a general feeling for the concept without getting too specific. Then, a couple of weeks later, I come back with, for example, the actual bench fabric that was spawned from that ripped-out page of *Vogue.*

Then I have to make sure that these ideas function. Not only must it be beautiful and the look the client wants, but the marble, glass, fabrics, etc., all have different demands. They must be durable based on the projected usage, must meet the legal codes, and so on. Will the material be available in the quantity we need in the time necessary? Will it go on the walls properly? Will the stone we are looking at for the entry be too exposed to the elements and start chipping off in a few years?

Q Where do you find this information?

A Partially, I depend on my past experience. But once we are done with the concept collages, we have to get real, and I usually go to our library, which is 1,700 square feet of sample materials and catalogs and see what is available that fits all the needs. We have a full time librarian who makes sure that it is all up to date. I may have manufacturers' reps come in to show me the latest products—furniture, fabric, etc. We also subscribe to most of the design and trade magazines. But we are always looking for new products, suppliers, and craftspeople. There was a designer here who once chased a truck that had a great sign on its side for some decorative plaster work. She invited them to our offfice to do a presentation, and they have since done wonderful work for our projects.

Q How do you find the suppliers who have the appropriate furniture for your projects?

A We have a lot of information—catalogs, samples, and such in the library here, but to keep current I also look through magazines, both trade and popular. I keep tearsheet files.

Q Do you ever have the need for historical research?

A When we did the Equitable, it was a Jefferson-inspired interior. The whole firm was buying books, taking field trips to Virginia on weekends, to the Metropolitan Museum period rooms; we took pictures, bought postcards, more books. The funny thing was that in the end the color scheme for that project came from a postcard portraying a porcelain vase from the Asia Society. The architects and interior designers were, of course, more faithful to the period detail from all those historical sources.

Q Does almost every project have a point of departure as specific as that postcard?

A Yes. In the work that I do there usually is a scrap of metal, a piece of lichen, a postcard, a stone, or something that the ideas were based on—they usually don't just materialize independently.

Q Is your approach different when you begin a renovation than it is when you start from scratch in a new space?

A I can think of one project where, when we walked into the main building lobby, we saw the most gorgeous mosaic floor and, surrounding the elevator, there was elaborate bronze work. We were inspired by this, took a lot of photographs, and ended up using those colors and shapes. Unfortunately, we could not save the mosaics on our specific floor, as they were too damaged.

Q How do you approach a project that doesn't have a point of inspiration like that mosaic and bronze lobby?

A In our group of designers that do furniture and finishes, I hire painters, graphic artists, sculptors—people who are trained in many different ways. I came from a textile design background. So we are a diverse group and get our inspirations in many different ways and from each other. How a shadow falls on the walls of a building, an exhibit at the Metropolitan, a piece of saved broken glass; anything may contribute to a concept.

Q Do you keep a collection of potential visual sources?

A Yes we do; we always have. In the eighties, we used to spend a fair amount of time looking for sources of inspiration; now things have become more economical, and we must come up with ideas very quickly. So it is particularly helpful having things in our materials library.

Q Do you keep a personal collection?

A I keep files of book and magazine illustrations; exhibition pamphlets; exceptional graphics on invitations, postcards, or announcements; articles on artists; photographs—any visual image that may provide inspiration.

Q What do you look for when hiring someone to work on a project?

A When I interview people, I of course want to see their professional portfolio, but I also tell them to bring their "bag of goodies." I don't care what is in the collection, but you can tell what and how a person thinks by what they show you and how they talk about those objects. One woman came in with wonderful puppets. Everything she approached had the most creative and unique touch, and she was able to translate her style to our work with furniture and finishes.

I look for people who can think on their own, have an excellent eye for color and composition, are organized, have a passion for their specific art, and can communicate that passion in our designs.

Q How does a concept for a design get executed? As an example, let's use a custom-designed boardroom table.

A The designer or architect develops the concept into a drawing. With my expertise in finishes, I come in and give ideas about types of wood and stains. Then the drawing is detailed, so that the woodworker has a complete scaled plan of the structure, as well as the types and layouts of veneers, how the woods are matched, etc. We also work directly with the woodworker in determining the stains and final finishes.

Sometimes, with larger projects, we actually go to Italy to choose marble or visit a veneer warehouse to select a whole tree for the veneer. (The tree is known as a flitch when sliced for architectural veneer). On these jobs, the architectural team confers with me to decide how and in which materials the designs will be executed and, in that process of choices, samples are labeled and drawings are done for each wall, floor, and ceiling in the space.

Q When you approach a project with many decorative components, such as wall coverings, paint, wood, and marble surfaces, how do you keep track of all the different elements?

A All the drawings are coded and specifications written in great detail before they go to the general contractor, who will subcontract the work to plumbers, electricians, stone contractors, etc. Once the contractor gets those drawings, coordination continues between our firm and all subcontractors awarded portions of the project throughout the course of the project. Besides the general contractor, there is also a furniture manager.

We also use many consultants on every project. One is the specification writer. For all the finishes and materials attached to walls, ceilings, and floors, I give him a page of specifications that describe each finish and material in fine detail—the color, product name, fire code information—everything. Each spec page is matched with a code for that material on the drawings. He then compiles a book that covers everything from how to take down the existing walls to every detail about how to install every material I have specified, as well as all the details the architects have drawn. We have in the office a library of control samples for all those coded materials so that we can quickly deal with the shop drawings and samples submitted by the individual subcontractors who work for the general contractor.

Q What happens to the specification book and the samples when the job is completed?

A We do a documentation book which has a two-inch-square of every material along with the sheet of specifications. Then, if the client calls years later about replacing upholstery, we have the order numbers. Sometimes clients will want a copy of this book for their own files. While we never completely repeat a design, we may refer to these books when developing other projects.

Q Where do you find the technical information necessary to do the spec sheets?

A When I first started working in this business, I would accompany a senior designer to the woodworker, where, for example, we would pick the general wood, bring back samples, and then work with the woodwork-

er on the stains until we found what was wanted. At that time in my career, whenever I began a project I would have to spend hours calling suppliers, contractors, anyone who could fill in my information gaps. It has taken years of watching and noting how all these different designers and craftsman do this work to have a repertoire of information.

Of course, I use the library we have here, and I keep my own files, which are broken down into subjects of different materials. I have glossaries of marble and wood terms, photographs, technical information I have collected, things like that. However, building and fire codes change, and it is very important to stay current with that information.

Q How much does your work draw from your general observations and your daily experience?

A You really don't get many ideas sitting in an office all day. All of us here try to go to galleries and other installations. We are in contact with New York and other places and try to be aware of the styles around us. When we travel, we take pictures and then catalog them for future reference. We look at restaurant interiors and collect interesting menus, remember interesting shop windows, keep collections of things that are visually exciting. You don't get clients too interested by just going to their office and showing them little samples. You have to be excited—it is a whole image that has to be in your head that you try to convey.

Sometimes I do wonder. When we finish a project, you know that all the colors work together, and you hope that you have made all those finishes and textures feel as good as they can. To do that, did I really need to find that perfect postcard or do all that other research? Maybe not, but that's how I work.

INTERVIEW WITH WACLAW GODZIEMBA-MALISZEWSKI
ÉBÉNISTE, OWNER OF LONDON JOINERS

Waclaw (Willy) Godziemba-Maliszewski fell in love with woodworking while studying history in England, and then worked for a variety of cabinetmakers and *ébénistes* throughout Europe. At his shop in Pound Ridge, New York, he uses the formal techniques of classical cabinetmaking, gold leaf, *boulle* (marquetry), *jeux de fond* (geometric inlay), *frisage* (the joining of larger panels), *pietre* dure (stone-inlaid wood), and *chinoiserie,* as well as the rustic techniques found in French Provincial and Early American cabinetry. Mr. Godziemba-Maliszewski's projects include the conservation, restoration, and authentication of antiques, and the construction of custom contemporary furniture and interior woodwork.

Q Would you describe your work?

A I work in two general areas: fine woodworking—the building of new cabinets, boardroom tables, bankers' suites, and that sort of thing—and antique conservation and restoration. In both areas, I am known especially for my work with color and wood. I don't use stains, because a stain lies on the surface of the wood and does not penetrate the cells of the wood. It is basically a powdery oil. Therefore, light refraction is extremely limited, and you get a two-dimensional look. A walnut stain from the can will only give you a flat walnut color.

If, however, you color the wood with a chemical dye, such as one made with walnut hulls and cream of tartar, or other ingredients, it goes deeply into the wood and enhances the color potential of the wood rather than imparting its own color. It reacts with chemicals in the wood and, therefore, does not produce a solid color. The same technique applied to walnut lumber from different parts of the country will be different because of the different minerals and chemicals taken into the tree in various soil conditions. It is possible to achieve a desired color per specifications by use of certain chemicals derived from natural substances, such as cochineal (insect abdomen), alkanet root, cream of tartar, and potassium dichromate.

Q How did you learn this process of coloring wood?

A It is traditional. The fifteenth-century Italian artist Vasari wrote about these processes in his book on technique. In eighteenth-century Paris, in the artisan's quarter, people knew the techniques of the Low Countries' textile industry, which was renowned for its tapestries and lightfast colors. This knowledge influenced the *ébéniste*—the French term for a cabinetmaker, which really distinguishes between the cordon-bleu-chef cabinetmaker and the short-order-cook cabinetmaker.

The modern wood colorist, Georg Frank, working in Paris in the 1920s, collaborated with an *ébéniste* who had a commission to reproduce furniture from the Louvre for a middle-eastern emirate. The problem was how to color a piece to get the patina of ages into the wood. Frank studied the wood, the magnificent product of many years of sun fading the original chemical enhancement of the wood. He knew that when the furniture was made, knife grinders and tanners worked upriver, and he concluded that coming down into Paris via the river were large amounts of ferrous sulfate and tannic acid that had found their way into the wood during the finishing process. Frank had the idea that he would use ferrous sulfate and tannic acid as a base with other chemicals to treat the wood to get the look of the original furniture. He was perfectly successful.

Q How do you decide what dyes are needed to enhance a piece of wood?

A If it is a beautiful piece of wood, then it doesn't take much to get the wood to speak. But, then, not everyone can afford the finest woods in the world. These are scarce to begin with, and to use them for an architectural element that calls for lots of wood would be very difficult. But if you take poplar, which is less than the price of pine, but an extremely stable wood, and rub on to the wood first a 15-percent solution of water and cream of tartar, and then apply a solution of ferrous sulfate (white vinegar in which you have dissolved steel wool and brazilwood extract), it will chemically turn the poplar a rich leather brown that is very deep in the wood. Different cuts of poplar will react differently, and other chemicals, such as potassium dichromate, will turn the same board into faded English walnut.

Q If the process reacts differently in various conditions, do you have much control of the end result?

A Yes. You work first on sample boards to determine the exact proportions and steps in the process. When you buy a load of cherry, for example, with mixed parts of the tree, they will all show color a bit differently. Because these samples are from the actual wood lot, they also demonstrate to the customer the varying characteristics of wood. If the client picks a color on a two-by four-inch sample, and that piece happens to be quarter-sawn, it looks a certain way. So it is your duty to produce samples on all the types of wood that will be used on that job.

Q Is this technique applicable to larger commercial jobs?

A Yes. For the Roger Smith Winthrop Hotel in New York, the specifications were for stained wood. I did a series of samples using dye made with the cochineal insect, which is the base ingredient for many types of reds from golden reds to purple reds. The red is lightfast—the reason the British Redcoats' coats didn't fade is that they were dyed with cochineal. I was able to show that by dyeing, rather than staining, Honduran mahogany for the entire hotel lobby, we could achieve a multicolored wood with a deep color quality that glistened like a cat's eye stone—an effect called chatoyancy.

Q When the job is too large to do alone, how do you manage to get a crew to produce uniform coloring?

A Like a chef running up and down the range of a very large restaurant, tasting everybody's work. With something like French polish on large scale, you have to use some shortcuts. It is possible to bring it up purely in traditional methods and do an entire lobby or several floors of a hotel, but the cost would be prohibitive. The shortcuts make it affordable.

Q What was your training?

A I studied in several countries—England, Ireland, Italy. When I was young, I took Eurorail around different countries and worked in cabinet shops, boat yards. I practically swept floors for *ébénistes.* I worked for the Pietelli family of Florence. Their Italian version of French polish is superior, but the family would not tell me the process. In the artisan section of Florence, people pull down their blinds so that neighbors who are in the same business can't copy the techniques. The same families may have been neighbors for hundreds of years. Years after I had worked for the Pietellis, a young member of the family was hitchhiking around America, and he came to my shop in Pound Ridge, New York. He was penniless, and he wanted to go to Hawaii, so he worked for me for several weeks. I had him exactly where I wanted him—Hawaii demanded the Pietellis' technique.

Q Can you tell me, without betraying a confidence, what is the difference between French and Italian polish?

A The basic difference is the concentration of lac. Lac is the excretion of the lac beetle, different from what is commonly called shellac. Shellac is really a highly refined commercial product. I have "buttons" of lac from Kazakhstan. The French technique uses much more alcohol and a thinner concentration of lac. The Italians have a very thick mixture, which requires more mineral oil. The application process is more difficult, but the results are much better. There is a controversy about where French polishing started. Most furniture historians say it began in France, caught on in England in the early 1800s, and reached America by 1840. But there is evidence of lac finishes in fifteenth-century Italian work. So you wonder when it really did come in. Did it come to the West with Marco Polo? It was used in the Orient for hundreds of years before Polo.

Q You restore important pieces of furniture. How do you approach this work?

A If actual pieces are missing, I have the antique tools to replicate the missing part. And I use wood that is as old as the piece. I have a whole collection of antique veneers and woods of many species taken from other pieces of unsalvageable furniture. I don't believe in stripping the finish unless it is absolutely necessary. You must determine what the original finish is, to see if it can be built up on the existing finish.

Q How do you decide what that original finish was?

A There are several techniques. Experience usually tells you. But a drop of a certain chemical turns a different color for various finishes. Oil is the most difficult to determine—is it linseed oil, cottonseed, fish oil? You use a combination of chemistry and instinct. Again, it is a little like being a chef.

Q How do you authenticate an antique piece of furniture?

A First of all, there are dealers selling an amazing amount of English and French eighteenth-century furniture, much more than was ever made. Where are all of these pieces coming from? A lot of reproduction furniture was made in the nineteenth century. Beginning in the 1840s, the Industrial Revolution produced a wealthy middle class that desired the objects that the landed estates already had. Many pieces were made over again. They are old, but not authentic.

So how do you determine authenticity? There are many things that make the piece speak to you. Saw cuts tell. Lazy spots tell: underneath a lock you find areas where the reproductionist wasn't very diligent in covering the trail. At first you may have the impression that you are looking at an original. Great artists are producing reproductions as we speak. In some cases, the piece may be old, or it may be made out of old wood in shops that change and embellish certain features. They are so good at what they do that it is extremely hard to spot. You look for band-saw marks. But one of the first band-saws was working in Paris in the eighteenth century. So seeing those saw marks doesn't necessarily mean a piece is modern. You catch them in their lazy areas—inside a joint, under a hinge. I have actually seen intentional things underneath hinges—messages from forgers who want their work to be known.

Q How do you approach a commission for custom-designed woodwork?

A I have a collection of rare woods, and the piece may be designed around one of these. More often, the client comes in with drawings or just a verbal description. For example, a real estate developer's office, Peter Friedman Ltd., that deals primarily with European clients buying property in New York, wanted an Old World look for their office. This could be done in two ways—by using traditional woods and joints, which would have cost a lot of money, or by taking some commercial shortcuts, such as using carpathian elm veneer on a solid substrate, biscuit joints instead of mortise and tenon. We took that approach. I did the drawings and executed the work. This was basically a trust relationship.

In another case, a project for a hotel, the contract was as big as a book. The signing took three or four months and, before it was signed, the clients had a panel of various outside experts review every detail. This contractual process had little room for the artisan. It was very hard to deal with the process they set up and not just open cans of wood stain. However, I do understand that it can be very dangerous for a client to give the artisan free rein. In my experience, other than having a direct reference, the best thing to do is to look at the artisan's truck or workshop. If the place looks like a rats' nest, or if the cabinetmaker has a sloppy kit with only generic tools, that is the kind of work you are going to get.

Q How do you strike a balance between showing a client enough to be sure that they know what they are going to get and still having the artistic freedom to do more than a merely competent job?

A The customer has to rely to a great degree on the artisan's reputation. It is also the artisan's responsibility to educate the customer. I had one customer pick out wood for an apartment that overlooked a park. The color samples were done in the winter when there was no green foliage. When the actual work was done, in the summer, an enormous amount of green was going to be reflected into the room from the park and affect the color. It was my responsibility to tell the client what would happen. You also have to know how stable the color is. Wood will change as it matures, and take on a life of its own. I show customers samples of wood that has been dyed and aged.

Q Have you ever advised clients not to use specific woods?

A Yes. An old building heated by radiators can produce havoc with the pines. There are a lot of environmental factors. If there is a sun-drenched exposure—in modern architecture, there are a lot of windows—this can destroy not only antiques, but any sort of paneling. I then recommend that the windows be covered with a protective film.

Q What are your most important research sources?

A Specific books include Bruce Hoadley's *Understanding Wood* and Vasari's *Vasari on Technique.* A number of old books, such as the *London Guild on Joiners and Cabinetmakers,* would comprise a several years' apprenticeship in the very old methods of joinery in everything from a staircase to a church door. The antique restoration aspect of my business has given me the opportunity to see everything that can go wrong with wood construction and to apply antique finishing techniques to modern work. I have learned a lot from old artisans. One fellow told me a simple trick to remove a screw that has been in something for two or three hundred years: just heat it up with a soldering iron. When I heard that I thought, "Of course, you can break the bond without breaking the screw." Much of what one knows is just picking up things over the years.

INTERVIEW WITH DICK VENTRE
SCENIC ARTIST

Dick Ventre has painted scenery for Broadway productions and the Metropolitan Opera in New York, and he has been the master scenic artist on more than forty-five feature films. He has worked with directors Paul Mazursky, Sidney Lumet, and Mike Nichols, and designers Tony Walton, Philip Rosenberg, and Jane Musky. As master scenic artist, he was responsible for executing the final finishes for the films *Running on Empty, The Glass Menagerie, The Secret of My Success, The Prince of the City,* and *Death of a Salesman.*

Q What type of research do you use in the preparation of film scenery?

A Mostly photographic. The photos are supplied by the art director or I take them myself, and they generally have to do with adding to or duplicating an existing location. What happens is that the art director sees something he wants, and then my job is to realize the look of that place so that it can be filmed.

Q How would you describe the photographs you use?

A Everyone involved in preproduction takes photos. The location department, which is responsible for finding the locations necessary to the script, takes general pictures—panoramas that often become the master shot for a scene. Then the art department will zero in on particulars they think will be featured, such as specific walls, signs, a front stoop. As the scenic artist, I will take pictures similar to the other departments, but am often more concerned about the exposure or how the light strikes a surface, and I often need more detailed pictures. It isn't uncommon for me to drag out the 200 mm lens to get a shot of a gargoyle on the top of a building that will appear in an exterior location shot, if the sculpture is going to be seen outside the window when we do the studio interior of a room associated with the location. In that case, the gargoyle forms a visual link between the exterior establishing shot and the interior scene and, to make a convincing match, I need to know how that piece of cast concrete reflects the light. It isn't enough just to duplicate the proportions and color of a location piece; you have to understand the layers of a surface.

Q Do you take into account what the film camera will see when executing scenery?

A You have to, because there are always time and budget considerations. If you are sure it is going to be a long shot, your only concern is that the desired graphic impact is there. You don't need to dwell on particulars. But if it is a tight shot of an actor leaning against a door frame, then you must be religious about the character of the surfaces of that piece of architecture, because the camera will be unforgiving.

Q How do you approach a shot in which the location is set in a historical period? As an example, take *Angel Heart*, where New York City streets were made to look as they did in 1950.

A You have to understand how things were made then as opposed to now. Materials we use extensively today didn't exist. For example, vinyl letters have changed the look of signs. Everything then was done by hand, so each letter had a different individual structure. To get the look of a street of shop windows, you must understand the anatomy of those letters. To achieve the flat visual appearence of something is not enough for the camera. It is being lit a specific way and filmed from different angles; the reality won't hold up if, in the process of creating the scenery, the surface doesn't reflect light in the same way as the actual material.

Q How do you begin the process of creating believable scenery?

A The trick to camera-perfect faux surfaces is to understand the actual materials so thoroughly that you always remember the real surface as you go through the paint process. If you are reproducing marble for instance, and one of the steps in the process leaves visible brush marks, you will probably be in trouble. Brush marks don't exist in the real world of marble. You can use that brush, but it must be in tune with the character of marble.

Q How are those steps in a technique determined?

A A lot has to do with how much will be seen on camera, and how much time you have to accomplish the shot. An example where we had the time and demand for detail is a scene for *The Secret of My Success,* in which marble in a location elevator had to be duplicated for a studio close-up shot. In the scene, we see Michael J. Fox get into the real elevator, and then change clothes between floors. Of course, the cameras didn't fit in the real elevator. I found the technique for reproducing the marble by studying the elevator walls to understand the depth and character of the veining, the scale of the fractures, the color. I took a lot of pictures from as many angles as possible, and I realized we couldn't go with a standard paint technique, because the surface was so reflective that there had to be something actually dimensional under the gloss for it to read properly. I could then decide on the materials and process—a spackle bas-relief layer that built the character of the real marble, under a two-part polymer coating.

Q How do you decide which materials to use in fabricating scenic surfaces?

A Most choices are based on my experience with various materials—how their physical properties respond to the different demands of workability and drying time, whether it will be used on an outside location or in the studio. I keep a file of materials research consisting of instruction and data sheets of products I have encountered on jobs or while perusing hardware and art supply stores. File boxes that go back for years are trucked from movie to movie. You must have a craftsman's command of the right materials for the job. Those requirements often include being able to combine a look of complete permanence with the ability to restore the location to its original state. So having a wide range of information is vital.

Q What research does the art director provide?

A Information may be only a verbal description or as specific as photos and detailed scaled drafting. For example, in *Ghostbusters,* New York's Central Park West had to open and swallow a police car. So four or five feet of archaeological strata of asphalt, concrete, rubble, dirt, and pipes had to be recreated. After taking a trip to a Con Edison excavation site with cameras, we received scaled section and front-view draftings, as well as photographs from the art department.

Q What type of color information does the designer provide?

A Often, the accuracy of color print film is suspect, so we are given paint chips, pieces of tin roofs, or bricks from the location. In other situations, it may be Pantone color swatches or color samples mixed on the location site. I always try to visit the location myself.

Q What research do you use when doing a studio set for a locale that cannot be visited by the production staff?

A My library has a general selection of local, national, international, and period information, books that show great paintings, great sites around the world. Although I probably won't be duplicating a specific location, the pictures and paintings give me an overview of the location. Books on Mexico or the Southwest, for example, give me an insight into how adobe is constructed, how light falls on the walls, how things in the place weather, and thus how duplicating the walls should be approached. Sometimes I can even find information about the tools that were used. The art director may give me a photo or drawing of a specific piece of sculpture he wants reproduced. If I have additional information on other statues on that period and place, then the artist who executes that sculpture has a more complete idea of what needs to be done. Research is almost like

what a long-shot is to a close-up. Some research gives the general picture, and other information defines the details.

Q How do you organize your research?

A I usually assemble composite research boards with photos and pieces of actual material. Accompanying those boards may be acetate overlays that indicate color, detail drawings, and scale notations that were made on site. All of this is used back in the studio to determine how things need to be fine-tuned to make the studio set match the location. What has worked well during a film is to keep folders with individual photos, taped together panorama shots, sketches, and draftings in boxes for each set, so that they can be pulled out at a moment's notice. This reference is particularly useful in the case of reshoots because then I have not just photos but information about techniques and materials. I keep some of these folders in my permanent files. Sometimes you return in subsequent films to past locations or remember sets that have the right look for future jobs.

Often, photos of past scenic reproductions are actually preferable to photos of the real thing. The needs of the camera have already been satisfied. It refreshes your understanding of what the film does and what the camera focus does, and helps you determine what is important and what is not critical.

Q Besides recording information, does your photography of research affect your work in preparing scenery to be filmed?

A When I am behind a camera and photographing a location for surface detail, it is as if I am sitting inside the camera and that visual information is being absorbed into me as well as the film. The photo that I take is not only a picture, but is like putting that first-hand experience on file. When I need to refresh that experience, I have the photo to remind me or to pass on to others on the project.

INTERVIEW WITH TAREK NAGA
ARCHITECT

Tarek Naga, currently working in Venice, California, has designed or been a principal architect for private residences, academic facilities, office buildings, libraries, hotels, and mixed-use developments in the United States, Egypt, and Saudi Arabia. Among the projects with which he has been involved are the United States Embassy in Cairo, the Red Sea Villas and Hotel in Hurghada, Egypt, the Oceanside Amphitheater in Oceanside, California, and the Centrum Tower in Worcester, Massachusetts. He served as senior project architect for the renovation and expansion of the Egyptian Museum in Cairo. Mr. Naga also teaches at Art Center College of Design in Pasadena, California.

Q What are your responsibilities as an architect?

A I am responsible to the client and to the site, if you will. There's a certain direct relationship between the architect and the site developed during the process, which is inseparable from the relationship with the client and the program, and society at large.

Q What do you mean by responsibility to the building site?

A I mean that forces are impacting the site. The natural conditions of the place—the wind, the social setting—which are specific only to that site. All these layers must be interwoven.

Q How do you go about collecting the information about the site?

A I visit the site, live in it, and develop a very intimate relationship with it. I make observations each time I visit the site, and I take a lot of photographs. Sometimes when I come back and try to match the memory and the photographs, they don't correspond.

Q Could you give an example?

A A residential design in the desert outside Cairo, within sight of the pyramids, which will be part of a large development. This is a unique situation, because the site started out as empty desert but is metamorphosing constantly, with the addition of ponds, plantings, and roads. Photographs of the site revealed that the layering of the intense yellow and reddish sand at the site is different from the whitish sand in the distance. I didn't see that when I first walked there. I was looking for something else. Our perceptions are affected by a mental agenda for certain things, and sometimes you overlook other things. When I sat on top of that hill and looked around me, it was an absolute desert, and the piece I first had in mind would actually sit in a very different place, green with plantings. But at a distance the desert is still there, so it will not be severed from the original setting.

Q When beginning this project, you saw a desert and took photographs of that site; what other information did you need to design the building?

A I started the process with interviews with the clients, a husband and a wife, to talk about what the house meant to each of them. How many rooms did they want? What did the kids need? How did they feel about the ever-present desert sun? Using this information I came up with a design program created from a sense of what the house means to them, individually and together. The whole notion would be very different if we were building in a densely populated urban setting.

Q Are there times when the site dominates the design?

A Another project was right on the water, the Red Sea, with the site literally screaming to be untouched, "I don't want anybody to build here. Period." So, do you say, "Okay, I can't touch it"? If I do that, the client will have another architect. But throughout the whole process that sense of the site was very present in my mind. The architecture that came at the end reflected that it was nomadically visiting the site because it is really only there temporarily. It wasn't temporary or cheap construction, but it almost excused itself, as if it was touching the site without really digging in, without settling in. It is impossible to say how you go about researching that. It's really almost a psychological set of observations. There's a lot of material written about genius loci. A lot of it is based on the context and stylistic historical information that are part of the site. For instance, in Florence all those churches are part of the genius loci. But there is other necessary information that cannot be described by preexisting architectural conditions.

Q Building materials are very important to you. How do you approach them?

A I try as much as possible not to have a set of preconceived notions. We all fall in love with certain textures and materials. I resist that, so that architectural condition dictates the materials. The materials are important, but are really driven by the process; they do not drive the process.

Q How did you decide on the materials for the Red Sea project?

A There was the beautiful white sand, blue-green water, and in the background the incredibly red, almost moonscape mountains—huge rocks. It was a combination of the very harsh and very serene and we were caught in between. The building was all designed in galvanized metal. It hovers. It floats. It reflects light. Visually and structurally, you can work with metal and make it look like it's floating. If I had used masonry or concrete or any material of that sort of plasticity, it would have sat heavily on the site. The structural demands of the materials would have made visual demands, and evoked a sense of being rooted in the site. And that's the exact opposite of what I was trying to do.

Q As you are looking for the right material for a design, what sources do you use?

A I find looking through the traditional catalogs and books and all is limiting because the materials are presented to you as a package. So I try to mentally reinvent materials every time I do a project. The set of circumstances of a site and the program dictate the role of the materials. In the desert project, I thought that because the site was surrounded by sand, that thin slabs of sandstone might clad the building. Cut into very thin veneer slabs, it becomes an artificial skin. This way it would be possible to visually sculpt—to bend and follow the contours of the architecture as if the whole piece were carved out of stone. Stone is a very dignified material and it ages beautifully. The older it gets, the more powerful it becomes. Sandstone had the possibility of disappearing at first because everything on the site seemed to be like sandstone. But when the whole site is covered with green, will the building recover part of that memory of the land covered with sand, and reflect the surrounding hills? That question is directly related to the process of metamorphosis that the whole site will continue to experience.

Q If you chose stone veneer, how would this affect the structural aspect of the house?

A The stone would literally be hung, suspended with anchors, on the building. The structure would be cast concrete, so you would have, in the concrete, steel

anchors that will become hooks—the same way you construct a curtain wall on a skyscraper. The weight of a stone facade is so great that the pieces are hung independently per floor, so they are manageable. And this would be the same concept, but because it is going on very unusual shapes and planes, it requires innovative detailing and some interesting structural techniques.

Q So that surface treatment dictates the structure?

A Yes. And the technique can be double-used. Instead of the stone hanging directly against the concrete, if the surfaces are separated, air pockets are created between the concrete surface and the stone slabs. The stone and concrete touch at points. But there remains an air gap with some holes in it to circulate the air, and this thin layer of air is natural insulation from the harsh sun, so the heat never penetrates to the inner structure because the air constantly is circulating. So the use of cladding solves another problem, which is the desert heat.

Q We've been talking primarily about residential projects. How do you approach a commercial project?

A It's identical. It's all about behavior patterns and aspects of the site.

Q But if you're designing an office building, it's hard to question everyone who uses the space in the way that you spoke to the two residential clients.

A If the building is something like a museum and the end user is a public citizen, then I can think how I would use the space. When the client is a builder or developer and the end user is personally unknown, it is more problematic because the architect is left to invent the individual. We really have to play the roles ourselves. If I work in this environment, what would I do? How would I behave? What if I were a doctor in this hospital? You have to wear many hats. But the more specific your client, the more accurate your programming.

Q How do you respond to a list of demands from a client?

A You write it down and give it back to them. "That's what you said, and that's what I think." "That's what I heard you say. And that's what you mean, but I have a suggestion." You recommend what would fit in with their needs. And then you suggest other things.

Q What do you first show your clients?

A Sketches, drawings, models. I never really push the design process too far before they see the three-dimensional aspects of the space because certain things look puzzling when they only see drafted plans. A model is always a vital part of the design and presentation process. Then I give them samples throughout the whole process.

Q Once you have arrived at an approved design, it is translated into construction drawings. What information do you give the people who are building the project?

A A set of construction documents, which are very difficult to read. Architects do their best to translate their ideas into graphic drawings, but it is impossible to document the entirety of a three-dimensional structure, no matter what you do. You detail it to death, but no matter how many drawings you have, there are always areas that are impossible to cover. So, in most cases, I prefer to build a large-scale model to aid the builder. They can turn it around and look under a model, and then they can pinpoint the problem and look at the drawings. It is important to help the builder understand the process. I document for them, as much as possible, the process and the ideas behind the structure. Often, by the time you give the builder a set of construction drawings, the conceptual aspect behind the project is completely removed. It helps to show some of the early material—the first photographs of the desert, for example.

Q What information do you give an interior designer?

A Everything, from the very first sketch. I take them through the entire birth process, instead of just giving them a set of drawings and saying, "Here it is, that's the space, go for it." To be able to really understand what they see when they are looking at various spaces and surface textures, I think they have to understand how it came about. I show them the first set of photographs, materials that have been chosen, and those that have been discarded, so they will understand the evolution of the piece.

Q How do you organize your project files of materials and processes?

A I file them by project, not by materials, because the application of this material within a project becomes different from just the index of stone. So you have to cross-reference how this stone behaved on this project. I also go back and document the project, after having built it, to see how well it has held up and how it has behaved, because there are surprises. You want to see how the clients used it, how it behaved on the site. Did it really do what you thought it would? You review the various applications in terms of the site. If you are building in Boston, the behavior of sandstone is not the same as in Cairo.

Q Do you keep a file of how the project evolves from beginning to end?

A While working on a design, I keep all the old models and sketches around. It is amazing how often you are looking for an answer, and the answer is somewhere in a very old sketch where you've actually explored that very same notion from a very different point of view. The solution is there, right in front of you. You almost did it before but you discarded it, but for different reasons.

Q What is the importance of research to your development as an architect?

A It is really the method of inquiry that's more important. Every time you start a new project, you have to think of it as the first one ever built. You start almost from scratch, asking all the simple, almost irrelevant questions. You have to learn to ask the right questions, and you are always looking for clues to the answers. Being an architect is also a little like being an actor—you are the doctor today if you are building a hospital. It is like living a role. Once you succeed in entering the role, you ask yourself, "Do I have to design a casino the way they do in Vegas?" It then has to be architecturally investigated and developed with all seriousness.

INTERVIEW WITH MARTIN CHARLOT
MURALIST, PAINTER, ILLUSTRATOR

Martin Charlot has spent most of his career in Hawaii; he currently lives in California. His works are usually site-specific commissions executed in oil, fresco, acrylic, ceramic tile, relief porcelain, or etched glass, and they vary widely in scale and subject. His clients include Consolidated Theaters, McDonald's Corporation, Westin Maui Hotel, Dillingham Corporation, and the State of Hawaii. Mr. Charlot is the author and/or illustrator of eight books. He studied with Ansel Adams, and apprenticed with his father, Jean Charlot.

Q Tell us something about your work.

A When you are a muralist, you are always looking for walls. I've done murals for private residences, prisons, high schools, police stations—wherever there's a wall and someone wanted a picture. Most of my murals are public. I am usually working with people who have never worked with an artist before. I don't want to spring things on them, so I try to have them follow me along the process. Many artists resent having the client look over their shoulder, but I've found that communication with the people the mural is for doesn't hold me back. It gives me freedom, in that trying to include them actually makes the mural richer than if it all came from me.

Q How much information do you get from your client before you begin a project?

A As much as I can, because murals are for an audience, and I want to find out who this audience is. I talk to as many people as possible. If you are doing a state or city job, there is usually a committee. For a high school, for example, the committee is made up of people who work at the school, perhaps students, people from the community, some hired experts. Even beyond that I want to get out into the community and get a feel for the place. I want to sponge up every bit of information.

Q How do you do that?

A It depends on the subject matter. If the subject matter is in our own time, I cruise around the neighborhoods, around the places that people frequent. I take lots of photographs. Make sketches. Soak up as many feelings about the community as possible. I also do drawings to present to the committee for them to approve or disapprove, so they can make choices.

Once I did a mural for a prison in Kauai, Hawaii, where there also is a place called the Alakai Swamp, a refuge for birds. I thought this was a good subject for the prison because it was very beautiful and because the idea of refuge as sanctuary was meaningful to the situation. So for the presentation I painted rare Hawaiian birds flying through the Alakai Swamp, and around each bird I put a circular rainbow.

The prisoners and everybody on the committee looked at the presentation carefully, and they oohed and they aahed. Just as I thought it was all approved, one of the prisoners said, "We really like it. Can you do one thing for us? Can you not have the rainbows go all around the birds? Can each of the rainbows have an opening?" Having the rainbows encircling the birds was like a prison, something I never thought of. Listening to them, I became aware of the sensibility that was needed for the mural.

Q Do you have a standard form of presentation or does it change with each client?

A It changes. Usually, I first do rough little sketches. I try to leave things pretty open at the beginning, so I can get input. From experience I know you can't expect people who haven't worked with artists to translate a rough sketch into a finished product. So you really have to show them something that is quite finished. For example, I was commissioned to do a painting, and on the canvas I sketched out every detail. The group looked at it for the longest time while I explained what the colors were going to be. After half an hour, the first question was, "Is there going to be color or are you going to leave the canvas empty like this?" They could not translate my verbal explanation of color onto the line drawing.

Q What sort of visual information do you receive from a client?

A If it is a historical subject, I usually request photographs. If I am doing a community mural, I look for a photographic collection in the local library; if there is none, I'll ask if somebody has a personal cache of photographs. Usually, though, I have to research the images myself.

Q What sources do you use?

A For a historical piece, I go to every book I can find about the subject in libraries, archives, private homes, bookstores. I study the subject and how other artists have approached it in the past. I'm currently doing a mural for a restaurant on a Western subject. I have looked at all of the Western art and at every photo I can find and have visited four different museums in Los Angeles. I've been to every bookstore and to the libraries. I grab the books and photocopy them, or photograph them on the copy stand, and build a file of visual images for each subject in the mural.

Q When you look at work that other artists have done on a topic, does it affect your style?

A Usually it frees me. Because when you find that other people have approached something in a certain way, then you are free from having to go in that direction yourself, and you can find your own way.

My father, Jean Charlot, was a muralist very much in the cubist style; he taught Diego Rivera to do frescoes. When I was growing up, I'd go through my father's art books, and it was Rubens and artists of that period who really turned me on.

Q Do you have a certain process you use when you first approach a mural?

A I try to vary it to keep it interesting for myself. If I nail it down completely at the beginning, I don't have the opportunity to come up with new ideas during the process of actually making it. So I leave little empty spaces. I don't have an idea now for that corner, but I will later. You have to trust that the ideas will come; you don't have to have everything all worked out at the beginning.

Q Would you detail the preparation you did for a specific mural?

A I did a mural called *Stars in Paradise* for a theater in Hawaii. I flew to L.A. to research it. I went to the library of the Academy of Motion Picture Arts and Sciences, found a list of movie stars who were connected with Hawaii, and researched every visual I could about those artists. I wanted to have photos that would work together as a composition. A lot of the figures were drawn from their own publicity photos. I did Tom Selleck from life, but portrayed him with his arms at his side. When he saw it, he said, "No, no, I really..." Any time someone points a camera at Tom Selleck, he puts his hands on his hips, so I redid his picture to make him happy.

I like to use the mural expanse as one composition rather than treating it as a collage of different locations. So I decided to locate it in old Waikiki and place the stars in a composite of buildings from that area. I went to Waikiki and photographed the floors, the stairways, the old theaters, the hotels—all that distinctive 1920s and 1930s architecture—and then created a space, and set my people within the space. Doing that mural I thought, "Gee, this isn't going to be my style. This isn't going to be my picture. It is really going to be their picture, with their faces." Although I thought I was losing myself and my style to the subject, the result still came out looking like a painting I had done.

Q How do you get ideas for a project?

A It really depends on the situation. For instance, in Hawaii, everybody wanted the same thing: a pastiche of all of the races together, loving each other. Happiness. Well, that's kind of a cliché, so I try to steer clients towards other, more interesting ideas. But then I got the commission for a telephone book cover. Because of those past experiences, I knew what people in Hawaii wanted, so I did a beautiful landscape with all the different races at a luau.

In *Fruits of the Spirit,* a mural that was painted in a public place for a large art gallery, I knew that by the time the painting was finished, thousands of passers-by would have watched me work. So I chose a subject I believed everyone could relate to—flying dreams and children at play. In these dreams children are portrayed flying and swimming through the lush landscape of Hawaii. I did six or seven quick, playful paintings, sketches of all those fantasy things I wanted to do as a kid—zooming through trees and so forth. Some things worked and other things didn't. When I had a pretty good idea of what poses I wanted, I photographed children jumping on trampolines; I photographed my son swimming in a local stream. This gave me details I could never make up in my own mind: hair flowing in the air, water splashing, clothes rippling in the wind—all details that make the painting richer. But everything grew out of those original sketch paintings.

Q How do you translate all these researched images to the canvas?

A I draw directly on the canvas from models or project a photo or a sketch on the canvas. With a slide projector I can juggle the images around or change the scale to see what works. The classical way of squaring the drawing and the canvas and enlarging it by hand also works really well. (In this method a grid is laid over the preliminary artwork, and a corresponding grid is drawn on the canvas—for example, one square inch on the drawing will equal one square foot on the canvas. The smaller-scale line drawing is transposed to full scale by transferring where the lines intersect the small grid to the grid on the canvas.)

Q Do you keep research from past projects?

A Sure. I have files of photocopies on different subjects: slides of water, rocks—so many rocks that I never need to paint the generic rock. One picture of a flower from a certain angle has found its way into probably six projects. I also keep files of ideas. There are ideas you have for a project that you want to do but that don't quite work out for that piece, but you may be able to apply them to something else. Research for an American Indian mural I am currently working on will end up in my files. It has been very hard to find the necessary images; most of the photos done in the 1800s are very stiff, people looking straight at the camera or in profile. It took me a week of research just to find the right photo of a face in three-quarters view. In this face was the nobility and pain of someone who had survived the terrible history of war and near genocide.

Q Once you find the right historical research, how do you combine the sources to make a scene that lives on the canvas?

A The people I paint need to look relaxed—as if they are really living in the space they occupy on the canvas. It is important for me to determine the feeling the painting will have before I begin. When looking at all the books and picture files, I start to juxtapose certain photographs of faces, people, horses, and other impressions. In the 1950s, my father was doing a mural about the Hopi Indians, so I spent time as a child around that tribe. At that time, the villages and the people looked exactly the same as these research photographs taken in the 1880s. Having been there as a child, playing with Hopi children and getting to know the families, gave me a memory that made the research familiar.

Q How are you affected by the location of your murals?

A That brings up another sort of research very important to my work—experiencing the space and surface I am to paint. Whenever possible, I walk around that space. Feel what it is like to approach that wall from every possible angle. Get a real three-dimensional image in my head. Go and touch the wall, make friends with it. I am going to be caressing it for maybe a year or two. So there is going to be kind of a love affair here. I look at

the architecture of the space—where the doors are. It tells me where lines should go, how the eye should be led. I take into account the actual perspective of the room, the lighting.

Q How do you work with architects?

A Architects are usually very suspicious of muralists. They are afraid that you will impose something detrimental to the space they worked on so hard. You often feel as if you are in enemy territory. So I try to provide everything I can—scale drawings, models of the mural in the space, sight lines—to assure them I will be sensitive to their work and will try to incorporate the movement of their building into the movement of the mural.

Q How do you deal with the technical problems of exterior installations?

A It is important to use exterior media whenever possible. I like painting with glazes on tiles, relief ceramic work—anything other than paint, because the sun is just too hard on paint. The glazes of course are different colors after they are fired than when you apply them. Fresco, another durable medium, is the same. When you do a fresco, you are basically painting on lime mortar, which is very gray. You paint your colors on the wet gray mortar, and it takes up to two years for the colors to become fully brilliant in the dry white mortar. You learn to deal with this.

Q Is your work affected by sources other than visual ones?

A Sometimes. When I was painting a portrait of Hawaii's King Kamehameha IV, I researched the period and found a great picture of him. With the photo was a letter written by the photographer that played in my mind the whole time I worked on the piece. It told a story of a man in tattered clothing who sat for a photo portrait. The photographer, an American, asked where he worked. He said, at the palace. The photographer said that he really wanted to photograph the king, and the man said he could help, and of course he came back later that day dressed as the king. It gave me a sense of who the king was—he dressed regularly as a commoner and had a mischievous Hawaiian sense of play in dealing with outsiders.

Q How do you research portraiture?

A I like to do portraits from life but if that is not possible, I work from photographs—preferably ones I take myself. Even if I am working from life, I like to go to the sitter's home and photograph objects that are important. Some will appear in the painting, some won't. Portraits can be difficult if clients have ideas of themselves that differ from how you see them.

Q Aside from gathering necessary background and source information, what do you think is the importance of research to an artist?

A It enriches the piece. If you think everything that is needed is within you, you are cutting off your nose. All the lives gone before, the history of a community, bring strength. I always liked the sense of drama, the sense of time and place, of people reacting to each other within the image. All of those things seem to be good emotional colors to use for art.

INTERVIEW WITH MEGAN MEADE
RESOURCE LIBRARIAN/PROJECT ASSISTANT, BUTLER ROGERS BASKETT

Overseeing the interiors and architectural libraries, Ms. Meade selects, updates and classifies applicable information; she maintains the slide and photo library; organizes manufacturer presentations to the firm, and conducts specific project-related research. Her responsibilities also include pricing, selecting, and assembling materials for projects and presentations. (When Ms. Meade was interviewed, she was employed by Kohn Pederson Fox Interior Architects, so all specific examples in this conversation refer to that firm.)

Q Would you describe the work you do?

A I oversee the library at Kohn Pederson Fox Interior Architects in New York City, which means that I organize, update, and augment the architecture and design research collection. In order to do this, I meet with manufacturers and representatives who show me new products. I also set up presentations for the firm so that everyone can learn about the products that are available as well as issues that may affect their design choices, such as endangered vs. renewable woods. Sometimes I am also called upon to help research materials and sources for the selection of furniture and finishes on design projects.

Q How do you go about researching materials?

A It depends on the job. For example, for the Bronx District Attorney's new offices, a government job, we were given a very specific list of products and manufacturers who are on contract to work with New York City. I collected catalogs or samples of all the materials specified in their contract. Then, if we weren't pleased with those colors or textures, we found the products similar in quality and price, which we preferred for aesthetic values.

We also introduced materials that were not on their list. For example, we suggested quarry tile in a lobby area subjected to high traffic and consequent abuse. The quarry tile came up when the design partner on the project, Judy Swanson, presented me with a piece of brick from our materials library made of cement and flecks of colored stone. She wanted a rough-hewn material for the high traffic areas, but the brick was too heavy to use for an interior wall surface. After contacting various tile distributors and seeing many samples, we decided that quarry tile was the best solution.

Q Was most of the information necessary to find these materials in your library?

A Well, yes and no. If the samples and catalogs were not here, all the information I needed was only a phone call away. We have one of the bigger in-house libraries in New York City, but of course we don't have the room to keep everything. I have a computer Rolodex system with the names and numbers of manufacturers, representatives, and distributors we work with. And we have source books: *Sweet's Catalogs,* the *Thomas Register,* and the *Interior Designers' Handbook.* Most manufacturers in those listings will send samples by next day air if they know they are in contention for a project.

Q What else is in the library?

A Catalogs for everything from manufacturers of hardware to companies that make lighting fixtures, furniture, and accessories; the list goes on and on. A great deal of space is dedicated to physical samples. Large bulky things, like pieces of wood, are stored on rolling carts. Marble and stone samples are kept on fixed metal shelving. We have shelves and shelves of fabric. We also have catalogs with complete information about these materials, so even if we have only one piece of Cold Springs granite, we can see what other types are available.

Q Besides catalogs and samples, what else?

A We have files of literature on products for which we have no catalog. We have "cut files" filled mainly with pictures of the furniture we use for presentations. We have fabric price lists.

One section of the library was a result of the Green Committee. We collected information about recycled construction materials and products that were environmentally sound with fewer VOCs (volatile organic compounds), lists of endangered woods, energy-efficient lighting, information about ergonomics, source books such as the American Institute of Architects' *Environmental Resource Guide,* and anything conducive to green design.

The firm has a collection of art and architecture books on specific architects, places, and periods; on craft furniture, styles of ornament, and office design. We subscribe to many trade and related magazines. The staff refers to them frequently for everything from new products and finishes to keeping tabs on the competition.

Another area of the library contains files on artwork, art consultants, and craft artists. The *Avery Index to Architectural Periodicals* allows you to look up articles on specific topics and projects. And of course we have a section where all the building codes and graphic standards are kept. These must constantly be updated to keep up with new regulations. An extension of the library is a large collection of slides and photographs of the firm's work, used for purposes of marketing as well as reference.

Q How do you organize the material in this library?

A The catalogs are organized first by product category. In one section are architectural product binders, such as acoustical ceiling tile, access flooring, and hardware. I labeled each of these catalogs with a number that relates to the product; for example, 08700 is hardware, and three letters under that number represent the first three letters of the manufacture's name. That way I can keep all the hardware catalogs alphabetically. The numbers come from the master format put out by the CSI (Construction Specifications Institute). When specifications go out on a specific job, they are usually based on that numbering system. I organize the information in my loose files by the CSI number. *Sweet's Catalog* also roughly adheres to that system.

I keep catalogs for furniture, lighting, and accessories in a different area. These I have arranged by style and given my own color coding system. Furniture, for example, is broken down into categories: contract, decorative, traditional, and outdoor furniture. And then each binder is given a colored strip according to which section it belongs in.

Loose samples are kept on rolling carts or fixed shelving and are organized by type, species, or style. For example, wood is grouped into cherry, maple, and so on. Our large collection of wool carpet samples are organized by color, separately from nylon carpet. Small fabric samples are kept in plastic boxes cataloged by manufacturer, and larger samples are organized by color and kept on adjacent shelves.

Q What about photographs?

A We have some photographs of heavier materials like stone and marble for convenience of presentation. Sometimes we keep a photo record of presentations we have done for certain projects.

Q Do you keep files of suppliers and craftspeople?

A We have a file filled with slides, photos, and resumes of craft artists who design furniture, glass, metalwork, and mosaics. We have a file of architectural woodworkers. I consult either a catalog or my computerized Rolodex for suppliers. The designers also have their own files, sources, and contacts.

Q What are the research demands on your library when a design team begins a project?

A The designers reference as many sources as they need. For instance, if they need to locate a certain type of movable partition and don't find the information on the catalog shelf, they then look at *Sweet's.* I'm not necessarily asked to supply lots of general research, but someone may ask me for a certain building code, or to help find information on metalwork or spiral staircases. Sometimes a designer has an idea and can't locate the necessary specific material or information; I research it or help steer the designer in the right direction. By working together and pooling our resources, designers come up with an idea, look at different materials, and maybe find something that they didn't even know they were looking for.

Q What other sources do you use?

A What is dictated by the job. There may be a technical aspect for which we need an outside consultant—a mechanical engineer or lighting consultant, for example. Sometimes we may want to use a particular fabric that we have seen, but change it to a different scale and color. In that case, we might work with the manufacturer to develop just the right look for our project.

There are endless sources outside our office, from the New York Public Library to the American Institute of Architects' library in Washington, an oriental rug showroom, or an art exhibition.

Q What do you think are the most important research materials in a design firm?

A The most important thing is probably to have a good Rolodex and contacts, so that if what you want is not in house, you can get samples and information quickly. The fax, the telephone, and next day air are indispensable. Computers are critical: not only can they help you keep track of your inventory, but more and more manufacturers are including discs or CDs with their catalogs, so you can look up details and even print them out. *Sweet's Search,* a CD-ROM, lets you conduct your search in the computer right at your desk. It's the wave of the future.

INTERVIEW WITH STUART R. MORRIS
PROGRAM MANAGER/ARCHITECT, BOVIS

Stuart R. Morris has been involved in the construction and design for a range of commercial, residential, academic, medical, and recreational projects. He deals with both new construction and renovation; his assignments include the largest theme park in Europe, a 140,000-square-foot commercial office building in New York City, and the renewal program for an Ivy League university. In the course of these projects he has been responsible for coordinating international contracts, supervising and training construction teams, design development, bid documents, coordinating construction programs, and establishing the Bovis Internet web site.

Q Would you describe your work as a program manager for an international program and construction management company?

A I have been involved in everything from commercial office buildings to theme parks, hospitals, universities, and other institutional projects. We are the link between the owner and architect in construction projects. With them, we develop the building values, costs, and schedules, and recommend materials.

Q What is your primary responsibility on a project?

A Our information serves as a guide to the construction, and this means taking into account all those factors that affect design and construction choices—climate conditions, environment, accessibility, site conditions, market factors. The architect and the client make the final decision, but the creative process grows much easier in a climate of factual, well-organized information.

Q When do you begin to work with the client?

A Sometimes we are hired by an owner in the early planning stages, and then we may recommend architects. Sometimes we come into a project after the planning stage to manage the construction; we have been hired to evaluate an ongoing construction project, and we have been brought in at the end of construction to tie up loose ends and do the "post-mortem" evaluation—why a project was successful or unsuccessful.

Q What type of information do you get from the client when you begin a project?

A We start with an overview. For example, if a client has a building program with 200,000 square feet, a percentage will be retail, a percentage will be parking, and a percentage will be residential. We assign a cost-per-square-foot value based on the percentage of floor area ratios. We have to know what is going to happen in that building before we can start.

Very often the information necessary to determine the floor area ratios (and subsequently the cost per square foot) is gained from a historical data base of similar facilities, built under similar conditions, with similar finishes. In addition, there are three factors that drive projects: scope (what is the level of material or type of finish?), schedule (how long will the project take?), cost (how much does the client want to spend?). If the budget is high, you can do things in more expensive materials or in a shorter time frame.

Q Where does the function of the building fit into this scheme?

A The function is the overall determinate factor for the scope, schedule, and cost. A "Class A" office building offers a number of amenities and higher levels of finish with more expensive materials and perhaps a sophisticated communications system. The clients define their requirements, and it is our job, along with the architects, to maximize the quality of information regarding these requirements. If we can't get enough information at the beginning, we advise a contingency or incorporate some cost allowances. We qualify and quantify those unknowns, and at the early stages of the preconstruction estimate, we develop a list of items which may have been overlooked.

Q You mentioned a "historical data base." What does that mean?

A We have a company data base of budgeted items, and when we do projects, we document certain basic standards and building systems—for example, how much a certain facade costs per square foot based on the type of finish used. Over the years, we have accumulated indicators, and often there is written documentation that accompanies the cost and schedule history. You can see that a building took two years from concept and design approval. Then, as you get into the details, you will find that this was a complicated facade which had a combination of punched windows, or a curtain-wall combined with a conventional loadbearing masonry wall with stone panels. The method of installation is defined, as are the materials. By having all the information about how the work was contracted and how the costs were accrued, you get a very clear picture of all the components necessary to the making of that particular construction. This information is entered in the project data sheets on a computerized data base, which works on various levels of detailed information. The main categories are very general—was it a concrete structural building or was it a steel building? Was it a conventional facade or was it a window curtain-wall system? Then, in more detail, if it was a window curtain-wall system, was the glass reflective or was it clear? What was the frame material? As we continue in the computer age, we are able to keep more information at each level. Another important factor is the people who run these projects. We may go back to contractors who have performed the work and installed the material, or to people who were involved in the early planning with the architect, to determine which material provided a better life cycle, which material is more readily available, which material was a truer color match.

Q How do you work with architects and designers?

A When an architect or designer is planning the project, a lot can be seen in the thumbnail sketches. Recently, a client showed us some basic conceptual drawings, and from those we were able to provide the developer with a fairly comprehensive budget based on experience with similar buildings that we had worked on with the architect. For example, we knew that of the total million square feet, 50 percent would be for the office facility and 50 percent would be allocated to parking. Then we focused on the office and went on to determine the floor area ratio, and so on. With thumbnail sketches, you begin to define the product. Eventually you get to an overview budgetary guide. The architect then knows what needs to be designed from a financial standpoint. The documents we put together at this stage describe what the mechanical systems costs should be, how efficiently the building will function, what the usable tenant space is.

Q Do architects find this restrictive?

A No, usually not at all. Many architects keep similar records on how efficiently they have designed buildings. The material we develop gives them a guide. Sharing this information up front prevents the architect from putting together a set of plans and documents that cannot be executed for the proposed budget. My training as an architect helps me, as program manager, to guide the project from a cost and quality aspect as the architect continues to design the building via the drawings. It actually can free the architect. In this day and age, the cost and project budget are critical to producing a successful project.

Q How do you get from thumbnail sketches to cost per square foot?

A An architect goes through various stages, and at each of those stages the program manager for the team continually refines what is required information. The architect develops a design and produces conceptual drawings, schematic drawings, design development documents, and finally construction documents. At each phase the architect presents the documents and defines further the level of finish, color, and the quantities of material. We provide the costing and scheduling information and confirm the level of scope based on the drawings and specifications of each phase.

Q Do you also coordinate the interior design?

A In some projects the interior finish is considered part of the entire project. But in many new constructions the base building is separate from the tenant interior work. The developers put up the facility and the basic level of finishes, and then the tenants determine the level of finish for their space. There are many different combinations. An architect may have someone design only the lobby; in another situation the interior designer may design all of the tenant spaces as well as the common spaces.

Q Part of your job is to help clients choose materials. How do you go about this?

A Some clients physically point to a material in a existing installation and ask us to provide the same product. We then research that installation. When was it constructed? By whom? Where was the specific material fabricated? Is it still available, and does it fit into the cost model? If not, can we come up with a suitable substitute?

Q How do you evaluate materials for their suitability?

A There are many qualitative factors—durability, maintenance, aesthetic qualities. We use these as well as cost, installation time, etc., to evaluate materials. For instance, there are options for a flooring material—ceramic tiles of various sizes, marble, terrazzo, wood, vinyl. All of these have initial qualitative ratings. Aesthetically, what is the most pleasing? What feels the best? Which can be walked on barefoot? Which can be walked on in high-heel shoes? Then we must deal with the maintenance. Which is easier to clean? Which has the most porous surface? Which will absorb less dirt? Smaller tile requires more grout joints, and grout has a higher porosity, so that floor will show more dirt. But smaller tile is denser, and will break less easily. We compare the initial installation cost to the life-cycle cost based on how long the material will last. The combination of all these factors, which define the look, the feel, and the functioning of the space, allows us to contribute to the final decisions made by the architect and the client. This sort of analysis is applied to every element of the construction from the choice of wall fixtures and ceiling finishes to the basic structure.

All of these factors are reviewed in terms of the current industry cost rates, the availability of the material, ease of working with the material at that site, local labor practices, and so on. Let's say that steel is currently less expensive than a concrete structure, and can be easily brought into the site; then steel may be the material of choice. But maybe the cost of steel is increasing, and the construction won't begin for another eighteen months.

We may advise the client to reevaluate any decision based on the cost of steel.

Q What types of research do you use to get this information?

A We get material from various societies that gather industry information. We follow market information. We get trade publications and very often are invited to participate in seminars about current trends within the industry. Early on the Bovis Construction Group set up in-house technical services to research technical and materials information. The group is broken up into various disciplines: structural, mechanical, electrical and communications specialists, and architectural specialists. These employees focus on new products and techniques. They also stay current with ways of conveying and organizing information. It is research and development from the standpoint of practical application. We are an international organization, and we electronically transfer information between America, Europe, and Asia so we can share the data base, and adapt the information via annually published indexes to the appropriate country.

Q You have served as a project manager for theme park installations. Do these themed structures differ from more regular construction?

A Construction is still construction. The same style of working early on with the design group works well. A wide data base becomes particularly important because the job often involves translating designs evolved for one site to other states or countries. We keep track of building code requirements and availability of materials, which vary from place to place. Structures that appear to be themed can usually be created through the same principles that have always been used in the construction industry, and the difference happens in the finishes. The final look often misrepresents the actual product. In other words, how do you make concrete wood? A designer may incorporate trees that cannot be grown and must be sculpted, or, because concrete is more durable outdoors, it may be the choice for executing old wood planking. In one installation, stone walls spanned the exterior and interior spaces. Some of the stones were real, some were made from molded reinforced fiberglass, and some were precast man-made stones. All of the stones were painted to look the same, and we gave the interior space the same look as the exterior, without dealing with the structural problems of the weight of real stone on an interior floor. We needed to repeat the installation at different locations, so we had molds made of the walls—by this time it was hard to tell which part of the wall was made of which type of stone—and the subsequent installations were all reinforced fiberglass.

In these situations, you have to find people who can create a believable concrete tree. Our job is to bring together the designer or architect who has a vision for the look and the artisan who has worked with possible ways to produce that look. Because we deal with a number of large construction projects, we are constantly shown new products that we in turn suggest to artisans and contractors. They will do mock-ups or samples with the materials and often come up with applications never dreamed of by the manufacturer.

I was recently the Deputy Director of Operations for the 1995 Special Olympics World Games, and encountered a problem that at first seemed unsolvable. We had a moderate budget based on the donated time and materials of contractors, a limited time schedule, and the design for the Olympic torch put the open flame in a fifty-foot-tall, freestanding structure with a high-gloss paint finish. Obviously, the flame had to be very large—larger and more colorful than we could get from the planned pressurized gas line. A pyrotechnical specialist came up with the idea that using lava rocks (the barbecue gas grill product) suspended over the gas source would spread the gas, allowing for a larger flame. This worked, but the amount of heat projected would still play havoc with any high-gloss paint. One of the contractors talked to a metal supplier who suggested we fabricate the inner part of the torch exposed to the flame from a special heat-resistant metal, which would shield the outer metal, which was a different type of metal that was receptive to a high-gloss finish. The torch was a product of a team brainstorming based on what practically could be done in the time frame, for the budget, with available materials, to achieve a desired effect.

Q Are there any specific research sources or facilities you find essential?

A People. The access to people from a contracting standpoint. From designers and architects and tradespeople to the contractors and suppliers who have managed materials and products. One of the jobs of the construction manager is the guiding of clients to contractors who can best perform their work. Certain contractors not only work better with stone, but some work better with certain types of stone in different applications. I have used different contractors to install the marble on the floor and interiors of a building from those I chose to apply the stone on the exterior, and then we had a third contractor who painted wood to look like marble. You can research the information from product guides, manufacturers' catalogs, and numerous trade publications, but some of the best information comes from hands-on experience; from people who have actually used materials to satisfy a requirement in an anticipated or an unexpected role. It is through the discussions with those who actually performed the work you find out the best indication of what was successful, what was unsuccessful, what was cost effective, what was time consuming, or what was expedient, and finally, most important of all, were the client and the eventual users of the space satisfied?

GLOSSARY

Abrasive finish. A flat, nonreflective surface finish.

Adobe. (1) Unfired brick, often containing straw, dried in the sun. The oldest form of brick. (2) The structures made from adobe brick.

Adobe mortar. *See* Mud mortar.

Agglomerated stone. A product made from quarry waste and binder.

Aggregate. Granular material mixed with cement to form concrete or mortar. Fine aggregate includes sand or other fine particles. Coarse aggregates are gravel, pebbles or other hard materials usually between ¼ inch (6.3 mm) and 1½ inches (38 mm) in diameter. Heavyweight aggregate, like barite or steel, is of high density and is used for heavyweight concrete. Lightweight aggregate, like natural pumice, cinder, or perlite, is of low density and is used for lightweight concrete. Both lightweight and heavyweight aggregate are used in the manufacture of concrete block.

Alabaster. Fine-grained, translucent variety of gypsum, generally white in color, which can be cut and carved easily with a knife or saw. The term is often incorrectly applied to fine-grained marble.

Alloy. A metallic material formed by combining two or more metals or a metal and a nonmetal.

Aluminum. A lightweight, very malleable metal, muted silver in color but capable of taking a high polish, used for sand-casting, mold-casting, and die-casting. Its strength is increased by rolling. It is easily alloyed with other elements such as chromium, iron, nickel, zinc, manganese, copper, silicon, and magnesium. When exposed to air, it forms a protective oxide. Anodizing (an electrochemical process) causes a thickening of the oxide, and during this process the metal can be colored with dyes.

Arris. In masonry, the edge of an external angle. It can be unfinished or shaped. *See* figure G-3.

Artificial stone. A building material that is a mixture of stone or marble chips embedded in a matrix of cement or plaster and finished like stone by polishing, carving, etc.

Ashlar. A cut block of stone, usually square or rectangular in shape.

Ashlar masonry. Construction consisting of square or rectangular units of stone or concrete bonded with mortar. *See also* Bonds, masonry.

As-fabricated. Metal finishes resulting from the normal production process. They include *unspecified*, an uncontrolled finish produced by casting, rolling, etc., which varies from dull to bright and may contain stains or residues; *specular*, a mirror-like cold-rolled finish; and *matte*.

Asphalt. A naturally occurring dark brown to black substance that becomes viscous at relatively low temperatures and hardens when cool.

Asphalt block. A paving block made from asphaltic concrete.

Asphalt cement. Asphalt that has been refined for use in paving and construction.

Asphaltic concrete. A mix of liquid asphalt cement and aggregate that, when hardened, is used as a paving and construction material.

Backing veneer. The layer of veneer used on the reverse side of a piece of plywood from the face or decorative side.

Balanced match. A way of aligning wood veneer pieces of equal width so the patterns match on the face. *See also* Book match, Slip match, Veneer matching.

Basalt. A dark-colored igneous rock commercially known as granite when used as dimensional stone, it is used extensively for paving.

Base. The bottom course of a stone wall or the first horizontal member above grade of a finished floor.

Basketweave. A decorative masonry bond, often used as paving, formed by laying pairs of units perpendicular to adjacent pairs. *See* figure G-1.

Beach pebbles. *See* Riverbed aggregate.

Bed. (1) Term describing the relation of the grain in a stone to the direction it is set. If the grain runs horizontally to the course joints, it is set on a "natural bed." Stone set with grain running vertically is on "edge." (2) The bottom horizontal surface of a masonry unit, covered when the masonry is set in place.

Bedding. The prepared base for concrete and masonry.

Bed joint. The layer of mortar between courses of masonry units.

Bending. A mechanical process for forming metal with the metal at room temperature or at elevated temperatures, accomplished with the aid of rollers, bending shoes, and mandrels. Primarily used to produce curved sections from straight lengths of tube, rod, or extruded shapes.

Bevel. A sloped surface contiguous with a vertical or horizontal surface.

Beveled glass. Glass that has a tapered polished edge.

Bird's eye. A wood figure in lumber and veneer in which small areas of the wood fibers are contorted, forming wavy and circular figures that resemble bird's eyes.

Bleed. In brick, staining caused by corrosive metals, oil-based putties, or other manmade or natural materials.

Blending. The positioning of adjacent stone veneer panels, floor slabs, or tiles to visually harmonize their predominant colors and or patterns. *See* figure G-12.

Blister. A wood figure in which an uneven contour of the growth rings causes the appearance of raised spots.

Block. A unit of masonry material.

Bluestone. A fine- to medium-grain metamorphic quartz-based stone, ranging in color from green and lilac to dark gray and blue.

Boasting. Cutting stone with a chisel, resulting in a surface characterized by roughly parallel chisel marks of various widths.

Bond. (1) The adhesion of mortar or grout to masonry. (2) The adhesion of cement paste to aggregate. (3) The adherence between plaster coats. (4) The pattern formed by the interlocking of masonry units. *See also* Bonds, masonry.

Bonder. *See* Header, Rowlock.

Bonds, masonry. An arrangement of units in a pattern, which may be structural or purely decorative, as illustrated in figure G-1. Masonry that does not form a pattern is called a *random bond*. General patterns are *basketweave, coursed ashlar, diagonal bond, herringbone, running bond, stack bond*. Brick patterns are *common (American) bond, English bond, English cross* or *Dutch bond, Flemish bond*. Stone patterns are *coursed broken-bond ashlar, coursed rubble, mosaic (cobweb), random ashlar, random rubble, uncoursed rubble*. *See* individual entries.

Book match. A technique of aligning sheets of wood veneer in which one leaf is turned over and aligned with an adjacent leaf (as in facing pages of a book), producing a face with a symmetrical pattern that is a balanced match. Marble veneer may also be book matched. *See* figures G-12 and G-13.

Brake forming. A mechanical method of bending metal, usually performed on sheet, strip, or plate. *See also* Roll forming.

Brass. A yellow, green, or brown alloy in which the chief constituents are copper and zinc. Alpha brass is usually only copper and zinc, while alpha-beta brass may contain other metals. Brass is soft and very workable, polishes to a high luster, is often plated with chrome, nickel, or silver, and casts easily. It is hard to distinguish visually from bronze, and some materials referred to as bronze are technically brass. *See also* Bronze.

Brazing. An intermediate-temperature method of joining metals using a nonferrous filler metal with a melting point lower than that of the metals to be joined; the filler metal is then drawn between the closely fitted surfaces of the joint by capillary action.

Brecciated marble. Any marble composed of angular fragments.

Brick. Small, usually rectangular masonry units made of clay or shale, formed while in a plastic state, and dried or fired in a kiln. Brick nomenclature depends on the orientation of the unit, as illustrated in figure G-2. *Common brick* or *building brick* are intended for use in both structural and nonstructural masonry where appearance is not a consideration, and are used as a backing material. *Facing brick* are intended for use in both structural and nonstructural masonry when appearance is a consideration. *Hollow brick* are identical to facing brick but have a core or cell area of 25 percent to a maximum of 60 percent. Larger cores or cells in hollow brick allow use of reinforcing steel and grout. *Paving brick* are used to support pedestrian and vehicular traffic and are vitrified. Old paving brick are called brick pavers. *Ceramic glazed brick* are units with a ceramic glaze fused to the body and are used as facing brick. *Thin brick* are fired clay units with normal face dimensions but a reduced thickness. They are used for veneer. *See also* Extruded brick, Modular brick, Molded brick, Nonmodular brick.

Brilliant-cut glass. Beveled glass into which various shapes, such as oval and fluted facets, are notched into the bevel by means of an engraving technique, enhancing the play of light on the glass to give it additional sparkle or texture. *See also* Engraving (glass).

Broached. A stone finish with broad parallel grooves.

Broom finish. The texture produced by stroking a broom over freshly troweled concrete.

Broken stripe. A wood figure in quarter-sliced veneer in which a stripe runs parallel to the length of the veneer and appears to go under the surface and then out again, hence appearing broken.

Bronze. A yellow, green, or brown alloy in which the chief components are copper and tin, but which may contain other metals. In reality, many alloys referred to commercially as "bronze" contain no tin, and are technically brass, making it difficult to distinguish visually between the two. Like brass, bronze is soft and very workable, polishes to a high luster, is often plated with chrome, nickel, or silver, and casts easily. *See also* Brass.

Brown coat. The second coat, about ⅜ inch (9.5 mm) thick, in plaster or stucco work, applied over the scratch coat.

Brownstone. Trade term applied to dark brown and reddish brown sandstone extensively used for construction in the United States in the nineteenth century. The characteristic brownstone fronts of New York City came from the Connecticut River Valley in Massachusetts, southeastern Pennsylvania, and New Jersey.

Brushed. (1) A skid-resistant finish produced by brushing freshly troweled concrete. (2) A stone finish produced by a wire brush.

Buffed finish. A reflective metal surface texture resulting from grinding, polishing, or buffing processes. Buffed finishes include smooth specular, which is bright and mirror-like, and specular, which is less bright, showing evidence of scratches and imperfections.

Building brick. *See* Brick.

Building stone. Rock that has been cut for use as dimension stone or for general use in construction.

Bullnose. Finishing trim tile with a convex radius on one edge, used on the top of wainscoting or on outside corners.

Burl. (1) A wartlike growth on a tree trunk which contains abnormal growth patterns, typically caused by damage to that portion of the tree. Larger burls are valuable for use as veneer and decorative woodwork because of the intense figuring. Also called burr. (2) The figure resulting from a burl.

Burr. *See* Burl.

Bush-hammered. (1) A finish produced by bush-hammering on cured concrete. (2) A corrugated stone finish with interrupted parallel markings produced by bush-hammering. The markings vary from very subtle to rough: fine (8-cut) has markings not over ³⁄₃₂ inch (2.4 mm) apart; medium (6-cut) has markings not more than ⅛ inch (3.2 mm) apart; coarse (4-cut) has markings not more than ⁷⁄₃₂ inch (5.6 mm) apart.

Bush-hammering. A mechanical process that produces textured surfaces varying from subtle to rough.

Butt. A wood figure from sections of stump wood in which dis-

BASKETWEAVE

COURSED ASHLAR

DIAGONAL BOND

HERRINGBONE

⅓ RUNNING BOND
(OFFSET BOND)

RUNNING BOND

STACK BOND

COMMON (AMERICAN)
BOND/SIXTH COURSE HEADERS

COMMON (AMERICAN)
BOND/SIXTH COURSE
FLEMISH HEADERS

ENGLISH BOND

ENGLISH CROSS (DUTCH BOND)

FLEMISH BOND

COURSED BROKEN-BOND ASHLAR

COURSED RUBBLE

MOSAIC (COBWEB)

RANDOM ASHLAR

RANDOM RUBBLE

UNCOURSED RUBBLE

FIGURE G-1. MASONRY BONDS

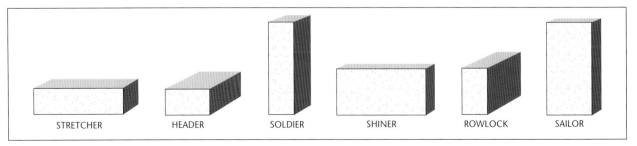

STRETCHER   HEADER   SOLDIER   SHINER   ROWLOCK   SAILOR

FIGURE G-2. BRICK NOMENCLATURE, BASED ON POSITION OF FACE WITHIN COURSE (FACE IS LIGHT-TONED RECTANGLE)

GLOSSARY

tortion of the fibers causes the grain to appear to crinkle and fold into wavy ripples. Also called stump figure. *See also* Stump wood.

Butt joint. (1) An end-to-end square joint between two members. (2) An external corner formed by two stone panels.

Calcium-silicate brick. *See* Sand-lime brick.

California finish. *See* Knocked-down skip-trowel.

Came. The strip of cast lead or zinc used to hold pieces of glass together in a stained glass design, or to hold the panes of glass in a window casement. Also called window lead.

Cant. *See* Flitch.

Capital. (1) A top piece, as of columns, doors, and moldings. (2) The masonry units on the top of a wall (also called cap). (3) The architectural element between the shaft of a column and a beam, arch, etc.

Capstone. The stone at the top of a masonry structure.

Casting. Forming an article by solidification of molten or plastic material in a mold.

Cast iron. A corrosion-resistant material produced from the casting of crude iron. There are various grades of malleability, compressive strength, etc.

Cast stone. A concrete building material intended to imitate stone.

Cathedral grain. *See* Plain-sliced, Flat grain.

Cell. A hollow air space in building tile, concrete block, or hollow brick.

Cement (hydraulic). An adhesive made from a burned mixture of clay and limestone that sets by virtue of a chemical reaction when mixed with water, and is capable of doing so under water. *Natural cement* is made from clayey limestone, which, after burning, is ground into a fine powder. *Portland cement* is produced by burning a mixture containing hydraulic calcium silicates and calcium sulfate, and grinding the resulting clinker. *White cement* is Portland cement that hydrates to a white (instead of the normal gray) paste because it is made from raw materials of low iron content and fired by a reducing flame.

Cement mortar. A mortar made from cement, lime, sand, and water. *See also* Mortar.

Cement paste. The bonding material that results from a mixture of cement and water.

Ceramic glazed brick. *See* Brick.

Ceramic tile. A surfacing unit, usually thin, made from clay or a mixture of clay and other inorganic, nonmetallic materials heated to cause conversion to a solid, glassy state. The face may be glazed or unglazed.

Checks. (1) Short adjacent cracks in the surface of a glazed ceramic unit. (2) Fine splits or separations running parallel with the grain in wood. End checks are separations in the plane of the wood rays on the end-grain surface.

Cladding. Exterior stone veneer.

Clapboard. Wood board siding installed horizontally to cover timber framing. *See also* Siding.

Clay. A natural mineral aggregate that becomes plastic when combined with water, hardens when dried, and becomes vitrified when fired to sufficient temperatures. Clay used in brick-making generally comes from an area near the manufacturing facility, so the color and mineral makeup of the local clay will affect the color and other properties of the finished units.

Closure. (1) The last brick or part of a brick built in to complete a course of masonry. (2) A brick or part of a brick used to break bond at quoins and openings in brick walls. (3) A specific size of modular and nonmodular brick.

Cluster. A wood figure in a rotary or half-round veneer cut from the trunk of trees that contain scattered clusters of burl figures intermingled with plainer grain.

Coarse grain. Wood texture resulting from large and widely spaced growth rings. The term also applies to wood with large pores as found in oak or ash. Also called open grain and coarse texture.

Cobble. A small, naturally smooth rock used for building and paving.

Cobblestone. A dimension stone used in paving. Generally used to describe paving blocks (usually granite) cut into rectangular shapes.

Cobweb. *See* Mosaic bond.

Cold-painted. *See* Painted glass.

Colored glass. The result of natural impurities present in unrefined glass-making ingredients, like the green of bottle glass. Color is also achieved by adding metallic oxides or other elements to colorless molten glass, or by tinting the hard surface with substances such as copper salts or silver compounds and then reheating in a kiln. Also called stained glass. *See also* Painted glass.

Combed. A plaster or stucco finish that is the result of going over the wet finish coat with a comblike tool.

Common (American) bond. A structural brick bond consisting of courses of stretchers only with a course of headers only at regular intervals, usually every sixth or seventh course. *See* figure G-1.

Common brick. *See* Brick.

Concrete. A composite material that consists essentially of a binding medium with embedded aggregate. *Portland cement concrete* is a mixture of portland cement, aggregate, and water. *Lime concrete,* the earliest form of concrete, is mixed from sand, stones, lime, and water. It sets more slowly and is not as strong as portland cement. *Rubble concrete* is made by adding building rubble, small rocks, or other filler to the concrete as it is being poured.

Concrete finishes. The final surface textures applied to the material. Commonly used finishes are *broom, brushed, bush-hammered, float, gun, rubbed, rock-salt, sack-rub, swirl float,* and *trowel. See* individual entries.

Concrete masonry. Hollow or solid building units molded from concrete-based materials; for example, concrete block and concrete brick.

Copper. A reddish brown soft metal that is highly resistant to corrosion because of the green chemical film it develops on exposure to air. Copper is the basis of the alloys bronze and brass.

Coquina. A coarse-textured and porous limestone composed of shells loosely cemented by calcite. It is quarried primarily in Mexico and Texas, the Mexican variety being denser. Also known as shell stone (particularly the Texan variety). Fossil stone (also called fossil rock) and keystone are technically coquina, but are so coarse that they are considered separate products. Nomenclature may vary in different parts of the United States.

Core. (1) Relatively thick veneer, lumber, or chipboard that forms the center ply of a panel. (2) Hole in brick used to aid in the manufacturing process and shipping.

Corrosion. The chemical reaction that causes the deterioration or change of metal or any other material as a result of exposure to air or water.

Course. (1) A horizontal row of masonry units. Coursed masonry consists of units assembled in visible layers, with or without mortar. See also Bonds, masonry. (2) A row of shingles or other such construction unit.

Coursed ashlar. A masonry bond consisting of ashlar units assembled in visible courses that form a horizontal line the length of the field. See figure G-1.

Coursed broken-bond ashlar. A bond particular to stone; ashlar stone of random shape and size are set in full horizontal courses, but with a variety of sizes of vertical mortar joints. See figure G-1.

Coursed rubble. Fieldstone and roughly dressed stone assembled to give a sense of courses with or without mortar. See figure G-1.

Cove. A concave molding. See figure G-5.

Crazing. Cracking in the glaze coat of a ceramic piece caused by tensile stresses.

Crossfire. A general term describing various types of wood figure markings that cross the grain of a piece of wood.

Cross grain. Wood grain that does not run parallel to the length of the lumber.

Cross set. See Flashed brick.

Crotchwood feather. A wood figure formed when the grain comes together at the crotch of the tree where two limbs meet to form a "Y". The resulting flitch is called a crotch block. The center slice from the crotch block is where the feather, or plume, is obtained. Also called flame figure.

Crotchwood swirl. A wood veneer figure revealed in the slicing from either side of the crotch block from the center feather section.

Crowhop. Descriptive term applied to joints between tiles that are out of alignment.

Curly. A wood figure resulting from distorted growth of fibers in the trunk of the tree, giving a wavy or curly appearance.

Curtain wall. An exterior nonbearing wall built between structural supports. Also called enclosure wall. See also Veneer (masonry).

Cut glass. Glass that has been cut into by means of a rotating wheel, a lathe, or grinding. See also Beveled glass, Brilliant-cut glass.

Cut stone. Stone that has been precut to specified dimensions for a specific installation.

Dab. See Dash.

Dash. An even pebbled plaster or stucco two-step finish produced by dipping a whisk broom or bundle of reeds in stucco and stippling or slapping the wet finish coat with the tool. A color different from the under coat may be used. Also called dab or stipple.

Diagonal bond. A decorative masonry pattern, generally used as paving, that is a variation of running bond with the units set on a diagonal in relation to the edges of the area being covered. See figure G-1.

Die-skin finish. See Extruded brick.

Dimension stone. Natural building stone that has been cut and finished to specifications. The surfaces of dimension stone are named as illustrated in figure G-3.

Directional textured finish. A satin-smooth metal texture produced by wheel- or belt-polishing with abrasives, resulting in tiny continuous parallel scratches on the surface of the metal. Standard finishes include fine, medium, coarse satin, uniform, handrubbed, and brushed. See also Metal Finishes.

Divider strip. A strip used in terrazzo work to divide the panels. The strips are made from either a white alloy of zinc (silver in color), half-hard brass (gold in color), or plastic. Strips vary in width, and are embedded in depths from ⅝ inch to 1¼ inches (16 to 32 mm), depending on the requirements of the installation.

Dog tooth. A line of brick that protrudes from the rest of the wall.

Dolomite. A crystalline variety of limestone, containing over 40 percent magnesium carbonate.

Door stock. Veneers suitable for doors, usually 86 inches (218 cm) or longer.

Draped glass. Glass which has been formed, when in a hot plastic state, into folds similar to those in drapery. When the glass cools, the folds remain.

Dressed stone. Stone that has been cut to shape and worked on the face.

Dry stone. Stone laid without mortar.

Dry-press brick. Brick made by forcing powdered damp clay into molds under high pressure, producing a very dense, smooth unit that may later be sandblasted or textured. This was the predominant method of brick manufacturing from 1880 to 1930. Also called semi-dry brick.

Durex blocks. Roughly cubed 2¾ inches to 3½ inches (69 mm to 89 mm), usually granite blocks used for paving. Often placed in concentric circles with half-inch (13 mm) joints.

Dutch bond. See English cross bond.

Edge grain. See Quarter-sawed.

Efflorescence. A whitish powder sometimes found on the surface of masonry, usually caused by the deposition of soluble salts carried through or onto the surface by moisture.

Eggshelling. A fired ceramic glaze that resembles the texture of an eggshell.

Enclosure wall. See Curtain wall.

End grain. A piece of lumber cut transversely across the fibers.

Endwood. An effect found in wood (to be used as veneer) where the fiber direction is perpendicular, or nearly so, to the surface. It is responsible for much of the pattern in crotch, burl, broken stripe, and mottle figures.

English bond. A structural brick bond with alternating courses of headers and stretchers. *See* figure G-1.

English cross bond. A structural brick bond which differs from English bond only in that vertical joints between the stretchers in alternate courses do not align vertically. These joints center on the stretchers themselves in the courses above and below the header row. Also called Dutch bond. *See* figure G-1.

Engraving (glass). The cutting or scratching of a design into a glass surface by means of a sharp pointed tool or a rotating wheel.

Etched glass. Glass treated with hydrofluoric acid to produce surface changes ranging from almost clear to frosted to pitted, depending on the strength of the acid and length of the application.

Exposed aggregate. A concrete finish produced by scattering an aggregate, usually ½ to ¾ inch (13 to 19 mm) over the wet, troweled surface, patting it into the concrete, and finishing with a float to completely embed the aggregate. The effect can also be achieved by washing away the outer skin of mortar before the concrete has fully hardened, thereby exposing the aggregate. *See also* Terrazzo.

Extruded brick. Brick formed by pushing wet clay (or a mix of clay and shale) through a die to form a ribbon that is cut into appropriate sizes and shapes by a wire-cutting process that produces various marks particular to the manufacturing plant. Specific textures and finishes (such as bark, comb or pin-scratched, rolled relief patterns, incised and sand finishes) are executed before the ribbon is cut. Texturing is considered unique to modern extruded brick. A smooth surface, also called die-skin finish, is produced if the skin is left intact as it passes through the die.

Extrusion. The process of shaping heated metal into a form by forcing it from a closed container through a die of the desired shape. Corners are sharper than those formed by brake forming or roll forming.

Face. (1) In masonry, the exposed surface of stone, brick, or other masonry on a structure. *See* figure G-3. (2) In woodworking, the decorative veneer on the exposed side of paneling, furniture, cabinets.

Facing brick. *See* Brick.

Faience. Tile made with variations in the face, edges, or glaze, intended to give the appearance of hand-made tile.

Fiddleback. A wood figure similar to curly figure with a tight and uniform ripple appearance across the grain of the wood.

Field. (1) The main part of a masonry wall. (2) The tile that covers most of a wall or floor, excluding the trim or other detailing.

Fieldstone. Stone found on the ground (i.e., not quarried) that is a suitable size and shape for use as dry wall or rubble masonry.

Figure. The specific term used to refer to unique patterns occurring in individual trees, regardless of the method of cutting. Figure falls into three basic categories: crossfire, as in fiddle-

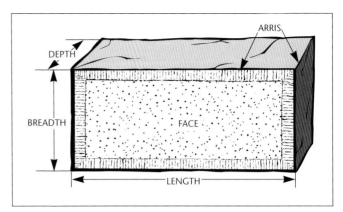

FIGURE G-3. DIMENSION STONE NOMENCLATURE

back; lineal direction, as in ribbon stripe; and nondirectional, as in bird's eye. Specific figures include: *bird's eye, blister, broken stripe, burl (burr), butt (stump), cluster, crossfire, crotchwood feather (flame), crotchwood swirl, curly, fiddleback, flake, ghost figure, Karelian burl, knotty, mottle, olive character, plum pudding (raindrop), quilted, ribbon stripe, roll (herringbone), spalted, wormy. See i*ndividual entries.

Fine grain. Wood texture resulting from annual growth rings that are narrow and closely spaced. Applied to wood with small pores, like maple and cherry. Also called close grain, dense grain, narrow grain.

Finishes. *See* Concrete finishes, Metal finishes, Plaster and Stucco finishes, Stone finishes.

Finish coat. The last coat, usually about ⅛ inch (3 mm) thick, in the application of plaster or stucco. It is applied over the brown coat. It is the surface that is textured or colored with pigment.

Firebrick. Brick manufactured to withstand high heat for use in fireplaces, furnace linings, and flues.

Firing. The process of heating ceramic units in a kiln to the temperature necessary to produce the desired qualities.

Flagstone. Thin slabs of stone used for wall veneer and paving.

Flake. A wood figure found in species of wood that have a very heavy medullary ray growth, such as oak. In veneer, when the cut is on or near to the radial, it is close to parallel to the medullary ray and passes in and out of the uneven growth, resulting in the flake effect. In lumber, the effect results from quarter-sawing.

Flame figure. *See* Crotchwood feather.

Flamed. A rough stone finish produced by the application of intense heat. Also called thermal finish.

Flashed brick. Brick that has been intentionally burned unevenly in the kiln by a flash of flame. When the bricks are cross-stacked (bricks in the kiln are stacked with spaces between them and with alternating layers placed in alternating directions), the part of the brick under the top brick remains unburned, resulting in a mark on the surface of the brick called a cross set.

Flat cut. A cut across a half- or quarter-log. Also called a tangential cut. See Flat grain, Plain-sliced.

Flat grain. Lumber that exhibits oval or loop patterns bracketed by straighter grain (resulting from a flat cut). Also called plain sawn, flat cut, or cathedral grain.

Flemish bond. A structural brick bond consisting of alternate stretchers and headers, with the headers in alternate courses centered over the stretcher. *See* figure G-1.

Flitch. (1) The section of a log or piece of wood ready to be cut into veneer, commonly a quarter- or half-log. Also called cant. (2) The sheet that results from veneer cuts, kept together and usually applied consecutively.

Float. (1) A wooden or metal hand tool with a smooth broad blade used to finish concrete, plaster, or stucco. (2) A medium rough texture produced by finishing concrete with a float.

Foil. *See* Metal leaf.

Forging. The process of forming metal by heating and/or hammering. *Cold forging* is a modern process of forming metal in which the metal is shaped as desired by repeated blows. *Hot forging* is a modern process of forming metal parts by pressing a heated slug or blank cut from wrought material into a closed impression die.

Fossil stone. *See* Coquina.

Frog. A depression (not a hole) in a brick, usually located on one surface, used to aid in handling, manufacturing, and shipping. The name of the manufacturer is often found here. Also called panel.

Gauged brickwork. Brick that has been cut and shaped to an exact size or shape to fit into arches, panels, ornamental bands, etc.

Gauging plaster. A quick-drying finish coat that is a mixture of gypsum ready-mixed plaster and lime putty.

German silver. *See* Nickel silver.

Ghost figure. Term generally applied to wood figure that is not prominent but is noticeable from certain angles or as a result of a finish.

Glass. A rigid transparent or translucent material made by fusing sand with potash under heat.

Glass block. Masonry unit made from glass molded in two sections and sealed together, the trapped air between serving as an insulating feature.

Glass concrete. Translucent glass castings set into a concrete wall panel or sidewalk.

Glass tile. Glass cast 1 to 2 inches (25 to 50 mm) thick, used as tiles joined with mortar.

Glaze. A ceramic coating, or the material applied to a ceramic piece, which forms the coating when the piece is fired.

Glazing. The process of fixing pieces of glass into windows and doors with glazier's putty.

Gneiss. A granite composed of silicate minerals with interlocking granular texture and alternating layers of mineralogical composition.

Gold. A yellow, very malleable, soft, and ductile metal, capable of a taking high polish, and not affected by air, moisture, or acids. Usually hardened with alloys.

Gold leaf. *See* Metal leaf.

Grain. The general description of the pattern or character in wood that results from the configuration of the growth rings. The manner of cutting determines how the grain is revealed. Types of grain include *coarse (open) grain, cross-grain, fine grain, flat grain, plain-sliced, quartered, rift-sawn, straight grain, swirl. See* individual entries.

Granite. A visibly granular igneous rock that comes in a wide range of colors and consists mostly of quartz and feldspars accompanied by one or more dark minerals.

Gravel. Small, rounded particles larger than sand-size, resulting from the breakdown of rocks.

Greenstone. A general term for a metamorphic rock, typically dense and compact with poorly defined granularity, ranging in color from medium or yellowish green to black. It fractures irregularly, which limits its use as a dimension stone.

Grout. A cement-based or other chemically activated filler thin enough to pour and used to fill tile joints.

Grouting. The process of applying grout.

Growth rings. The annual layers of springwood and summerwood that appear as rings when a log is cut crosswise.

Guastavino tile. A masonry unit used in the construction of ceilings.

Gun finish. The undisturbed final layer of concrete applied from a spray nozzle.

Gunmetal. A variety of bronze.

Gypsum. Mineral composed of calcium sulfate and dihydrate. The primary ingredient in plaster of paris.

Gypsum ready-mixed plaster. A plaster in which the necessary materials are mixed with gypsum during manufacture and only require the addition of water.

Half-round cut. A veneer cut in which flitches of the log are mounted off center on the lathe. This results in a cut slightly across the growth rings, and produces a grain pattern between sliced and rotary cut. Half-round is considered a variation of a rotary cut. *See also* Veneer (wood) cuts.

Handmade brick. Fired or unfired brick fashioned in a manner that is not predominantly mechanized. Early brick was fashioned from clay into loaf shapes and allowed to dry in the sun. The Romans cut sheets of clay into individual bricks. *See also* Molded brick.

Hand-tooled. *See* Tooled.

Hardwood. Common classification of all broad-leaved trees. The physical hardness or texture of the wood has no bearing on the classification.

Header. A masonry unit placed in the course with its smallest surface dimension facing out and with the rectangular shape in a horizontal position. It is used to interlock with the wall behind. Also called bonder. See figure G-2.

Heavy-duty tile. Tile deemed suitable for use in areas of heavy pedestrian traffic.

Herringbone. An interlocking V pattern resembling a fish skeleton, used in parquet, wood veneer layout, and as a masonry bond. *See* figures G-1, G-8, and G-13.

Hewn stone. Stone shaped with hand tools.

Hollow brick. *See* Brick.

Honed. A satin-smooth stone finish.

Honeycombed concrete. Cast concrete with trapped air bubbles, usually resulting from inadequate vibration of the mold during the pouring. It may be induced intentionally for its textural effect.

Hydroforming. A process of shaping metal in which sheet metal is formed by a punch or male die against a rubber part subjected to hydraulic pressure.

Iron. A dull gray metal that rusts slowly, and is the most magnetic of metals. The principal alloy of iron is steel.

Ironspot brick. Brick with small random dark spots or flecks naturally caused by iron oxide in the clay. Applied ironspot is artificially achieved by sprinkling metal flecks over the clay before firing.

Italian finish. *See* Knocked-down skip-trowel.

Joint. (1) The space filled with mortar between masonry units, as illustrated in figure G-4. (2) A construction joint is the surface where two successive placements of concrete meet.

Karelian burl. A wood figure that is not really a burl but rather an individual characteristic of birch growing in Karelia, Finland.

Key stone. (1) The uppermost and last set stone in an arch, which locks the units together. (2) A coarse-textured and porous limestone composed of shells, coral, and other marine life loosely cemented by calcite. Quarried in the Florida keys and the Caribbean. Also called fossil stone.

Kiln. A furnace or oven constructed for the firing of brick, tile, terra-cotta, etc.

Knocked-down. A plaster or stucco finish produced by drawing a trowel over a partially set texture so that the high points of the dashed, spattered, or sprayed finish are "knocked down."

Knocked-down skip-trowel. A plaster or stucco finish produced by troweling over a previously applied spatter-dash finish, leaving patches of the spatter dash untouched. Also called Italian or California finish.

Knot. A section of wood where the veneer slice or lumber cut was made through part of a tree where a limb intersects. A *loose knot* is one not held in place by growth. A *sound knot* has been incorporated into the surrounding grain and wood. A *pin knot* is less than ¼ inch (6 mm) in diameter and shows a distinct center portion. It is a branch growth that did not develop. A *tight knot* is held in place by growth. An *unsound knot* exhibits decay.

Knotty. A wood figure resulting from the presence of sound knots, appearing in an intermittent fashion in a portion of the wood.

Lath. The metal mesh or wood strip substructure that holds the scratch or mortar coat in plasterwork.

Lamination. (1) The bonding of thin sheets of wood or veneer panels around a core material to form plywood. Laminated wood is composed of several layers joined tightly by means of an adhesive or fasteners. (2) The bonding of sheet or strip metal to various substrates such as steel, plywood, aluminum,

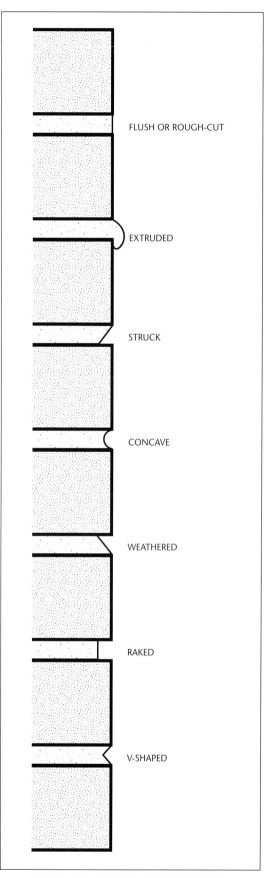

FLUSH OR ROUGH-CUT

EXTRUDED

STRUCK

CONCAVE

WEATHERED

RAKED

V-SHAPED

FIGURE G-4. TYPICAL MORTAR JOINTS

Formica, or mineral board under pressure, occasionally at elevated temperatures.

Leaded glass. (1) Pieces of glass, often colored, combined into a single unit by means of lead or zinc muntins or cames. Also called leaded light. (2) Glass made with lead.

Leaded light. *See* Leaded glass.

Lime. (1) Calcium oxide, in the form of a grayish-white solid, which is the basis of some mortars. (2) The general term for various forms of quicklime. (3) Hydrated lime is a dry product made from slaked lime.

Lime paste. Lime that has been mixed with water to a paste consistency.

Lime putty. Thick lime paste.

Lime plaster. One of the earliest plastic coatings for walls, made by mixing water, lime, sand, and additives such as horsehair.

Limestone. A sedimentary rock composed primarily of calcite or dolomite. The varieties used as dimension stone are usually well consolidated and exhibit a minimum of graining or bedding direction. Commercially used limestone are calcarenite, coquina, dolomite, microcrystalline limestone, oolitic limestone, recrystallized limestone, travertine.

Limestone marble. A compact, dense limestone that will take a polish and is classified as marble as trade practice. It may be sold either as limestone or marble.

Lime wash. One of the oldest house paints, made from lime mixed with water. It is naturally a brilliant white, but may be tinted with appropriate pigments. Also called whitewash.

Machine-tooled. *See* Tooled.

Majolica. Decorated earthenware or tile with an opaque glaze.

Marble. A category of dimension stone that includes a variety of compositional and textural types of metamorphic rock composed largely of calcite or dolomite. All stone in this category must be capable of taking a polish. Varieties include limestone marble, serpentine marble, travertine marble.

Masonry. (1) Construction with units that can be bonded together with mortar, such as stone, concrete block, tile, or brick. (2) The area of the construction industry that works with masonry units or with applications of cement-related materials such as plaster, stucco, and concrete. (3) The structures built from masonry units.

Masonry cement. A factory-mixed cementitious product that requires only the addition of sand and water to make mortar.

Matrix. The bonding material, usually portland cement paste, used in artificial stone and terrazzo to hold the aggregate in place. Where applicable, it may be a noncementitious binder.

Matte. (1) A dull surface finish. (2) An as-fabricated metal finish.

Medullary ray. In a tree, the cellular structure that radiates from the center of the log. Medullary ray growth is perpendicular to the growth rings. When intense, it is what causes the conspicuous figures in species such as oak when the veneer is quarter-sliced or lumber is quarter-sawn. Also called pith ray.

Metal. A member of a group of materials that are conductors of electricity and heat, usually malleable, capable of being hammered thin, fusible, and that exhibit some luster. Base metals are aluminum, copper, iron, lead, nickel, tin, and zinc. Alloys include brass, bronze, pewter, gar-alloy, steel, and nickel silver. Precious metals are gold, silver, and platinum.

Metal finishes. The final surface textures of the material, produced by mechanical means or as a result of the normal production process. Metal finishes include *as-fabricated, buffed, directional textured, nondirectional textured,* and *patterned. See* individual entries.

Metal leaf. Very thin sheets of metal (they can be 0.000004 inch) applied to the surface of metal, wood, plaster, or glass, usually used for decorative purposes. Also called foil.

Mexican paver tile. Handmade terra-cotta tile used for floors. The tile is very porous, and must be sealed to be practical. Also called Mexican floor tile.

Mirror finish. *See* As-fabricated, Buffed finish.

Miter. The junction of two units at an angle, usually 45 degrees.

Modular brick. Brick made to fit within a module, usually 4 or 8 inches, which forms the base unit of modular brick construction. In the United States, the nominal dimensions are 4 x 2⅔ x 8 inches (dimensions given are width, height, length). *Closure or econo,* 4 x 4 x 8 inches. *Engineer,* 4 x 3½ x 8 inches. *Utility,* 4 x 4 x 12 inches. *Norman,* 4 x 2⅔ x 12 inches. *Roman,* 4 x 2 x 12 inches. Ancient roman brick is the same general proportion (although the height is often relatively smaller), but may be a variety of specific dimensions. *See also* Nonmodular brick.

Molded brick. (1) Hand-molded brick is made by pressing soft clay into a two-part mold dusted with sand (which remains on the surface after firing) or water as a release. (2) Sand-struck brick is made by a mechanized process in which wet clay, known as "soft mud," is forced into a mold using sand as a release. Different colored sands are used for various effects. (3) Water-struck brick is made by a mechanized process and uses water as a release, resulting in a smooth finished surface.

Molded glass. Glass shaped by a variety of techniques, including pouring molten glass into a mold, allowing a hot plastic sheet of glass to slump into a mold or to sag around a form, and making impressions in hot, plastic glass.

Molding. A shaped member, usually ornamental, used to accent an architectural or decorative element or to conceal construction joinings and intersections. Commonly used moldings are illustrated in figures G-5 and G-6.

Monolithic concrete. Concrete building units cast with no joints.

Mortar. (1) A plastic mixture usually consisting of portland cement paste, lime, and sand. (2) Any cementitious aggregate; old mortars were a mixture of lime, sand, and water. (3) In fresh concrete, the material occupying the spaces between the particles of coarse aggregate.

Mortar bond. The adhesion of mortar to masonry units or to reinforcing steel.

Mosaic. A designed finish composed of small units called tesserae, usually mounted on paper to form mosaic sheets, which are then set in mortar.

Mosaic bond. Irregularly shaped stone with dressed face set with a regular width mortar joint and used for either solid or veneer walls. Also called cobweb. *See* figure G-1.

Mosaic tile. (1) Small tiles, usually less than 6 inches (152 mm) square, or pieces of ceramic tile, glass, marble, or other stone, arranged and grouted in place. (2) Ceramic mosaic tile is unglazed, mounted on paper or mesh sheets for use as mosaics, floors, counter surfaces, walls, etc.

Mottle. A wood figure in which broken up cross markings are intermingled with stripe. Broad cross markings produce a patchy effect called block mottle. A very small fine figure is known as bees-wing mottle.

Mud. Slang terminology for mortar.

Mud mortar. A mixture of screened (sifted) earth and water used as a binder for aggregate; the resulting paste is used to bond adobe brick. Also called adobe mortar.

Mud plaster. Plaster made from a mixture of screened (sifted) earth and water that is used to cover structures made from adobe brick.

Mullion. The vertical member dividing door panels or multiple windows in a common frame.

Muntin. A strip that is part of the framing structure that holds glass panes in place in a window.

Muntz metal. A variety of brass composed of 60 percent copper and 40 percent zinc.

Nailable concrete. Concrete composed of a lightweight aggregate, enabling nails to be driven into it when set and cured.

Natural cement. See Cement (hydraulic).

Natural cleft. A stone finish formed when slate is split into sheets.

Natural wood. A general descriptive term indicating a wood surface that exhibits desirable or acceptable characteristic markings of that species (e.g., knotty pine).

New-used brick. A proprietary term used to describe brick that appears old because it has been intentionally distressed after manufacture.

Nickel. A dark-silver to green-gray metal that is strong, hard, and resistant to corrosion. It is used as a plating material and in alloys.

Nickel copper. A dark gray copper-nickel alloy that is harder than nickel and resistant to corrosion.

Nickel silver. A copper-zinc-nickel alloy that is bright silver and can be soldered, formed, tempered, and cast. Also called German silver.

Nogging. Filling the open spaces of a wood frame structure with masonry.

Nominal dimension. Describing masonry or tile, the measurement that is equal to the specified unit size plus the intended mortar or grout thickness.

Nondirectional textured finish. Matte metal finishes of varying degrees of roughness that are produced by spraying sand or metal shot against the metal.

Nonmodular brick. Brick referred to by its specified dimensions because it does not fit into a modular system. Dimensions given are width, height, length (USA). *Standard*, 3½ to 3⅝ x 2¼ x 8 inches. *Closure standard*, 3⅝ to 3½ x 3⅝ to 3½ x 8 inches. *Engineer standard*, 3½ to 3⅝ x 2¾ to 2¹³⁄₁₆ x 8 inches. *King,*

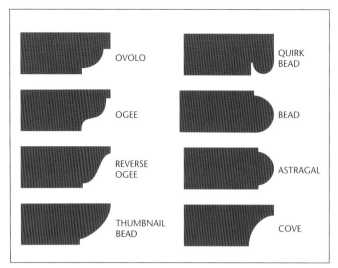

FIGURE G-5. MOLDING PROFILES

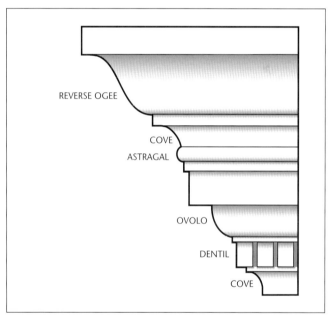

FIGURE G-6. TYPICAL COMBINATION OF MOLDINGS

3 x 2⅝ to 2¾ x 9⅝ inches. *Queen,* 3 x 2¾ x 8 inches. *See also* Modular brick.

Offset bond. *See* Running bond.

Ogee. Molding with a reverse curved profile—concave above, convex below, or vice versa. *See* figure G-5.

Olive character. A wood figure, originally describing the heartwood of ash, that is bright tan with olive markings. The actual log is so rare that the term is now one of description, not classification.

Onyx. A translucent stone, generally layered, having a crystalline structure not discernable under a microscope, in pastel shades, particularly yellow, brown, and green.

Oolitic limestone. A limestone composed largely of spherical or subspherical particles called oolites or ooliths.

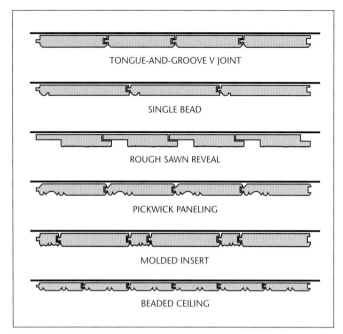

**FIGURE G-7. SOLID LUMBER PANELING PATTERNS
(SECTION VIEWS)**

Opalescent glass. Glass manufacturered with additives, resulting in an oily, yellow-green quality. It was frequently molded.

Ordinary rubble. *See* Rough rubble.

Ormolu. A gilt cast bronze used for ornament.

Painted brick. Fired brick that has been painted (usually by a random spray) to give the appearance of old brick.

Painted glass. Colored or clear glass that has been painted with special enamels and fired in a kiln, gilded with metallic powder or foil, or cold-painted (oil- or lacquer-based paint applied to the glass without subsequent firing). *See* Colored glass.

Panel. *See* Frog.

Paneling. Solid lumber made in a variety of profiles and used to cover interior walls. Commonly used profiles are illustrated in figure G-7.

Parquet. Wood flooring made from small strips or blocks, usually forming a geometric pattern or design, as illustrated in figure G-8.

Parquetry. An ungrouted, usually geometric pattern or design composed of contrasting materials or colors.

Patina. (1) The aura of aging on a surface. (2) The green film formed on metal by natural or artificial oxidation. The film is protective, usually an oxide or sulfate of the metal involved. When produced artificially, the purpose is to hasten the natural weathered effect. Also called Verde antique and verdigris.

Patterned finish. A textured or embossed metal surface texture produced on light-gage sheet metal by passing an as-fabricated sheet between either two engraved matched-design rolls (embossed) or a design roll and a smooth roll.

Paver. A paving brick or stone, unglazed natural tile, quarry tile, or porcelain tile intended for either pedestrian or vehicular traffic.

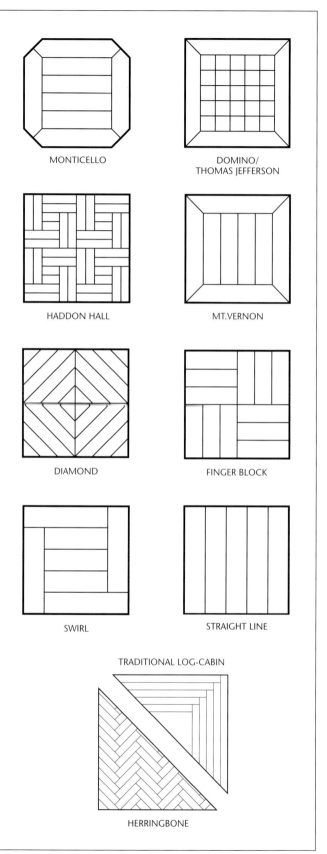

FIGURE G-8. TYPICAL WOOD PARQUET PATTERNS

Paving brick. *See* Brick.

Paving stone. Stone shaped or intended for paving.

Peeled veneer. Veneer cut by centering a log on a lathe so as the log revolves, the cutting knife moves toward the center, slicing a continuous sheet.

Pebble dash. A variety of exposed aggregate in which pebbles are pressed or blown into the finish coat of stucco. Also called pebble wall.

Pebble wall. *See* Pebble dash.

Pewter. Traditionally, an alloy of tin and lead that is dull gray but polishes to bright silver, is soft, and casts well. Contemporary pewter, called Britannia metal, is composed of tin, antimony (a white metallic element), and copper.

Picked. A stone finish of small pits produced by the point of a pick or chisel.

Pith ray. *See* Medullary ray.

Plain sawn. *See* Flat grain.

Plain-sliced. (1) A veneer cut in which the half-log, or flitch, is mounted with the heart side flat against the flitch table of the slicer, and the slicing is done parallel to a line through the center of the log. Also called flat cut. (2) The grain resulting from flat slicing.

Plank match. *See* Random match.

Plaster. (1) A cementitious material or combination of cementitious material and aggregate that, when mixed with water, forms a paste that hardens chemically. When applied to a surface, it adheres and hardens, preserving the form or texture it had when plastic. (2) The hardened mixture.

Plaster of paris. Gypsum from which three-quarters of the previously chemically bonded water has been evaporated, so that when mixed with water it reacts quickly.

Plaster and stucco finishes. The final surface texture of these materials often described as fine, medium, or heavy texture or smooth finish. Specific terms for some commonly used finishes are *combed, dash, knocked-down, knocked-down skip-trowel, sand finish, skip-trowel, spatter-dash, sprayed, troweled. See* individual entries.

Plastic. Term describing a spreadable or pourable consistency that results from a material's ability to hold water.

Platinum. A grayish white precious metal that is malleable and ductile and can be polished to a lasting high gloss finish. It is corrosion resistant and used as an alloy.

Plinth. (1) The block at the junction of the stone base and trim around a door or other opening. (2) The bottom stone block of a column or pedestal.

Plucked. A rough stone finish produced by small pieces of the stone splitting off as it is machine planed.

Plum pudding. A wood figure that is the result of scattered growths or wood grain distortions that look like raisins or raindrops. Also called raindrop.

Pointing. The final filling and finishing of mortar joints that have been raked out.

Polished. A glossy stone finish.

Porcelain. A glazed or unglazed vitreous ceramic material.

Porphyritic. A texture of granite defined by relatively large grains (phenocrysts), typically of feldspar, that are distributed in a distinctly finer-grained matrix. The phenocrysts of porphyritic granites generally are rectangular or partly rounded, and may be as large as several centimeters in size.

Porphyry. Igneous rock characterized by distinct and contrasting sizes of coarse- and fine-grained crystals, used as a decorative building stone.

Portland cement. *See* Cement (hydraulic).

Precast concrete. Concrete formed at a site other than the installation site.

Proprietary. A specific finish, technique, product, or manufacturing process that belongs exclusively to one or a few companies or individuals.

Quarry block. Generally a rectangular piece of rough-cut stone as it comes from the quarry readied for shipment.

Quarry tile. Unglazed tile made from natural clay or shale, which is a minimum of 6 inches (152 mm) square, with the color throughout the tile.

Quarter cut. A veneer cut that saws or slices as near as possible to the radius of the log.

Quartered. Wood veneer grain that results from a quarter cut.

Quarter flat. A method of slicing veneer from a quarter of a log where the slices are approximately perpendicular to the radius of the log.

Quarter-sawed. (1) Lumber that has been cut as close to the true radial of the log as possible. (2) A characteristic lineal grain that is the result of quarter-sawing a log. Also called edge grain or vertical grain.

Quarter-sliced. A type of quarter-cut wood veneer. The quarter-log or flitch is mounted on the flitch table so that the growth rings of the log strike the knife at approximately right angles, producing a series of stripes, straight in some woods, varied in others.

Quartz-based stone. Stone that may be either sedimentary (e.g., sandstone) or metamorphic (e.g., quartzite) in formation.

Quartzite. A metamorphic quartz-based stone formed in exceedingly hard layers.

Quicklime. Calcium oxide lime in its most active state (in comparison with hydrated or slaked lime, which is less reactive).

Quilted. A wood figure in which spots result from wavy interlocking growth rings. The spots are larger and denser than in blister.

Quoin. (1) One of the masonry units forming the external corner of a wall, contrasting with the rest of the wall in shape, material, etc. (2) A brick cut for use as an exterior corner.

Raindrop. *See* Plum pudding.

Raised grain. A weathering or wearing of wood in which the softer part of the grain is worn away, exposing the harder parts.

Random ashlar. Bond of ashlar-stone of random shape and size set with mortar joints that form partial horizontal courses but not a continuous line. Also called random coursed broken bond. *See* figure G-1.

Random coursed broken bond. *See* Random ashlar.

Random match. The arrangement of veneer aligned with no

attempt to match grain. Also called plank match. Marble may also be random matched. *See* figures G-12 and G-13.

Random rubble. Roughly shaped rubble bonded with mortar and set without regard to coursing. *See* figure G-1.

Reinforced concrete. Concrete that has metal rods, wire, or some other appropriate material embedded in it during the pouring or casting process to increase its structural integrity.

Ribbon stripe. A wood figure that results from quarter-slicing where the grain is parallel with the length of the veneer and with a minimum of distortion. A straight, uniform, stripe effect results.

Rift. A description of grain in lumber or veneer cut from species having a heavy medullary ray growth (like oak). The wood exhibits a straight grain and no flake figure because the method of cutting does not intersect the medullary ray.

Rift cut. A veneer cut made on a lathe, rotating the flitch and positioning the slicer at an angle of about 15 percent off the quartered position, cutting the log into layers perpendicular to the medullary ray.

Rift-sawn. Lumber quarter-sawn with selected boards that do not exhibit flake figure.

Riverbed aggregate. Naturally smooth stones or pebbles used as an aggregate. Also called beach pebbles.

Rock. A naturally occurring aggregation of one or more minerals from the earth's crust. *Igneous rock* has solidified from a molten state; for example, granite. *Metamorphic rock* has been altered in appearance, density, and crystalline structure, and in some cases mineral composition, by high temperature or intense pressure, or both. For example, slate is derived from shale; quartz-based stone from quartzitic sand; and true marble from limestone. *Sedimentary rock* is composed of sediments laid down in successive layers composed of preexisting rocks or the skeletal remains of sea creatures; for example, limestone.

Rock-salt. A pockmarked finish in horizontally poured concrete resulting from sprinkling rock salt over the surface while soft and pressing it into the surface. After curing, the salt is removed by hosing with water.

Roll figure. A wood figure in which large visual twists usually run on a diagonal to the edges of the board. Book matching this figure results in a herringbone pattern. Also called herringbone figure.

Roll forming. The process of shaping metal from a flat product by passing it between multiple stands of contour rolls. Generally, the corners are not as sharp as those formed by the extrusion method.

Rotary cut. A veneer cut in which a log is centered on a large lathe; as the log revolves, the cutting knife moves slowly toward the center and a continuous sheet of veneer is peeled.

Rough-hewn. A rustic or very rough wood surface finish.

Rough rubble. *See* Uncoursed rubble.

Rough-sawn. *See* Sawn.

Rowlock. A brick which is placed in the course with its smallest surface dimension facing out, with the resulting rectangular shape in a vertical position. It is used to interlock with the wall behind. *See* figure G-2.

Rubbed. (1) A concrete finish obtained by using an abrasive to remove surface irregularities. (2) A very smooth, but not satin, stone finish.

Rubble. Stone consisting of fieldstone and irregular or partly dressed stone, often with one split or roughly finished face, used chiefly for exterior walls and foundations.

Running bond. A structural masonry bond formed when all masonry units are laid in stretcher positions, with a half-unit overlap. Headers are not used in this pattern. Also called offset bond. A variation is ⅓ running bond. *See* figure G-1.

Rustic terrazzo. *See* Terrazzo.

Rustication. Masonry in which corners, rough stone faces, and face plane shifts are emphasized. Rustication exaggerates the natural look of stone because it creates shadows, and it is often used to give the appearance of weight to the lower part of a building.

Sack-rub. A technique used on formed concrete surfaces designed to fill pits and air holes. It is produced by rubbing mortar over the surface and, before it dries, applying a mixture of dry cement and sand with a sponge float.

Sailor. A brick placed in a course in a vertical position with the widest and longest dimensions used as the face. *See* figure G-2.

Sandblasted. A coarse (coarse-stippled) or slightly pebbled (also called fine-stippled) stone finish produced by sandblasting.

Sandblasting. Process in which a surface is bombarded by a stream of abrasive at high pressure.

Sand finish. A matte stone surface resulting from the application of a steady flow of sand and water under pressure.

Sand-float (sand) finish. A plaster and stucco finish produced by drawing a wet trowel evenly over a finish coat that contains a coarse enough sand for it to be visible on the surface.

Sand-lime brick. A concrete masonry unit in the shape of a brick, often colored with pigment, made principally from sand and lime and hardened by autoclave curing. Also called calcium-silicate brick.

Sandstone. A sedimentary rock composed mostly of mineral and rock fragments within the sand size range (2 to 0.06 mm) with a minimum of 60 percent free silicate, cemented or bonded to a greater or lesser degree by various materials, including silica, iron oxides, carbonates, or clay. It fractures around (not through) constituent grains. Varieties include bluestone, brownstone, quartzite, and quartzitic sandstone.

Saw texture. A finish on siding that gives the effect of saw marks on wood.

Sawn. A term that describes a wide range of stone finishes produced with saw blades. Gang saws produce parallel scores; rotary or circular saws make circular scores. Also called rough-sawn or sawed finish.

Sawn veneer. Wood veneer cut with a saw, in contrast to veneer peeled on a lathe or sliced with a knife.

Sawtooth masonry. Brick arranged to resemble the teeth of a saw.

Scabble. To rough-dress blocks of stone, often for storage or

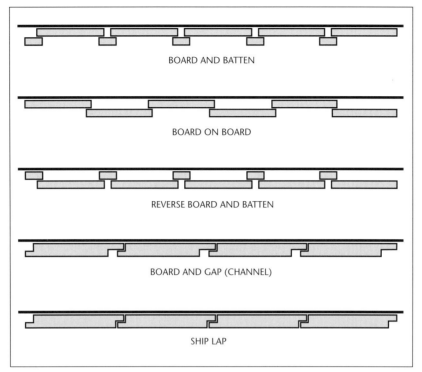

FIGURE G-9. VERTICAL BOARD SIDING (SECTION VIEW)

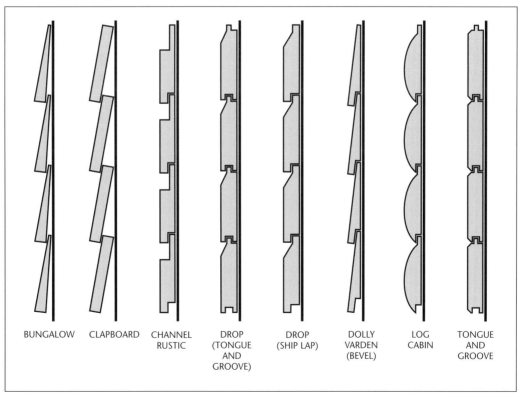

| BUNGALOW | CLAPBOARD | CHANNEL RUSTIC | DROP (TONGUE AND GROOVE) | DROP (SHIP LAP) | DOLLY VARDEN (BEVEL) | LOG CABIN | TONGUE AND GROOVE |

FIGURE G-10. HORIZONTAL BOARD SIDING (SECTION VIEW)

shipment. The product is a rustic finish designated as rough scabbling, medium scabbling, or fine scabbling, based on the texture.

Scagliola. An imitation of marble or stone produced by mixing marble or stone dust with a binder, adding pigments to the plastic medium to imitate veining, grain, or other features, and polishing the surface of the hardened material.

Scratch coat. The first coat of plaster or stucco, about ½ inch (13 mm) thick, applied to a substructure of metal or wood lath. Before setting, its surface is "scratched" with a rake or similar tool.

Screen wall. (1) A brick wall that consists of a pattern of open spaces between brick in the courses, resulting in light filtering through the wall. (2) Concrete block that is made with open spaces so that when assembled into a wall, a pattern is formed.

Sculptured tile. Tile with a raised and/or depressed design molded into the face.

Semi-dry brick. *See* Dry-press-brick.

Serpentine. A hydrous magnesium silicate material, generally dark green with markings of white, light green, or black. Commercially considered marble because it can be polished, it is not a true marble in the geological sense.

Shell stone. *See* Coquina.

Shiner. Brick placed in a course in a position with the longest dimension in both the vertical and horizontal planes facing out. *See* figure G-2.

Shot-sawn. A coarse, uneven stone finish ranging from a pebbled surface to a rippled surface with irregular grooves.

Siding. Lumber or specially finished exterior-grade plywood used to cover the exterior of a wood-frame structure. Commonly used vertically and horizontally applied siding patterns are illustrated in figures G-9 and G-10.

Silver. A very soft metal that is easily worked and cast and used for plating. Sterling silver is alloyed with 7.5 percent copper.

Skip-trowel. A plaster or stucco finish applied in a way that shows the trowel marks, which sometimes form a pattern.

Slake. To add water to quicklime to make putty.

Slate. Metamorphic rock most commonly derived from shale and composed mostly of micas, chlorite, and quartz. The rock can be split into thin but strong sheets and is used for roofing and paving.

Sliced veneer. Veneer cut by means of a slicer knife; the method used for cutting most fine face veneers.

Slip match. A technique of aligning sheets of wood veneer in which one leaf is "slipped" beside and aligned with an adjacent leaf, producing a repetitive pattern that is a balanced match. *See* figure G-13.

Smooth. Term used to describe the finish of dimension stone with a minimum of surface interruption. Also called smooth machine or smooth planer finish.

Smooth specular. *See* Buffed finish.

Softwood. Common classification of coniferous or cone-bearing trees. The physical softness or texture of the wood has no bearing on the classification.

Soldier. A brick placed in a course in a vertical position, with the edge used as the face. *See* figure G-2.

Soldering. A relatively low-temperature process of joining metal using filler metals that melt between 350 and 500 degrees Fahrenheit (177–260 degrees Celsius). The solder is drawn between the closely fitted surfaces of the joint by capillary action.

Spall. *See* Spalling.

Spalling. The delamination of the face of brick, stone, tile, or terra-cotta as a result of impact and/or weathering. A spall is the resulting chip or flake.

Spalted. A wood figure that exhibits areas of discoloration that resemble very dark thin ink lines shot through the wood, the result of a form of decay.

Spatter-dash. A plaster or stucco finish that is produced by spattering on the material using reeds as a brush, often used in combination with dash finish.

Special matches. The arrangement of veneer resulting in patterns such as box, checkerboard, diamond, herringbone, and custom designs. Also called sketch matches.

Specified dimension. A measurement referring to an actual manufactured size.

Specular finish. *See* As-fabricated, Buffed finish.

Split-faced. Stone that has a rough, natural finish resulting from being split rather than sawed.

Spinning. A process of forming sheet metal by bending or shaping it under pressure applied by a smooth hand tool or roller while the metal is revolving rapidly.

Sprayed. Plaster on stucco finishes resembling spatter-dash finish that result from the material being applied through a nozzle under pressure.

Stack bond. A decorative masonry bond formed when there is no overlapping of units. All vertical and horizontal joints are aligned. *See* figure G-1.

Stained glass. *See* Colored glass.

Stamped concrete. Concrete in which a pattern or design has been produced by pressing a shape into the concrete surface before it has fully set.

Stamping. Bending, shaping, cutting out, indenting, coining, or forming metal by means of shaped dies with a press or power hammer.

Statuary bronze. Term used to describe a range of naturally weathered or chemically oxidized brown to black bronze surfaces.

Statuary finish. A protective coating process in which the metal surface is converted to a protective film that is usually light, medium, or dark brown.

Steel. An alloy of iron and carbon, which may in turn be alloyed with nickel, chromium, cobalt, and other elements. Low-carbon steel is soft; medium-carbon steel is strong; high-carbon steel is hard and can be sharpened; all three rust easily. Stainless steel, the product of adding chromium, is strong, will not rust or corrode, and can be finished in a variety of ways.

Stipple. *See* Dash.

Stone. A piece broken or cut from a rock.

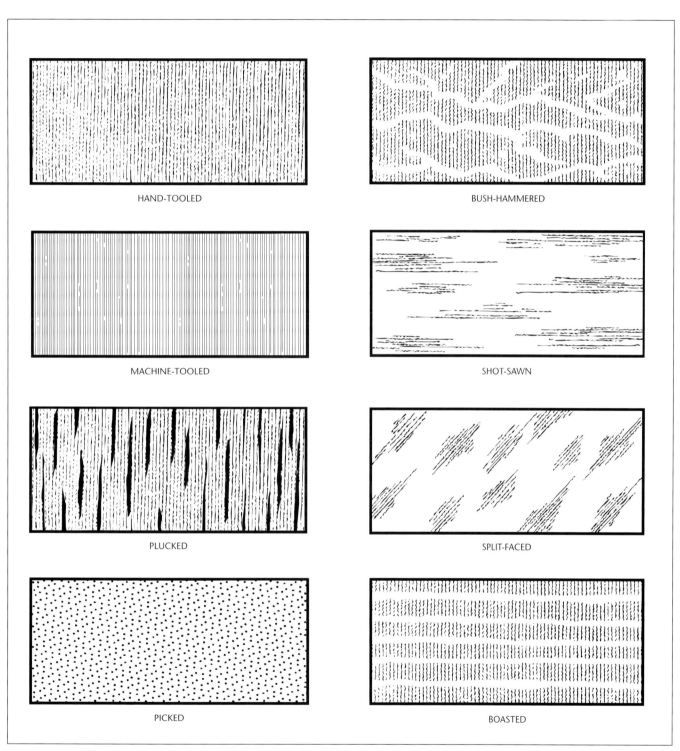

HAND-TOOLED

BUSH-HAMMERED

MACHINE-TOOLED

SHOT-SAWN

PLUCKED

SPLIT-FACED

PICKED

BOASTED

FIGURE G-11. STONE FINISHES

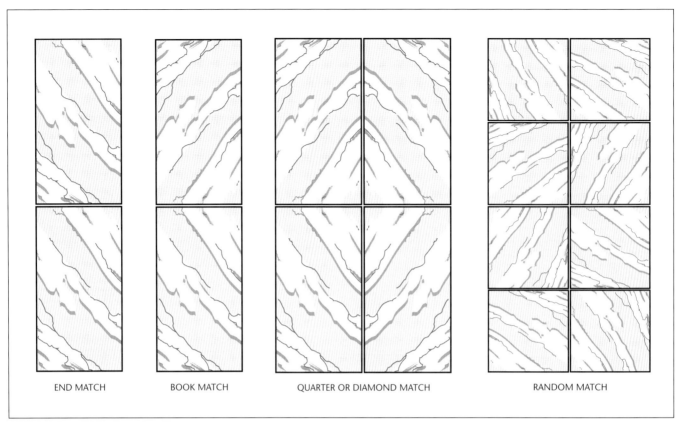

END MATCH	BOOK MATCH	QUARTER OR DIAMOND MATCH	RANDOM MATCH

FIGURE G-12. MARBLE VENEER LAYOUTS

Stone finishes. The final surface texture of a sawn stone, as illustrated in figure G-11. Finishes include *broached, brushed, bush-hammered, flamed finish, honed, natural cleft, picked, plucked, polished, rubbed, sandblasted, sand finish, sawn, shot-sawn, smooth, split-faced, tooled.* Not all finishes are applicable to all stone. *See* individual entries.

Stone tile. Stone or marble cut into tile sizes.

Straight grain. Grain that is revealed when the cut runs vertically parallel to the center of the log.

Stretcher. A brick placed in a course with the longest dimension in the horizontal plane and the edge facing out. It is the most common position for bricks in wall construction. *See* figure G-2.

Stucco. (1) A concrete plaster used to coat exterior walls. Because it is concrete and is permanently colored, it is resistant to weathering. Most applications involve three coats: scratch coat, brown coat, and finish coat. (2) Cement stucco or plaster is a mixture of portland cement, lime, sand, and water applied as a hard covering for textured walls or as decorative interior plaster work.

Stump figure. *See* Butt.

Stump wood. Wood from the portion of a tree where the roots join the solid trunk, characterized by distortion of the fibers producing butt or stump figure.

Swell bellies. (1) Areas of a brick wall that has bowed as a result of insufficient structural support or foundation. (2) Mortar joints in a brick wall which are not parallel or perpendicular to the base.

Swirl. A multipatterned wood grain marking, seen in veneer that has been peeled by a rotary cut, because this cut follows the log's annual growth pattern.

Swirl float. A nonskid finish in concrete produced during the final troweling by keeping the trowel flat and using a rotary motion.

Tangential cut. *See* Flat cut.

Tessera (plural, tesserae). Small piece of marble, stone, tile, or glass or other material used in mosaics.

Terra-cotta. Usually red, brown, or orange glazed or unglazed baked clay units made from a blend of various clays and additives. Architectural terra-cotta comes in a variety of clay colors with varied glazes. Traditionally made by pressing clay into a plaster mold, terra-cotta is also manufactured mechanically.

Terrazzo. Marble, granite, onyx, or glass chips in a cementitious or resinous matrix that is poured in place, usually between metal or plastic divider strips, and then ground and polished smooth. Typically a finish for floors, stairs, and walls, terrazzo can also be precast and installed. Rustic terrazzo is a variation; in lieu of polishing, the surface is washed prior to setting to expose the chips; riverbed aggregates are often used.

Texture, brick. *See* Extruded brick.

Thermal finish. *See* Flamed finish.

Thin brick. *See* Brick.

Tile. A surfacing unit less than 12 inches (305 mm) square, usually relatively thin in relation to its facial area. Types of tile

BOOK MATCH

SLIP MATCH

RANDOM MATCH

REVERSE OR END GRAIN BOX

PARQUET MATCH

HERRINGBONE OR V-BOOK MATCH

SWING MATCH

DIAMOND MATCH

8-PIECE SUNBURST

REVERSE DIAMOND

BOX MATCH

DRAWINGS FROM ARCHITECTURAL WOODWORK INSTITUTE

FIGURE G-13. WOOD VENEER MATCHING

GLOSSARY

include *ceramic, faience, Mexican paver, mosaic, quarry, sculpted,* and *stone. See* individual entries.

Tin. A blue-white silvery metal that is soft, malleable, and resistant to corrosion. Most tin in architectural use is tin-plated sheet steel. Tin is also widely used as an alloy.

Tooled. A stone finish with parallel grooves cut into it. Available with two to twelve grooves to the inch (254 mm), the finish may be executed by hand (hand-tooled) or machine (machine-tooled).

Travertine. (1) A variety of crystalline or microcrystalline limestone distinguished by its layered structure. Pores and cavities commonly occur in some layers, producing the characteristic open texture. (2) A marble that is a variety of limestone.

Troweled. A smooth or textured uniform concrete, plaster, or stucco finish obtained by using a trowel. The types are generally self explanatory: troweled smooth, directional skip trowel, etc.

Tumbled brick. Brick that has been distressed by rolling it around in a device that resembles a concrete mixer to produce the desired effect of old brick.

Uncoursed rubble. Fieldstone set in mortar with no regard to coursing. Also called ordinary or rough rubble. *See* figure G-1.

Underbed. The cementitious mixture that supports the divider strips and final layer in terrazzo.

Unspecified finish. *See* As-fabricated.

Vein. In stone, a layer, seam, or narrow irregular body of mineral material different from the surrounding formation.

Veneer (masonry). Nonloadbearing interior or exterior wall of brick or stone covering the structural layer. Appropriate marble veneer may be applied as illustrated in figure G-12. *See also* Curtain wall.

Veneer (wood). Thin layer of wood of uniform thickness produced by cutting a log in a specific manner on a lathe, slicer, or saw. *See also* Veneer (wood) cuts.

Veneer (wood) cuts. Methods of cutting a log into sheets of veneer either on a lathe or by slicing. In slicing, two flat parallel sides are necessary—the face side, which strikes the knife blade, and the back, which is clamped to the flitch table. As the face side strikes the blade in either a vertical or arch stroke, a leaf of veneer is sliced from the flitch. Types of cuts include *half-round cut, plain-sliced (flat cut), quarter-flat, quarter-sliced, rift cut,* and *rotary cut. See* individual entries.

Veneer matching. The process of aligning sheets of wood veneer to produce a specific design or effect based on the figure or grain, as illustrated in figure G-13. Common matches include *book match, random match, slip match,* and *special,* or *sketch, matches. See* individual entries.

Verde Antique. *See* Patina.

Verdigris. *See* Patina.

Vertical grain. *See* Quarter-sawed.

Vitreous. Term applied to brick or ceramic products with very low porosity, and therefore low water absorption, as a result of being fired to a sufficient temperature. Also called vitrified.

Wall tile. Glazed tile intended only for interior use, not to withstand exposure to the elements, pedestrian traffic, and other wear.

Waney-edged. Wood siding that is not milled on one edge, leaving an irregular edge that is exposed when installed. Originally applied to wood difficult to mill, like elm, when the edge was left uncut for ease of production, the term is now applied to any siding with a rustic, irregular edge.

Wear. The process that removes material from or breaks down a surface as a result of abrasion or impact.

Weathering. The process of change in a material's appearance, chemical composition, and/or structural integrity caused by exposure to climate and other natural forces.

Weathering steel. Steel chemically treated to weather to a certain condition and remain relatively stable, maintaining the visual effect of weathering without becoming unsound.

Welding. A high-temperature and/or pressure process of joining metal that fuses the base metal without the addition of filler metal.

White cement. *See* Cement.

Whitewash. *See* Lime wash.

Window lead. *See* Came.

Wormy. A wood figure that is caused by worms or borers attacking a log. It ranges from occasional holes to worm holes uniformly covering a sheet of veneer.

Wrought iron. Iron that has undergone a thermal process to drive out impurities, which allows it to be heated and forged into shapes. It is tough and ductile, has great tensile strength, and is resistant to corrosion.

Zinc. A bluish gray metal that is soft, brittle, and highly resistant to corrosion. Widely used for galvanizing and in alloys.

INDUSTRY REFERENCES: ARCHITECTURE, DESIGN, AND CONSTRUCTION

INSTITUTES AND ASSOCIATIONS

American Institute of Architects. 1735 New York Ave. NW, Washington, DC 20006-5292. A professional society for architects and others related to the building industry, the institute provides educational and information services, which include extensive publications, a telephone library service, and an on-line computer network.

American National Standards Institute. 11 W. 42 St., 13th floor, New York, NY 10036. The U. S. representative of the International Organization for Standardization, the institute coordinates national and international voluntary standards for products and processes. Its publications cover a wide range of topics, from surface-texture symbols used in architectural drafting to specifications for flame-retardant fabric.

American Society of Interior Designers. 608 Massachusetts Ave. NE, Washington, DC 20002-6006. A professional society that provides educational, marketing, and informational services.

Construction Specifications Institute. 601 Madison, Alexandria, VA 22314-1791. An organization founded in 1947 to standardize building codes, establish construction specifications, and study materials, practices, and techniques, CSI offers educational and technical resources.

UK SOURCES

British Standards Institution. 389 Chiswick High Rd., London W4 4AL. Draws up voluntary standards and codes of good practice. The organization also offers educational and technical resources, and publications on a wide variety of construction and architectural materials and techniques.

Institute of Materials. 1 Carlton House Ter., London SW1Y 5DB. An international forum for discussion, which offers information on materials, publication services, and a library.

Interior Decorators and Designers Association Ltd. (IDDA). Unit 1-4, Chelsea Harbour Design Centre, Lots Rd., London SW10 0XE. An international association for professionals.

Royal Institute of British Architects (RIBA). 66 Portland Pl., London W1N 4AD. A professional society for architects, it is concerned with the general advancement of civil architecture and provides educational and information services and publications.

PUBLICATIONS

ARCAT. The Architect's Catalog, Inc. Fairfield, CT: 1995. This directory lists building product manufacturers and industry associations, and includes key words used in the industry to refer to specific products.

Architectural Graphic Standards. 9th ed. Charles George Ramsey and Harold Reeve Sleeper. The American Institute of Architects. New York: John Wiley, 1994. Designed for architects, interior designers, and allied professionals, this is a detailed graphic and diagrammatic assembly of data, standards, and information. It contains extensive line drawings, charts, and data tables, covering most aspects of building design, construction, and materials.

Avery Index to Architectural Periodicals. Avery Library. Boston: G. K. Hall. Part of the Getty Art History Information Program, this is a comprehensive listing of journal articles on architecture, preservation, landscape architecture, and city planning. It produces some 15,000 citations per year from approximately 700 journals published in more than 45 countries. The printed version is updated annually; the CD-ROM version is updated daily, and is available from the Research Libraries Group, (800) 537-RLIN.

Construction Glossary: An Encyclopedic Reference and Manual. J. Stewart Stein. New York: John Wiley and Sons, 1980.

Construction Specifications Institute Manual of Practice. Construction Specifications Institute. This comprehensive reference source discusses construction document formats, specifications, product representation, and contract information. Additional specification manuals for construction specialties are published by the same organization.

Dictionary of Architecture and Construction. 2nd ed. Cyril Harris. New York: McGraw-Hill, 1993. Containing 22,500 definitions and 2,000 line illustrations, the dictionary provides broad coverage of the terminology of architecture and construction.

Exterior Details. Jocasta Innes. New York: Simon and Schuster, 1991. A consumer-oriented survey of house exteriors, the book covers a wide range of countries and historical periods. Color photographs accompany the text, which describes building materials and techniques, with particular emphasis on finishes.

Illustrated Dictionary of Building Materials and Techniques. Paul Bianchina. Blue Ridge Summit, PA: TAB, 1986. Through text and line drawings, this dictionary explains construction terms, materials, and techniques, with appendices of abbreviations, conversions, tables, and weights.

The Interior Decorator's Handbook. New York: Columbia Communications. This national buying guide and source directory of interior finishes, materials, furnishings, and services is published semi-annually.

Means Illustrated Construction Dictionary. Kornelius Smith and Howard Chandler. Kingston, MA: R. S. Means, 1991. This dictionary uses text and line drawings to define more than 12,000 terms, acronyms, and abbreviations used in the construction industry.

Sweet's Catalogs. Sweet's Group. 18 volumes. New York: McGraw-Hill. Regularly updated, this source listing of materials covers usage, applications, appearance, building code requirements, product manufacturers, industry associations, and sources for technical support. Listings are organized alphabetically by material and include current addresses and telephone and fax numbers of suppliers and associations.

Thomas Register. 29 volumes. New York: Thomas Publishing. This regularly updated registry of American manufacturers is organized alphabetically by product and by manufacturer.

Vasari on Technique. Giorgio Vasari. Translated by Louisa S. Maclehose. Unabridged republication of 1907 ed. New York: Dover, 1960. Originally published in 1550, this is a sourcebook for Renaissance methods and materials.

MUSEUM DIRECTORIES

American Art Directory 1995–1996. R. R. Bowker. New Providence, NJ: R. R. Bowker, 1995. A directory of art schools, organizations, museums, libraries, galleries, and corporations with art holdings in the United States and Canada, it is arranged alphabetically by region, as well as indexed by subject. Also included is a selected reference to international art museums and schools.

Cambridge Guide to the Museums of Europe. Kenneth Hudson and Ann Nichols. Cambridge: Cambridge University Press, 1991. An alphabetical, country-by-country guide to 2,000 European museums, it describes the collections and their accessibility, specifies museum hours, and includes a subject index.

The Official Museum Directory 1996. 26th ed. American Association of Museums. 2 volumes. New Providence, NJ: R. R. Bowker, 1995. Volume 1 lists 7,500 museums in the United States by category: aquariums, art galleries, botanical gardens, children's museums, historical sites and houses, museums of natural history, nature centers, planetariums, museums of science and technology, specialized museums, and zoos. Volume 2 is a museum product and service guide.

WOOD

INSTITUTES AND ASSOCIATIONS

Architectural Woodwork Institute. 13924 Braddock Rd., Suite 100, Centerville, VA 22020. An organization of manufacturers of architectural woodwork in the United States and Canada, the institute provides research, design, and technical information services. Its manual defines industry standards.

Fine Hardwood Veneer Association and American Walnut Manufacturers Association. 260 S. First St., Suite 2, Zionsville, IN 46077. The association provides design, educational, and technical information services; maintains a database of photo and reference files; and holds a current inventory list of available hardwoods and veneers.

Association of British Plywood and Veneer Manufacturers (ABPVM). Alma Rd., Ponders End, Enfield EN3 7BP.

British Woodworking Federation (BWF). 82 New Cavendish St., London W1M 8AD. A trade association for members of the timber industry, including those involved with architectural woodwork, which offers various publications.

Institute of Wood Science (IWSc). Stocking La., Hughenden Valley, High Wycombe, Bucks HP14 4NN. A professional and examining body concerned with wood science. It produces a journal and newsletter.

PUBLICATIONS

Architectural Woodwork Quality Standards. 6th ed. Architectural Woodwork Institute. 1994. This illustrated AWI publication provides the information necessary to set U. S. and Canadian standards for architectural woodwork. In addition to industry specifications, the manual details veneer layout, cabinets, joinery, and more.

Complete Manual of Wood Finishing. Frederick Oughton. Briarcliff Manor, NY: Stein and Day, 1985. This illustrated textbook covers the history of traditional application techniques for a wide variety of wood finishes. A glossary and list of materials and suppliers are included.

The Complete Manual of Wood Veneering. W. A. Lincoln. New York: Charles Scribner's Sons, 1984. This textbook is recommended by industry professionals.

Fine Hardwoods Selectorama: A Guide to the Selection and Use of the World's Most Popular Species. Fine Hardwood Veneer Association and American Walnut Manufacturers Association. An alphabetical list of some 300 woods is accompanied by color photographs and a brief description of the woods' characteristics, availability, country of origin, and price range. Additional technical charts explain terminology and treatment processes.

Gems of the World's Forests. R. S. Bacon Veneer Company, 100 South Mannheim Road, Hillside, IL. 60162. This book describes more than 200 hardwoods, and includes drawings of veneer cuts and layouts.

The Good Wood Handbook: The Woodworker's Guide to Identifying, Selecting, and Using the Right Wood. Albert Jackson and David Day. London: Harper Collins, 1991. A compact guide to the characteristics of wood that affect selection, identification, uses, and workability, it contains excellent color photographs of 74 wood species, a guide to manmade boards and veneers, and a glossary of industry terms.

Hardwood Floors. Don Bollinger. Newtown, CT: Taunton, 1990. Primarily a technical book, it illustrates layouts and veneer patterns of hardwood floors.

Identifying Wood: Accurate Results with Simple Tools. R. Bruce Hoadley. Newtown, CT: Taunton, 1990. This illustrated listing contains the practical information and techniques necessary to identify different (primarily American) woods in various situations.

The International Book of Wood. Hugh Johnson. London: Mitchell Beazley, 1976. A study of wood, from its chemical and physical properties to its history and uses, this book describes 144 species of wood with color photographs and text.

Know Your Woods. Albert Constantine, Jr. New York: Charles Scribner's Sons, 1975. This general guide to wood includes descriptions of more than 300 wood species, some with photographs.

A Reverence for Wood. Eric Sloane. New York: Funk and Wagnalls, 1965. An esoteric but informative look at American wood, this book contains excellent drawings of hand-hewn architectural woodwork, accompanied by text that describes the tools and methods used to shape raw timber into lumber and lumber into beams or clapboard, and so on.

Textbook of Wood Technology. 4th ed. A. J. Panshin and Carl De Zeeuw. New York: McGraw-Hill, 1980. This textbook is recommended by industry professionals.

Tropical Timbers of the World: National Technical Information Service. U. S. Department of Commerce, PB85 156017.

Understanding Wood: A Craftsman's Guide to Wood Technology. R. Bruce Hoadley. Newtown, CT: Taunton, 1980. This translation of scientific information about wood is geared to the craftsman and the artist. Text and black-and-white photographs aid in identifying, choosing, preserving, and working with wood.

Wood Handbook: Wood as an Engineering Material. U. S. Department of Agriculture Handbook #72.

The Woodworker's Reference and Guide and Sourcebook. John L. Feirer. New York: Charles Scribner's Sons, 1983. Text and black-and-white photographs describe the properties of wood, from general descriptions to cell structures. Also included are a table detailing 250 common woods, a complete glossary, and information on standards, publications, and materials sources.

World Woods in Color. William A. Lincoln. New York: Macmillan, 1986. This indexed handbook identifies various woods.

STONE AND MARBLE

INSTITUTES AND ASSOCIATIONS

Building Stone Institute. PO Box 5047, White Plains, NY 10602-5047.

International Masonry Institute. 823 Fifteenth St. NW, Washington, DC 20005. A trade association that provides educational and technical support services for the masonry industry, the institute maintains a data bank of masonry research materials dating back to the 1830s.

Italian Trade Commission, Marble Division. 1801 Avenue of Stars, Suite 700, Los Angeles, CA 90067. An information resource for Italian marble and other Italian stones, the commission deals with architects, contractors, importers, distributors, and other professionals in the natural stone industry.

Marble Institute of America. 30 Eden Alley #301, Columbus, OH 43215. The national trade association representing the marble and dimension stone industry, the MIA offers marketing, education, and technical research services, as well as a quarterly magazine and other publications.

National Terrazzo and Mosaic Association, Inc. 3166 Des Plaines Ave., Suite 121, Des Plaines, IL 60018. An association of contractors and suppliers, it offers technical services and publications.

UK SOURCES

National Federation of Terrazzo Marble and Mosaic Specialists. PO Box 50, Banstead, Surrey SM7 2RD. A trade association for terrazzo marble and mosaic specialists.

Stone Federation Great Britain. 82 New Cavendish St., London W1M 8AD. A trade association that provides support for the masonry industry and produces several publications.

PUBLICATIONS

Dimension Stones of the World: Color Plate Books. 2 volumes. Marble Institute of America. This color plate collection of dimension stone is indexed by color, type, primary names, and proprietary names. It includes information on country of origin, quarry location, geological age, color range, recommended usage, and available sizes for each sample.

"Guide to Selected Sources of Information on Stone Used for Buildings, Monuments, and Works of Art." Joseph Hannibal and Lisa Park. *Journal of Geological Education,* 40 (13), 1992. This exhaustive annotated bibliography covers a wide range of stone and marble topics, from historical works to quarry sites.

A List of the World's Marbles. Marble Institute of America. Containing the names and locations of historical marble quarries dating back to antiquity, this document also specifies those known to exist in the early 1920s.

The Masonry Glossary. International Masonry Institute. Boston: CBI, 1981. An illustrated compilation of terms used in the masonry industry, it contains more than 600 entries.

MIA Design Manual. Marble Institute of America. This illustrated manual contains specifications, definitions, and terminology for the stone and marble industry.

Stone through the Ages. This quarterly magazine published by the Marble Institute of America reports installations, technical developments, and industry activities.

The Stoneworkers' Bible. J. M. Nickey. Blue Ridge Summit, PA: TAB, 1979. Coverage includes stone classification; artificial stone; dressed, molded, and scrolled stone; mortar; stonework bonds; stone setting; lintels, arches, and walls; and stone construction.

Terrazzo: Ideas and Design Guide. National Terrazzo and Mosaic Association, 1994. A guide to specifications, installation and maintenance of terrazzo, it also defines terminology, techniques, and materials.

BRICK AND PLASTER, CONCRETE, AGGREGATES

INSTITUTES AND ASSOCIATIONS

Brick Institute of America. 11490 Commerce Park Drive, Reston, VA 22091. A trade association that is the national authority on brick construction, the Brick Institute of America provides education, marketing, engineering, and technical services, as well as research assistance.

Friends of Terra Cotta, Inc. 771 West End Ave. 10E, New York, NY 10025. This organization provides information, publications, and expert resources on architectural terra cotta and its preservation.

International Masonry Institute. 823 Fifteenth St. NW, Washington, DC 20005. A trade association that provides educational and technical support services for the masonry industry, the institute maintains a data bank of masonry research materials dating back to the 1830s.

Portland Cement Association. 5420 Old Orchard Rd., Skokie, IL 60077-1083. An organization of cement manufacturers, the PCA provides services in market development, education, engineering, research, library services and technical assistance. The association also has an extensive list of publications, including technical bulletins, books, videotapes, and slides.

UK SOURCES

Architectural Cladding Association (ACA). 60 Charles St., Leicester LE1 1FB. A trade association representing manufacturers of cladding and producing various publications.

Brick Development Association (BDA). Woodside House, Winkfield, Windsor, Berks SL4 2DX. A trade body for UK brick manufacturers, which provides technical literature and an information service.

British Cement Association. Sentry House, Telford Av., Crowthorne, Berks RG45 6YS. An organization that offers research facilities and training, as well as a library, events, and publications.

Concrete Society. 112 Windsor Rd., Slough, Berks SL1 2JA. A trade association that produces publications, including a bimonthly magazine, and brings together all those who are interested in concrete.

PUBLICATIONS

Adobe: Building And Living With Earth. Orlando Romero and David Larkin. Photography by Michael Freeman. Boston: Houghton Mifflin, 1994. Text and color photographs trace the multicultural history of adobe and mud plaster construction, and give some technical information.

The Adobe Journal. PO Box 7725, Albuquerque, NM 87194. A quarterly publication, the journal chronicles modern, as well as historical, adobe construction. The journal's resource directory lists advertisers ranging from adobe builders, publications, and preservation services to related furnishings.

The Brick Book. Robert Hayward. New York: Thomas Y. Crowell, 1977. Text on brick-making and construction with brick is accompanied by illustrations and a glossary.

Brickwork: Architecture and Design. Andrew Plumridge and Wim Meulenkamp. New York: Harry N. Abrams, 1993. Color photographs and text trace the history and techniques of brick-making and building with brick. A glossary is also included.

The Brickworkers' Bible. Charles R. Self. Blue Ridge Summit, PA: TAB, 1980. This illustrated textbook provides technical information about composition and construction with brick, concrete block, and stone, and defines industry terminology.

Handbook of Brick Masonry Construction. John A. Mulligan. New York: McGraw-Hill, 1942. Designed to convey technical information, this textbook explores construction with brick, concrete, cement, lime, mortar, structural terra-cotta, and more.

Masonry Design and Detailing for Architects, Engineers and Contractors. 3rd ed. Christine Beall. New York: McGraw-Hill, 1993. A textbook on brick masonry, this book includes detailed architectural information about masonry walls.

Masons' and Builders' Library. 2 volumes. Louis M. Dezettel. Indianapolis: Theodore Audel, 1977. Volume 1 deals with concrete, block, tile, and terrazzo; volume 2, with bricklaying, plastering, rock masonry, and clay tile. The illustrated volumes provide detailed information on types and characteristics of materials, layouts, terminology, applications, and construction.

Modern Masonry. Clois E. Kicklighter. South Holland, IL: Goodheart-Willcox, 1991. This illustrated textbook gives an overview of the properties and construction uses of brick, stone, and block. It includes a glossary.

Principles of Brick Masonry. Brick Institute of America. 1989. This abbreviated form of the BIA technical notes is geared to students.

Technical Notes on Brick Construction. Brick Institute of America. This regularly published bulletin discusses nearly every topic related to brick and is available in a bound set of 100 bulletins.

Terra Cotta: Don't Take It For Granite. Susan Tunick. New York: Friends of Terra Cotta Press, 1995. A guide to terra-cotta buildings in New York City, this book also provides general information defining terra-cotta: how it is produced and how it is identified.

METAL

INSTITUTES AND ASSOCIATIONS

Copper Development Association, Inc. 260 Madison Ave., New York, NY 10016. The marketing, development, and engineering services arm of the copper and copper-alloys industry, the CDA also provides educational and informational publications and services, including computer access to worldwide technical data.

UK SOURCES

Aluminium Finishing Association. Aluminium Federation, Broadway House, Calthorpe Rd., Fiveways, Birmingham B15 1TN. A trade association that provides support for the aluminium castings and anodizing industries.

British Construction Steelwork Association Ltd. (BCSA). 4 Whitehall Ct., London SW1A 2ES. The national organization for the constructional steelwork industry, which provides services in technical, commercial, contractual, and quality-assurance matters.

Copper Development Association (CDA). Orchard House, Mutton La., Potters Bar, Herts EN6 3AP. This trade association promotes the use of copper and offers technical information and publications.

Institute of Metal Finishing (IMF). 48 Holloway Head, Birmingham B1 1NQ. An international professional body representing the finishing industry whose main objective is the dissemination of surface engineering and materials finishing technology. It also offers information services, publication distribution, international conferences, and a journal.

PUBLICATIONS

The Colouring, Bronzing and Patination of Metals. Richard Hughes and Michael Rowe. New York: Watson-Guptill and London: Thames & Hudson, 1982. Text and full-scale color photographs convey historical information, as well as a wide range of recipes and techniques.

A Dictionary of Metallurgy. Arthur D. Merriman. London: MacDonald and Evans, 1958. Illustrated definitions detail industry terminology and manufacturing processes.

GLASS

PUBLICATIONS

Glass in the Modern World: A Study in Materials Development. F. J. Terence Maloney. Garden City, NY: Doubleday, 1968. This illustrated textbook describes the history, production methods, properties, and types of glass.

Phaidon Guide to Glass. Felice Mehlman. Englewood Cliffs, NJ: Prentice-Hall, 1983. An overview of functional and decorative glass, this guide includes a short history of principal glass-manufacturing regions, a description of production materials and methods, and a glossary of terms. Color photographs accompany the text.

TILE

INSTITUTES AND ASSOCIATIONS

Ceramic Tile Institute of America. 12061 Jefferson Blvd., Culver City, CA 90230. The institute maintains a technical library and offers technical support. Its publications include a regular newsletter and a glossary of industry terms.

Tile Council of America. P. O. Box 1787, Clemson, SC 29633-1787. This trade association includes ceramic tile manufacturers, accessories manufacturers, and materials suppliers.

UK SOURCES

British Ceramic Tile Council Ltd. Federation House, Station Rd., Stoke-on-Trent ST4 2RT. The trade association representing the UK manufacturers of ceramic tiles.

Tiles and Architectural Ceramics Society. Cathy Herbert, Membership Secretary, Reabrook Lodge, 8 Sutton Rd., Shrewsbury, Shropshire SY2 6DD. The national society responsible for the study and protection of tiles and architectural ceramics. It publishes a newsletter, illustrated magazine, and journal.

PUBLICATIONS

The Ceramic Tile Manual. Ceramic Tile Institute of America. This reference book explains the history of tile, types and styles, codes, standards and specifications, installation techniques, and industry terminology.

Handbook for Ceramic Tile Installation. Tile Council of America. This regularly updated installation guide covers materials and techniques with text and drawings.

Tiles: 1,000 Years of Architectural Decoration. Hans Van Lemmen. New York: Harry N. Abrams, 1995. This illustrated overview of tile manufacturing and usage spans Western European and North American architecture from the early history of tile to the modern era.

PHOTO SOURCES

Casatelli Marble and Tile Imports, 34 Riverside Avenue, Norwalk, CT: S-9 through S-31, S-33 through S-36, MA-8 through MA-43.

Capitol Glass, 641 Hudson Street, New York, NY: G-7, G-9 through G-12, G-15 through G-22.

Connecticut Stone Supplies, Inc., 138 Woodmont Road, Milford, CT: S-39 through S-44, S-61, S-62.

Country Floors, 12 East Putnam Avenue, Greenwich, CT: T-9, T-10, T-14 through T-21, T-24, T-26, T-29, T-32, T-33, T-34, T-36 throughT-41, T-43, T-44, T-47, T-55.

Lockwood-Mathews Mansion Museum, 295 West Avenue, Norwalk, CT: W-60, W-61, W-62, W-66, W-67, W-69, MA-80, MA-82, P-9, P-41, P-169.

London Joiners, Westchester Avenue, Pound Ridge, NY: W-24.

Milgo-Bufkin Enterprises, ltd. 68 Lombardy Street, Brooklyn, NY: ME-8, ME-14, ME-20, ME-25, ME-26, ME-31, ME-32, ME-34, ME-37, ME-120, ME-125.

Marble Modes, Inc. 15-25 130th Street, College Point, NY: S-32, MA-15.

Properties owned by the Preservation Society of Newport, 424 Bellevue Avenue, Newport, RI:
The Breakers: W-57, W-59, W-64, MA-88, MA-89, MA-92, ME-127, G-2, T-58, T-64.
Kingscote: G-36, G-37, G-41.
Marble House: W-3, W-58, W-63, W-65, W-71, MA-59, MA-77, MA-91, ME-2, ME-71, ME-135, G-38, G-39, G-41, G-52, G-76.

Plasticrete, 99 Stoddard Avenue, North Haven, CT: P-14, P-21, P-75, P-81.

The Pierpoint Morgan Library, 29 East 36th Street, New York, NY: MA-74, MA-78, MA-79, MA-81, MA-84, MA-85, MA-86, MA-87, MA-137, T-6.

Quality Woods, Ltd., 63 Flanders Bartley Road, Flanders, NJ: W-75 through W-83.

Tri-State Brick of Connecticut, Inc., 71 R Hillard Street, Manchester, CT: B-7 through B-21, B-23 through B-41.

Zsiba-Smolover Limited, 10 Sterling Place, New Milford, CT: G-23 through G-26, G-35, G-48, G-49, G-51.

ACKNOWLEDGMENTS

I would like to thank the individuals who so generously gave their time and support, which made this book possible, especially Lou and Julie Juracek, Guy Gurney, Barbara Braun, Nancy Green, Gilda Hannah, Duane Langenwalter, and those who participated in the interviews.

The technical services provided by the associations and institutes listed in the Annotated Bibliography and Sources were invaluable, as was the access to materials and locations provided by the organizations credited in the Photo Sources. My thanks go to the following organizations and individuals:

American Plasterers, Inc., Berlin, CT, James McCarthy
Architectural Woodwork Institute, Greg Heuer
R. S. Bacon Veneer Company, Tim Sampson
Brick Institute of America, Brian Trimble
Ceramic Tile Institute of America
Copper Development Association, Inc., Dan Sternthal

Fine Hardwood Veneer Association and American Walnut Manufacturers Association
Friends of Terra Cotta, Susan Tunick
London Joiners, W. Godziemba-Maliszewski
Marble Institute of America, Pennie Sabel
Milgo-Bufkin Enterprises, Ltd., Bruce Gil and Bill Sogher
Portland Cement Association, Robert Shurer
The Preservation Society of Newport, Paul Miller and Monique Panaggio
Tri-State Brick of Connecticut, Inc., Wayne Canfield and Len Rosati
Valley Marble and Slate, New Milford, CT, Michael Wiston

All drawings unless otherwise credited are the work of Duane Langenwalter.

Finally, for the interview transcriptions I thank Deborah Meisels, and for her help and encouragement I thank Jan Juracek.

INDEX

Acer saccharum. See Bird's-eye hard sugar maple; Hard sugar maple; Spalted maple.
Adobe, W-90, 35; B-75, 137; B-146, 152
    mud mortar, B-87, 139
    mud plaster, P-12, 160; P-145, 189
    stucco painted, P-94, 178
    with whitewashed plaster, P-35
Agglomerates of marble and stones, P-22, 162
Aggregates, 158–94
    colored stucco, P-36, 165
    concrete, P-14, 161; P-15, 161; P-16, 161; P-26, 163; P-27, 163; P-29, 163
        cast coarse, P-105, 180
        exposed pebble, P-20, 162
        marble chips in, P-28, 163
        pea gravel in, P-29, 163
        quartz chips in, P-26, 163
        trap rock in, P-27, 163
Alabama white marble, MA-119, 116
Aluminum; ME-48, 207
    anodized, ME-13, 198; ME-39, 205; ME-50, 207
    cast, ME-17, 200
    conduit, ME-3, 196
    facade, ME-40, 205
    hand-brushed directional finish, clear-coated, ME-23, 202
    lettering on stainless steel, ME-101, 219
    perforated and fluted, ME-29, 203
    sculpture, ME-105, 220
Amaranth, W-29, 21
Amazaque, W-19, 20
American beech, W-32, 22
American black cherry, W-18, 19
American black walnut, W-46, 23; W-49, 24
American chestnut
    veneer, W-45, 23
    wood, W-14, 19
American tulipwood, W-9, 18
American walnut, W-23, 20
American white oak
    veneer, W-47, 24
    wood, W-43, 23
Ancient Roman
    arch, B-128, 149; B-129, 149
    brick, B-77, 137
        hand-molded, B-4, 125; B-157, 155
    marble colonnade, MA-1, 90
    wall, B-158, 155; B-160, 155
Anigre, W-7, 18
Aningeria. See Anigre.
Anodized aluminum, ME-13, 198; ME-24, 202; ME-39, 205; ME-50, 207
    roof with gold-colored weatherproofing, ME-88, 21
    weathered, ME-156, 232
Antique glass
    See also Stained glass.
    frosted, G-16, 237
    tinted, G-58, 245
    windows, G-64, 246; G-67, 246
    in zinc muntins, G-56, 244

Antique Green, Turkey, marble, MA-25, 94
Arches
    bonded jack, B-122, 148
    bonded radial, B-118, 146
    carved marble, MA-101, 111
    gothic with concrete keystone, B-127, 148
    molded brick, B-105, 143
    nonmodular, old Roman, B-114, 145
    radial arch variation, B-120, 147
    segmental Roman, B-116, 146; B-117, 146
    terra-cotta decoration, T-94, 273
Architectural
    brickwork, 145–49
    marble, 106–15
    metalwork, 204–09
    stonework, 76–82
    terra-cotta, 270–73
Artificial stone, S-14, 54
    in concrete, P-70, 172
Ash, W-15, 19
Ashlar
    broken-bond, S-86, 70
    coursed bond, S-76, 68; S-79, 69; S-82, 70; S-84, 70; S-85, 70; S-89, 71; S-91, 71
    random bond, S-77, 68; S-80, 69; S-81, 69; S-83, 70; S-88, 71; S-97, 73
    rusticated in coursed bond, S-79, 69
Asian rosewood, W-81, 33
Asphaltic concrete. *See* Concrete.
Astronium fraxinifolium. See Gonçalo alves.
Averia Green, Greece, MA-16, 93
Azul Aran granite, S-22, 56

Baccarat crystal prisms, G-2, 234
Baltic Brown granite, S-23, 56
Bark texture
    brick, B-11, 126; B-50, 133
Barn, painted, W-100, 38; W-142, 48
Basement window, G-29, 239
Base molding
    Giallo Siena marble, MA-90, 109
Basketweave pattern, paving brick, B-97, 142
Beach pebbles, S-105, 75
    split-faced, S-71, 67
    in tinted concrete, P-25, 163
Bent-sheet roofing, ME-89, 217
Betula alleghaniensis. See Yellow birch.
Bevel glass windows, G-65, 246
Birch, W-10, 18
Bird's-eye hard sugar maple, W-11, 18; W-56, 25; W-61, 28
Black mortar, S-83, 70
Block wall, structural concrete, P-85, 176; P-90, 177; P-91, 177
Blue ("glazed") header brick, B-64, 135
Blue Pearl granite, S-21, 56
Bluestone, S-42, 59
Board-and-gap or channel siding, W-110, 41
Board-and-gap-joined boards, W-139, 48
Board siding, W-54, 26; W-108, 41;

W-110, 41
Boardwalk planks, W-128, 46
"Bonderized" bronze (proprietary), ME-72, 213
Book-matched
    marble layouts, MA-63, 103; MA-65, 103
    veneers, W-43, 23; W-44, 23; W-45, 23; W-46, 23; W-48, 24, W-49, 24
Border designs
    interior borders, sculptured glazed tile, T-39, 262
    in interior woodwork, W-76, 32
    rusticated border on tombstone, S-141, 83
    sailor course border, B-96, 141
Botticino marble, MA-55, 101
Boxwood inlay, W-60, 28; W-66, 29
Brass
    decorative entryway, ME-56, 209
    dividers, in terrazzo, P-7, 159
    hand-brushed finish, ME-11, 198
    lettering, ME-91, 218; ME-98, 219
    woven architectural mesh, ME-27, 202
Brecciated marble, MA-7, 91; MA-46, 98; MA-64, 103
    column, MA-85, 108; MA-86, 108
    weathered, MA-135, 121
Breccia Pernice marble, fountain, MA-118, 115
Breccia Tavira, Portugal, marble, MA-31, 95
Brick, S-1, 52; S-4, 53; S-115, 77; 124–56
    ancient hand-molded Roman, B-4, 125
    architectural, 145–49
    basketweave pattern, B-97, 142
    blue "glazed" header, B-64, 135
    decorative, 143–44
    general views, 124–25
    glass, 239
    glaze, black speckle, B-61, 135
    glaze, white ceramic, B-78, 137
    mortar, 139–40
    painted, 150–51
    paving brick, 141–2
    structural wall, P-171, 194
    types and layouts, 132–38
    wall with combed stucco inserts, P-116, 183
    under whitewashed stucco, P-95, 178
    worn and weathered, 152–56
Brocadillo marble blocks, striped, MA-58, 102
Bronze
    architectural detail, ME-7, 197
    "bonderized" bronze, ME-72, 213
    building plate, ME-123, 224
    chemical patina, ME-117, 223; ME-118, 23
    cleaning in progress, ME-139, 227
    copper painted background, ME-60, 210
    door knocker, ME-4, 196
    door panels, ME-36, 204
    facade detail, ME-41, 205
    fluted, ME-25, 202
    gilt details, ME-71, 212

grate with waxed protective coating,
ME-81, 215
hand-brushed finish, ME-32, 203
handles, ME-126, 224; ME-127, 224
hardware, ME-126, 224; ME-130, 225;
ME-132, 225; ME-133, 226;
ME-135, 226
lacquered sculpture, ME-108, 221
lettering, ME-92, 218; ME-93, 218;
ME-94, 218; ME-95, 218; ME-96,
218; ME-100, 219
natural patina, ME-16, 199; ME-59,
210; ME-66, 211; ME-68, 212;
ME-74, 213; ME-76, 214; ME-122,
223
weathered, ME-140, 228
ornamental metalwork, ME-60, 210;
ME-63, 210; 210–14
patinated, ME-1, 196
silicone, ME-8, 198
protective sealant, ME-68, 212
punched and fabricated, ME-75, 214
random etched surface, ME-9, 198
sculpture, ME-103, 220
patinated, ME-104, 220
stainless steel window, ME-43, 206
statuary finish, ME-66, 211; ME-67,
211; ME-73, 213; ME-77, 214
Brownstone
architectural stonework, S-121, 79
bush-hammered finish, S-52, 62; S-55,
62
ornamental stonework, S-145, 84
random ashlar pattern, S-90, 71
roughly squared, S-152, 86
rusticated quoins, S-87, 71
sawn finish, S-88, 71
severely weathered, S-152, 86
troweled cement stucco, P-92, 178
under stucco, P-102, 179
Bubinga, W-37, 22; W-48, 24
Burlap glass, G-10, 236
Bush-hammered finish
brownstone, S-52, 62
granite, S-45, 60
Butternut, W-16, 19

Calacatta, Italy, marble, MA-10, 92
in floor design, MA-66, 104
California Sunrise granite, S-17, 55
Campagna marble, MA-89, 109
wall panel detail, MA-92, 109
Canadian Sunset marble, MA-53, 101
Canopy, stainless steel, ME-47, 207
Capital, columns, S-113, 77; S-114, 77;
S-115, 77; S-116, 78; S-117, 78;
S-118, 78; S-119, 78; S-120, 78; 85;
MA-105, 112
ancient and weathered, MA-131, 120
detail, S-149, 85
terra-cotta, T-90, 273
Cardwellia sublimis. See Lacewood.
Carpathian elm burl, W-60, 28
Carrara marble, MA-106, 113
Carvings. See Sculpture.

Cast-in-place concrete, P-53, 169
Castanea dentata. See American chestnut;
Wormy chestnut.
Cast bronze. See Bronze.
Cast concrete, P-61, 170; P-62, 170; P-63,
170; P-67, 171; P-98, 179; P-101,
179
deteriorating, P-161, 193; P-165, 193
painted, P-153, 191
Cast iron, ME-21, 201; ME-61, 210;
ME-64, 210; ME-84, 216
exterior enamel, weathered, ME-154,
232
facade, ME-55, 208
grate, ME-84, 216; ME-86, 216; ME-87,
216
painted, ME-82, 215
hardware, ME-131, 225
incised detail, ME-62, 210
machine parts, ME-6
painted ornamental work, ME-65, 211
rusting, ME-114, 222
weathered, ME-144, 228; ME-137, 227
Cedar, W-30, 21
Cedar butt-joined rough-sawn siding,
W-113, 42
Cedar clapboard, W-5, 17
Cedar decking, W-52, 25
Cedar diagonal ship-lap siding, W-112, 41
Cedar diagonal tongue-and-groove board
siding, W-108, 41
Cedar shakes, shaped, W-105, 40
Cedar-shake siding, W-107, 40; W-118, 43
Cedar ship-lap siding, W-111, 41
Cedar tongue-and-groove board siding,
W-54, 26; W-116, 43
Cedrela odorata. See Spanish cedar.
Ceiling
ballroom, G-76, 248
gold glass, G-49, 243
Guastavino tiles, T-5, 255
mosaic tile, T-64, 267
Cement
heavily textured, P-19, 161
troweled stucco on brownstone, P-92,
178
Ceramic mosaic tile, T-64, 267; T-66, 267;
T-67, 267
Chain-link fence, ME-83, 215
Channel siding, W-110, 41
Chemical patina, ME-117, 223; ME-118,
223; ME-120, 223; ME-121, 223
Cherry, wood, W-18, 19
door frame, W-74, 31
Chicken wire glass, G-83, 250
Chip glass, G-7, 235
Circle rowlocks, decorative brickwork,
B-107, 144
Clapboard
construction, W-97, 38; W-104, 39
freshly painted, W-131, 46
siding, W-109, 41; W-130, 46
Classic Pecan, Jamaica, marble, MA-26
Clear-coated aluminum, ME-23, 202
Clock, spun bronze and stainless steel,
ME-125, 224

Cluster burl character, veneer, W-47, 24
Cobble
in concrete, S-63, 65
coursed rubble, S-70, 67
Cobble stone
granite, S-100, 74; S-101, 74
with Roman brick edge, B-99, 142
Cocobolo, W-22, 20
Colonnade, ancient Roman marble, MA-1,
90
Colored glass, 240-41
See also Stained glass.
window, G-5, 234
Columns, S-109, 76; S-112, 76; S-115, 77;
S-116, 78; S-117, 78, S-118, 78,
S-119, 78, S-120, 78, S-132, 82;
S-151, 86; MA-85, 108; MA-94, 110;
MA-96, 110; MA-97, 110
African or Italian marble, MA-87, 108
ancient Roman marble, MA-3, 90;
MA-103, 112
brecciated marble, MA-85, 108; MA-86,
108
Cremo marble flutes, MA-108, 113
dry-pressed brick, B-103, 143
Fior di Pesco Classico, MA-84, 108
fluted marble, MA-6, 91
molded brick, B-104, 143
spiral, MA-111, 114; MA-112, 114
Concave or V joints, in mortar, B-86, 139;
B-88, 139; B-90, 139; B-93, 140
Concrete, 158-94
See also Aggregate concrete; Cast
concrete; Concrete block; Poured
concrete; Precast concrete.
artificial stone, set within, P-70, 172
asphaltic, P-18, 161; P-124, 184; P-127,
185; P-130, 165
beach pebbles, set within tinted, P-25,
163
block wall, structural, P-85, 176; P-90,
177; P-91, 177
cast-in-place concrete, P-53, 169
cobble, set within, S-63, 65
decorative uses, 187–88
concrete block, P-87, 177
exposed reinforced, P-170, 194
floated-swirl finish, P-65, 171
fluted block, P-81, 175
glass concrete, G-43, 242; G-46, 242
gothic arch keystone, B-127, 148
honeycombed
cast-in-place, P-23, 162
fine aggregate, P-58, 170
painted asphaltic, P-124, 184
painted reinforced, P-147, 189
pavers covered with, S-99, 74
pebble aggregate concrete, T-48, 264
plywood texture, P-63, 170
precast, P-123, 184, P-69, 172
rough-cast anchoring concrete, P-68,
171
rubble concrete, B-157, 155
rust, P-166, 194
scored and broom textures, P-125, 184
sidewalk, P-59, 170; P-60, 170; P-65,

171; P-66, 171
    stamped paving units, P-21, 162; P-71, 172
    tile inlay, P-54, 169
    tinted quoins, P-107, 181
    walkways, P-65, 171; P-66, 171
    walls, P-73, 173; P-85, 176; P-89, 177; P-91, 177
    weathered paint on, P-4, 158
    window, concrete repair, G-86, 251
    wood texture, P-61, 170
    worn and weathered, 189–94
Concrete block, S-7, 53
    with concave mortar joints, P-6, 159
    custom, P-84, 176
    metallic bleed, P-164, 193
    mortar, fine-texture dark, P-76, 174
    natural, P-83, 176
    pea gravel texture in, P-79, 174
    pink mortar, P-78, 174
    precast rustic face, P-86, 176
    raked joints, concrete blocks, P-79, 174; P-82, 175
    screen block, P-74, 173
    split-faced, P-72, 173; P-75, 174; P-88, 177; P-90, 177
    travertine texture, P-80, 175
Condensation, on glass, G-90, 252
Copper, ME-22, 201
    bent-sheet roofing, ME-89, 217
    chemical patina, ME-121, 223
    dome, ME-57, 209
    drainpipe, ME-129, 225
    hand-brushed finish, ME-11, 198
    inlay in boat's hull, ME-152, 231
    painted with bronze, ME-60, 210
    roofing units, ME-90, 217
    sculpture, new, ME-110, 221
Cornice
    ancient carved detail, MA-116, 115
    terra-cotta, T-87, 272
        decorative brickwork, B-109, 144
        egg-and-dart, sandblasted, T-102, 275
    travertine marble, MA-110, 114
Corrugated steel, ME-157, 232
Coursed fieldstone, S-5, 53; S-58, 63
    granite, S-57, 63
Cracked veneer, marble, MA-136, 121
Crazing, architectural terra-cotta, T-103, 275
Cremo Delicato, Italy, marble, MA-9, 92
Cremo marble fluted column, MA-108,113
Creosote weatherproofing, W-128, 46
Crossfire figure, veneers, W-46, 23
Crotch figure veneer, W-49, 24
Crystal chandelier, G-2, 234
Cuenca decorated tile, T-19, 258
Cyanite window glass, G-3, 234; G-80, 249
Cylindrical surface, siding on, W-113, 42
Cypress, W-34, 22

Dalbergia retusa. See Cocobolo.
Dalbergia stevensonii. See Honduran rose-
    wood.

Danielle, marble, MA-49, 99
Decorative
    brickwork, 143–44
    cedar-shake siding, W-118, 43
    concrete block, P-87, 177
    tile, 258-59
Dentil, MA-93, 109; B-106, 143
Diamond pattern
    anodized aluminum, ME-24, 202
    parquet, W-75, 32
Die-skin finish, brick, B-79, 138
Dimension brownstone corner, S-69, 66
Dimensioned granite, S-5, 53
Dimension stone, S-3, 52; 68–73
Diospyros. See East Indian ebony.
Dog-tooth pattern, decorative brickwork, B-109, 144
Doorknocker, cast-iron, ME-124, 224
Doors
    ballroom, G-76, 248
    beveled glass, G-53, 243
    bronze panels, ME-36, 204
    cherry frame, W-74, 31
    detail, painted wood, W-59, 27
    galvanized steel, ME-44, 206
    gilt wood detail, W-59, 27
    handles, cast bronze, ME-126, 224; ME-127, 224
    mahogany panel, W-64, 29
    multiple joints, W-137, 48
    oak panel, W-84, 34; W-85, 34; W-95, 37
    paneling, W-57, 27; W-63, 28; W-64, 29
    pine panel, W-86, 34
    plywood construction-site, W-103, 39
    stainless steel, ME-54, 208
    weathered, W-146, 50
    wire glass grill, G-78, 249
    wrought iron, G-78, 249
Doorway
    See also Entryway.
    detail, W-1, 16; MA-107, 113
    Carrara marble, MA-106, 113
    limestone, S-113, 77
    stainless steel, satin-finish, ME-58, 209
Doublex glass, G-11, 236
Dove White, Greece, marble, MA-11
Dracontomelum dao. See Paldao.
Drainpipe, copper, ME-129, 225
Dry-pressed brick, B-1, 124; B-3, 124; B-70, 136
Dry wall, S-64, 65

Eastern white knotty pine, W-13, 19
East Indian ebony, W-42, 22
Ebonized hardwood inlay, W-61, 28
Ebony, W-42, 22
Econo brick, B-26, 129; B-54, 133; B-80, 138
Efflorescence, B-55, 134; B-93, 140; T-96, 274
8x8 brick, B-44, 132; B-45, 132
Elazig Cherry, Turkey, marble, MA-20, 94
Elm waney-edged siding, W-117, 43
Emerald Green, India, marble, MA-41, 97

Emperado Dark marble, MA-69, 104; MA-93, 109
Enamel paint, exterior, ME-111, 222; ME-112, 222; ME-115, 222
Engineer brick, B-74, 137
English bond, brick, B-65, 135
English brown oak, W-8, 18
English-Flemish glass, G-9, 235
English oak burl, W-60, 28
Entryway
    brass decorative, ME-56, 209
    glass brick, G-28, 239
    terra-cotta motif, T-85, 272
    stainless steel, ME-35, 204
Eucalyptus granite, S-18, 55
European olive ash, W-44, 23
European white, Turkey, marble, MA-8, 92
Expanded metal, ME-33, 203
Exposed aggregates, 163; P-13, 160
Exposed timber, with stucco, P-100, 179
Exterior woodwork, 34–39
Extruded brick, 126–38
    paving, B-96, 141; B-100, 142; B-102, 142

Fabricatti, marble, MA-45, 98
Facades, S-7, 53; S-8, 53; MA-105, 112; MA-115, 115
    aluminum, ME-40, 205
    anodized aluminum, ME-39, 205; ME-50, 207
    bronze, ME-41, 205
        over stainless steel, ME-45, 206
    cast iron, ME-55, 208
    carved stone under stucco, S-8, 53
    glass building, G-72, 248
    glazed terra-cotta, T-82, 271
    Muntz metal, ME-37, 204
    old dimension-stone, S-7, 53
    serpentine with white and rose marble, MA-109, 113
    stainless steel, mirror-finish, ME-49, 207
    terra-cotta, T-76, 270; T-77, 270; T-78, 270; T-79, 270; T-82, 271
Factory windows, G-66, 246
    painted, G-71, 247
Fagus grandifolia. See American beech.
Faience tile, T-15, 257
fanlight window, G-62, 245
Fantasia, Mexico, marble, MA-42, 97
Fences
    chain-link fence, ME-83, 215
    wood, W-19, 44; W-120, 44; W-121, 44; W-122, 45; W-123, 45; W-124, 45; W-125, 45; W-126, 45
Fieldstone, S-4, 53; S-5, 53; 63-67; S-121, 79
    See also Coursed fieldstone.
    dimension brownstone corner, S-69, 66
    in dry wall, S-64, 65
    under limestone, S-156, 88
Figured mahogany door panel, W-64, 29
Finger parquet pattern, W-81, 33
Finishes
    See also Picked finish; Plucked finish;

Sand finish; Sawn finish; Shot-sawn finish; Split finish; Statuary finish; Stucco, finishes.
aluminum
hand-brushed directional, ME-23, 202
satin, ME-29, 203
bronze
mechanical, ME-41, 205
statuary, ME-66, 211; ME-67, 211
bush-hammered
brownstone, S-52, 62; S-55, 62
granite, S-45, 60
column, metallic, ME-51, 207
flame, stone, S-96, 73
floated-swirl, concrete, P-65, 171
hand-brushed
bronze, ME-32, 203
copper, ME-11, 198
hand-tooled
limestone, S-47, 60; S-113, 77
sandstone, S-54, 62; S-158, 88
metals, hand-brushed, ME-11, 198
patination prevention, ME-68, 212
rusticated finish, sandstone, S-53, 62; S-123, 79
stainless steel
mirror-finish, ME-49, 207
perforated, ME-54, 208
satin, ME-20, 201; ME-32, 203; ME-35, 204
trowel-sweep, plaster, P-33, 164
Fior di Pesco Carnico marble, MA-73, 105; MA-138, 122
Fior di Pesco Classico marble, MA-7, 91
column, MA-84, 108
Fireplace, MA-79, 106; MA-88, 109
Fir lattice, W-53, 25
Flagstone patio, S-104, 75
Flame finish, S-96, 73
North Dakota granite, S-46, 60
Flat cut, wood. See Plain-sliced, wood.
Flat exterior paint, brick, B-139, 151
Flat-sliced veneer, W-49, 24
Flip-matched veneer, W-50, 24
Flemish bond, B-1, 124; B-2, 124; B-3, 124; B-7, 126; B-51, 133; B-56, 134; B-78, 137; B-84, 138; B-123, 148; B-149, 153; B-151, 153; B-156, 154
Flooring, 32-33
brecciated marbles, MA-64, 103
Calacatta and Rosso Levanto marbles, MA-66, 104
exposed aggregates, P-13, 160
faience tile, T-15, 257
inlay detail, MA-117, 115
limestone and black stone, T-32, 260
marble, MA-137, 122; MA-139, 122; T-30, 260; T-31, 260
mosaic tile, T-9, 256; T-58, 266; T-60, 266; T-61, 266; T-65, 267
natural clay tiles, T-52, 265
terra-cotta tile, T-53, 265; T-55, 265
Florentine glass, G-17, 237
Flush mortar joint, B-87, 139; B-90, 139
Fluted concrete block, P-81, 175
Fluted marble column, MA-6, 91
Flutex glass, G-18, 237

Forged iron, ME-19, 200; ME-146, 230
Formica laminate, ME-28, 202
See also Cast iron.
Fossil stone, S-38, 58
uncoursed rubble, S-65, 65
sawn finish, S-48, 60
Fountain
iron-discolored marble, MA-130, 119
white marble, MA-118, 117
4x8 paver, B-96, 141
Four-leaf veneer, W-49, 24
Frost crystals, glass, G-89, 252; G-91, 252; G-92, 252
Frosted glass, G-8, 235
Full-flashed brick, B-17, 127
with cross sets, B-8, 126; B-10, 126
Fraxinus americana. See Ash.
Frieze, ancient, MA-132, 120

Galvanized steel, ME-44, 206
chain-link fence, ME-83, 215
rust, ME-149, 230
welded, ME-128, 224
zinc coating, ME-155, 232
Garden
fence, W-120, 44; W-121, 44
walk, S-107, 75
Garden-wall bond, B-64, 135
Ghiandoe granite, S-24, 56
Giallo Siena marble, MA-78, 106
base molding, MA-90, 109
Gilt bronze detail, MA-89, 109; MA-91, 109
Gilt wood
carved detail, W-3, 16
door detail, W-59, 27
panel detail, W-58, 27
Glass, 234–52
See also Windows.
beveled facets, G-48, 243
broken and weathered, 249–52
burlap, G-10, 236
chicken wire, G-14, 236
colored and painted, 240–41
condensation on, G-90, 252
cut, 243
Doublex, G-11, 236
English-Flemish, G-9, 235
Florentine, G-17, 237
Flutex, G-18, 237
frost crystals on, G-89, 252; G-91, 252; G-92, 252
frosted, G-8, 235
antique, G-16, 237
glue chip, G-25, 230
hammered, G-15, 236
manufactured, 235–37
molded, 242
Puralite, G-19, 237
reflections, 248
ribbed, G-12, 236
rough wire, G-20, 237
smooth, rough, G-21, 237
specialty, 238
textured, G-6, 234
wired with hammered texture, G-13, 236

Glass brick, 239
window
basement, G-29, 239
concrete repair, G-86, 251
hole in, G-87, 251
patterned and clear, G-31, 239
shaped corners, G-32, 239
with white grout, G-30, 239,
in window wall, G-27, 239; G-81, 250
Glass concrete, G-43, 242; G-46, 242
Glazed tile, 256–57
weathered, T-96, 274; T-97, 274; T-98, 274; T-99, 274
Gold leaf, W-57, 27
Gonçalo alves, W-27, 21
Granite, 54–56
arch, S-142, 84
bush-hammered finish, S-45, 60
chiseled and polished, S-137, 83; S-138, 83; S-139, 83
cobblestones, S-100, 74; S-101, 74
column, S-115, 77
coursed random ashlar pattern, S-77, 68
fieldstone, S-57, 63; S-63, 65; S-66, 66; S-70, 67; S-77, 68
flame finish, S-46, 60; S-96, 73
honed finish, S-157, 88
North Dakota, S-46, 60
painted paving stone, S-98, 74
partially honed split finish, S-51, 61
pavers covered in concrete, S-99, 74
paving stone in pattern, S-106, 75
pedestal, S-126, 80
polished, S-46, 60
polished molding, S-110, 76
rusticated in coursed ashlar bond, S-79, 69
rusticated in random ashlar pattern, S-81, 69
sandblasted finish, S-111, 76
shot-sawn finish, S-45, 60
split-faced in roughly squared coursed rubble S-94
tombstone, rusticated border, S-141, 83
turned column, S-112, 76; S-132, 82
window detail, S-129, 81
Gray common screened mortar, B-85, 139; B-88, 139
Gray/tan mortar, B-86, 139
Grigio Carnico, Italy, marble, MA-22, 94
Gris Fossil, Mexico, marble, MA-40, 97
Guastavino ceiling tiles, T-5, 255
Guibourtia demeusii. See Bubinga.
Guibourtia ehie. See Amazaque; Shedua.

Haddon Hall parquet pattern, W-83, 33
Half-timber, wood peg construction, W-89, 35; W-96, 37
Hand-brushed finishes. See Finishes.
Handles, cast bronze, ME-126, 224
Handmade brick, B-56, 134; B-64, 135; B-71, 136
Hand-tooled finish, limestone, S-47, 60; S-113, 77
Hard sugar maple, W-12, 18

Hardware, metal, 224
Herringbone
    parquet pattern, W-79, 33
    pattern, brick, B-94, 141; B-95, 141;
        B-102, 142
        decorative brickwork, B-107, 144
        molded paving brick, B-163, 156
Holly, W-26, 21
Honduran rosewood, W-21, 20
Honed stone, S-51, 61; S-113, 77; S-117,
    78; S-119, 78; S-120, 78; S-128, 81;
    S-133, 82

Ilex opaca. See Holly.
Impression glass, G-23, 238
    with gold leaf, G-26, 238
Inlays
    boxwood inlay, W-60, 28; W-66, 29
    copper, boat's hull, ME-152, 231
    ebonized hardwood inlay, W-61, 28
    floor detail, MA-117, 115
    lapis-lazuli inlay, S-109, 76
    mahogany, W-61, 28; W-66, 29
    rose marble, MA-98, 111
    tile in concrete, P-54, 169
    white marble, MA-98, 111
        in serpentine, MA-114, 115
Interior woodwork, 27–33
Iron
    See also Cast iron.
    cut, weathered, ME-141, 228
    discoloration, on marble, MA-130, 119
    forged, ME-19, 200
Ironspot brick, B-25, 129; B-26, 129; B-35,
    130; B-42, 131; B-63, 135; B-65,
    135; B-68, 136
    in decorative brickwork, B-110, 144
Italian brickwork, B-119, 147

Jaspe, Mexico, marble, MA-18, 93; MA-43,
    97
Joints, in exterior woodwork, W-94, 37;
    W-102, 39; W-113, 42; W-115, 42;
    W-124, 45; W-135, 47
Juglans cinerea. See Butternut.
Juglans nigra, W-23, 20
Juniperus virginiana. See Red cedar.
Juperano Tigeretto granite, S-20, 55

Kewazinga, W-48, 24
    See also Bubinga.
Key stone, S-48, 60
Kiln-formed glass, G-23, 238
Kinawa granite, S-12, 54
Knotty cedar, W-98, 38

Lacewood, W-17, 19
Lapis-lazuli inlay, S-109, 76
Lauan, W-83, 33
Leaded window panes, G-4, 234; G-69,
    247
    colored glass, G-33, 240; G-36, 240
Lead muntins, ME-15, 199
Leaves, in veneer, 23-24

Lettering
    aluminum on stainless steel, satin finish,
        ME-101, 219
    brass, ME-91, 218; ME-98, 219
    buffed stainless steel, ME-99, 219
    cast bronze, ME-92, 218; ME-93, 218;
        ME-94, 218: ME-95, 218; ME-96,
        218
        on stainless steel, ME-100, 219
    chiseled, in marble, MA-120, 116
    graffiti on Norman brick, B-161, 156
    oil-based exterior sign paint, B-132,
        150; B-137, 151
    V-grooved letters, in stone, S-138, 83
    welded lettering, ME-219
Lilac Classic, Turkey, marble, MA-12, 92
Limestone, S-6, 53; S-33, 58; S-34, 58;
    S-35, 58; S-36, 58; S-37, 58
    architectural stonework, S-127, 81;
        S-131, 81
    bush-hammered wall blocks, S-124, 80
    carved capitals, S-118, 78; S-120, 78
    carved ornamental stonework, S-143,
        84; S-144, 84
    column, S-117, 78; S-151, 86
    demi-bullnose or pillow-cut arris, S-91,
        71
    doorway, S-113, 77
    with fieldstone underneath, S-156, 88
    hand-tooled finish, S-47, 60; S-134, 82
    repair, S-154, 87
    rusticated, S-78, 68
    shot-sawn finish, S-50, 61
    stucco wall, S-150, 86
        turned, honed, S-133, 82; S-135, 82
Liriodendron tulipifera. See Poplar; American
    tulipwood.
Luna marble, MA-4, 90

Mahogany, W-67, 29
    boxwood carving on, W-62, 28
    Honduran mahogany, quilted, W-24, 20
    inlay, W-61, 28; W-66, 29
    panel door, W-87, 34
    veneer, W-49, 24
    wood, W-24, 20
Majolica painted tile, T-20, 258; T-21, 258
Manufactured glass, 235–37
Maple molding, W-56, 26
Maple, W-11, 18; W-12, 18; W-40, 22
Marble, S-1, 52; 89–122
    See also Brecciated marble; Numidian
        marble.
    architectural, 106–15
    carved detail, MA-102, 111
    chips in fine aggregate concrete, P-28,
        163
    end-matched, MA-59, 102, MA-62,
        103, MA-65, 103
    floor tile, T-30, 260
    general views, 90–91
    layouts, 102-05
    quarried marble, 101
    sculpture, 116–17
    tiles
        in mosaic, T-6, 255; T-33, 261; T-34,
            261; T-35, 261; T-62, 267

    tumbled, T-29, 260
    worn and weathered, 118-22
Marquetry, W-65, 29
Marron Braun marble, MA-69, 104
Metal, 195–232
    architectural work, 204–09
    bleeding on marble, MA-129, 119
    expanded, ME-33, 203
    finishes and textures, 202–03
    formica laminate, ME-28, 202; ME-30,
        203
    grates, plates, and fences, 215–16
    hardware, 224–26
    lath, P-19, 161
    lettering, 218–19
    ornamental work, 211–14
    painted and patinated, 222–23
    roofs, 217
    sculpture, 220–21
    worn and weathered, 227–32
Mexican Violet marble
    exterior veneer, MA-67, 104
    rope molding, MA-75, 106
Microberlinia brazzavillensis. See Zebrano;
    Zebrawood.
Mildew and mold, P-168, 194
Milletia laurentii. See Wenge.
Ming Green, China, marble, MA-35
Mirror
    crystal and glass crest, G-52, 243
    stainless steel, ME-20, 201
Modular brick, B-6, 125; 126–138
Modular Norman brick, B-42, 131
    graffiti on, B-161, 156
Modular Roman brick, B-41, 131; B-55,
    134; B-130, 149
Mold. *See* Mildew and mold.
Molded brick, B-1, 124; B-4, 125; B-56,
    134; B-60, 134
    decorative brickwork, B-106, 143
    paving, 141–42
Molded glass, G-22, 238; G-24, 238
    window, G-47, 242
Molding
    carved marble, MA-74, 106; MA-93,
        109; MA-97, 110
    maple, W-56, 26
    Mexican Violet rope, MA-75, 106
    polished granite, S-110, 76
    sculptured bullnose, ceramic tile, T-14,
        256
Montclaire, Vermont Danby marble,
    MA-61, 103
Mortar, S-83, 70; S-107, 75; S-108, 75
    bricks, 139–40
    fine-texture dark, with concrete block,
        P-76, 174
    marble set in, MA-56, 102
    weathering, B-141, 152; B-144, 152
Mosaic bond, S-59, 63; S-60, 64; S-61, 64;
    S-62, 64
Mosaic tiles, T-4, 255; T-6, 255; T-7, 255;
    T-59, 266
    floor, T-9, 256; T-58, 266; T-60, 266;
        T-61, 266
    weathered, T-100, 274
Mt. Vernon pattern parquet, W-77, 32
Mud plaster, P-145, 189

Mullions, in tinted glass window, G-63, 245
Muntins in windows
    leaded, G-54, 244; G-61, 245
    metal, G-58, 245; G-63, 245; G-64, 246
    wood, G-55, 244; G-57, 244
    zinc, G-56, 244
Muntz metal
    brake-formed, ME-14, 199
    chemical patina, ME-120, 223
    entryway, ME-35, 204
    exterior molding, ME-46, 206
    facade, ME-37, 204
Mystique, China, marble, MA-24, 94

Nickel-silver plated bronze, ME-18, 200
Norwegian Rose, Norway, marble, MA-14,
    93
Numidian marble
    fireplace, MA-91, 109
    panels, MA-59

Oak panel door, W-84, 34; W-85, 34;
    W-95, 37
Oak, W-6, 17; W-43, 23; W-51, 25; W-134,
    47
Oil-based exterior paint, B-132, 150;
    B-137, 151; ME-116, 222
Old paint, layers of, W-133, 47
Old-used brick, B-70, 136
Olive character, veneer, W-44, 23
Onyx, S-32, 57
Opalescent glass, G-59, 245
Ornamental stonework, 83–85
    scroll trim, marble, MA-128, 119
Oxidizing paint, W-132, 47; W-147, 50

Padauk, W-35, 22
Painted
    brick, B-14, 127; 150-51
    plaster, P-1, 158
    stone, S-136, 83
    stucco, P-30, 164; P-32, 164; P34, 164
    wood, W-127, 46; W-130, 46; W-131,
        46; W-132, 47; W-133, 47; W-135,
        47; W-136, 47; W-141, 48;
        W-142, 48; W-143, 49; W-144, 49;
        W-145, 49; W-146, 50; W-147, 50;
        W-148, 50
Paldao, W-38, 22
Pane. See Windows.
Paradise Blue, Brazil, marble, MA-33
Paradiso, Italy, marble, MA-13, 92; MA-30,
    95; MA-38, 97
Parquet patterns, W-75, 32; W-77, 32;
    W-79, 33; W-80, 33; W-81, 33;
    W-82, 33; W-83, 33
Patina, W-140, 48
    bronze, ME-16, 199
    natural
        copper bay window, ME-53, 208
        painted and patinated, metal, 222–23
        protective sealant, ME-68, 212
        stucco with natural patina, P-152, 191
        white marble, MA-99, 111

Paving
    brick, herringbone pattern, B-163, 156
    concrete and aggregate, P-121, 184;
        P-122, 184; P-125, 184
    concrete block with pink mortar, P-78,
        174
    Mexican paving tile, T-54
    precast concrete, P-123, 184; P-128,
        185; P-129, 185; P-131, 185
    stamped concrete, P-71, 172; P-126, 185
    terra-cotta set in mortar, T-57, 265
    terrazzo, P-132, 186; P-133, 186;
        P-134, 186
    tile, T-2, 254; T-56, 265
Pea gravel
    in aggregates, P-29, 163
    texture in concrete block, P-79, 174
Pebble aggregate concrete, T-48, 264
Pebble dash, patterned, P-112, 182
Pedestal
    granite, S-126, 80
    marble, MA-80, 107
    Skyros Greek marble, MA-81, 107
Peltogyne. See Amaranth; Purpleheart.
Peperino stone, S-25, 56
Perlatino blue, Italy, marble, MA-34
Pewter, polished, ME-10, 198
Picea sitchensis. See Sitka spruce.
Picked finish
    limestone, S-156, 88
    sandstone, S-56, 62
    travertine, S-102, 74
Pilasters
    marble with tooled finish, MA-104, 112
    Numidian marble, MA-91, 109
    weathered, T-90, 273
Pillow-cut arris, limestone, S-91, 71
Pine, W-13, 19; W-25, 21; W-31, 22
    log cabin construction, W-101, 38
    panel door, W-86, 34
    pressure-treated, W-55, 26
    shutters and clapboard, W-104, 39
Pink Agento, Greece, marble, MA-36, 96
Pink mortar, B-85, 139; B-143, 152; P-78,
    174
Pinot Noir granite, S-9, 54
Pinus elliottii. See Southern yellow pine.
Pinus lambertiana, W-25, 21
Pinus strobus. See Eastern white knotty
    pine.
Plain-sliced, wood, W-44, 23; W-45, 23;
    W-46, 23
Plaster, 158-94
    decorative uses, 187–88
    exposed interior wall, P-171, 194
    painted, P-9, 160; P-30, 164; P-32, 164;
        P-34, 164; P-41, 166; P-44, 166;
        P-169, 194, P-37, 165; P-38, 165;
        P-39, 165
    relief with metal leaf, ME-2, 196
    whitewashed over adobe, P-35, 164
Plucked finish, S-97, 73
Plywood
    construction barrier, W-4, 17
    construction-site door, W-103, 39
    painted, W-136, 47
Poplar, W-9, 18

Porcelain tile, T-51, 264
Portoro, marble, MA-51
Poured concrete
    broom texture, P-121, 184
    brushed texture, P-122, 184
    impressed pattern, P-52, 168
Precast concrete
    See also Concrete.
    coarse, P-54, 169; P-119, 183; P-144,
        189
        decorative uses, 187-88
        painted, P-111, 182
    fine aggregate concrete, P-48, 168;
        P-49, 168; P-50, 168; P-51, 168;
        P-110, 181
    stucco covered, P-56, 169
Pressure-treated
    butt-joined lumber, W-115, 42
    piling, W-2, 16
    pine, W-55, 26
Proprietary finishes
    "bonderized" bronze, ME-72, 213
    stainless steel, ME-26, 202; ME-31, 203
Prunus serotina. See American black cherry.
Pterocarpus macrocarpus. See Padauk; Ver-
    milion.
Puralite glass, G-19, 237
Purpleheart, W-29, 21

Quarried marble, 101
Quarry tile, T-49, 264; T-50, 264
Quarter-cut wood, W-43, 23
Quartered red oak, W-76, 32
Quartz chips, in fine aggregate concrete,
    P-26, 163
Quartzite, S-43, 59; S-84, 70
    broken-bond ashlar pattern, S-80, 69
Quercus petraea. See English brown oak.
Quercus rubra. See Red oak.
Quilted pattern, on aluminum, ME-24, 202
Quoins, rusticated brownstone, S-87, 71

Raked joints, concrete blocks, P-79, 174;
    P-82, 175
Random-matched, marble, MA-58, 102;
    MA-68, 104
Random-matched wall veneer, MA-69, 104
Random rubble, S-73, 67
Random-troweled texture, stucco, P-34,
    164
Red brick diaper pattern, B-108, 144
Red cedar, W-30, 21
Red lauan, W-36, 22
Red oak, W-8, 18
    board floor, W-78, 33
Red Travertine, Pakistan, marble, MA-28
Redwood , W-28, 21
Reflections, glass
    ballroom ceiling, G-76, 248
    stainless steel, G-74, 248
    window, G-73, 248
Reverse board-and-batten siding, W-98, 38
Ribbed glass, G-12, 236
Rift-sawn white oak frame, W-62, 28
River stones, in mortar, S-107, 75

Rojo Alicante marble, MA-73, 105, MA-83, 107
Rojo Coralito, Spain, marble, MA-27, 95
Rolled texture, brick, B-62, 135
Roman
    See also Ancient Roman.
    brick, B-4, 125; B-58, 134; B-67, 136; B-142, 152
    paving brick, B-98, 142; B-99, 142; B-101, 142
    ruins, MA-133, 120
    screen wall, B-155, 154
Rondels, tinted windows, G-42, 242; G-45, 242
Roofs
    cleft edge slate, S-92, 72
    copper bent-sheet, ME-89, 217
    metal, 217
    modern roof tiles, T-69, 268
    natural-cleft slate, S-75, 68
    terra-cotta tile, T-1, 254; T-68, 268; T-73, 269; T-75, 269
    tiles, T-74, 269
Rosa Alhambra marble, MA-72, 105
Rosa Morada, Mexico, MA-17, 93
Rosa Porino granite, S-15, 55
Rose marble
    inlay, MA-98, 111
    serpentine facade, MA-109, 113
    weathered, MA-125, 118
Rosewood border, interior woodwork, W-77, 32
Rosewood marquetry panel, W-65, 29
Rosewood parquet pattern, W-75, 32
Rosso Levanto marble, MA-66, 104
Rosso Sicilia, Italy, marble, MA-23
Rotary-cut, veneers, W-47, 24; W-48, 24; W-50, 24
Rouge Griotté marble fireplace, MA-88, 109
Rouge Royal marble, MA-49, 99
Rough-cast anchoring concrete, P-68, 171
Rough-hewn, wood peg joint, W-102, 39
Roughly shaped stone, S-58, 63
Royal Vermont Danby marble, MA-61, 103
Rubberwood, parquet pattern, W-75, 32
Rubble
    concrete, ancient roman bricks, B-157, 155
    coursed, S-93, 72; S-94, 72; S-3, 52
    uncoursed, S-65, 65; S-67, 66; S-68, 66; S-73, 67
Ruby Red granite, S-16, 55
Running bond, B-2, 124; B-4, 125; B-5, 125; 126–38; B-100, 142; B-112, 145; B-113, 145
Rust
    cast iron, ME-114, 222
    concrete, P-166, 194
    galvanized steel, ME-149, 230
    metal plate, ME-150, 231
    steel, ME-153, 232
    steel siding, ME-151, 231
    tower, ME-158, 232
    zinc coating of galvanized steel, ME-155, 232
Rusticated limestone, S-78, 68; S-117, 78; S-130, 81
Rusticated granite, S-110, 76; S-141, 83
Rustic terrazzo, P-134, 186

Safety glass, G-79, 249; G-88, 251
Sailor course border, paving brick, B-96, 141
Salome, Turkey, marble, MA-39
Sandblasted finish, S-111, 76
Sand finish
    brick, B-8, 126; B-10, 126; B-12, 126; B-32, 130; B-37, 131; B-40, 131; B-57, 134; B-74, 137
    dimension stone, S-82, 70
Sandstone, S-41, 59
    broken-bond ashlar pattern, S-86, 70
    capital
        on hand-tooled blocks, S-116, 78
        surrounded by travertine, S-114, 77
    carved ornamental stonework, S-143, 84
    cleft finish, S-40, 59
    columns, S-119, 78
    coursed ashlar bond, S-76, 68; S-82, 70; S-84, 70; S-85, 70; S-89, 71
    coursed broken-ashlar pattern, S-122, 79
    hand-tooled finish, S-54, 62; S-158, 88
    mosaic or cobweb pattern, S-59, 63; S-61, 64
    ornamental stonework, S-148, 85
    picked finish, S-56, 62
    roughly squared
        in ashlar pattern, S-158, 88
        with black mortar, S-83, 70
    rusticated finish, S-53, 62; S-123, 79
    sawn finish, S-39, 59
    uncoursed rubble, S-66, 66
    window arches, S-146, 84
Sand-struck brick, B-18, 127; B-56, 134
Santiago Red granite, S-19, 55
Satin finishes. *See* Finishes.
Sawn finish
    brownstone, S-88, 71; S-145, 84
    Cedar butt-joined rough-sawn siding, W-113, 42
    fossil rock, S-48, 60
    granite shot-sawn finish, S-45, 60
    granite turned column, S-112, 76
    limestone, S-131, 81
    sandstone, S-39, 59; S-89, 71
Sawtooth
    edge, paving brick, B-102, 142
    pattern, decorative brickwork, B-106, 143
Scratch coat, stucco, P-31, 164
Screen block, concrete, P-74, 173
Scroll trim, marble, MA-128, 119
Sculptural surface finishes, MA-121, 116
Sculpture, 116–17
    aluminum, ME-105, 220
    bronze, natural patina, ME-106, 221; ME-107, 221; ME-109, 221
    cast stainless steel, ME-102, 220
    classic statuary bronze, ME-103, 220
    copper, new, ME-110, 221
    honed finish, MA-124, 117

    light sand finish, MA-123, 117
    marble, MA-119, 116; MA-121, 116; MA-122, 117; MA-123, 117; MA-124, 117
    stainless steel, ME-42, 206
Sculptured tile, 262
    embossed patterns, T-40, 262; T-45, 263
    encaustic relief, T-44, 263; T-46, 263
    exterior tile, T-42, 263
    glazed, T-43, 263
    interior borders, T-39, 262
Security door, galvanized steel, ME-44, 206
Sequoia, W-28, 21
Sequoia sempervirens. See Sequoia.
Serpentine, MA-57, 102; MA-95, 110; MA-98, 111
    weathered, MA-125, 118
Shedua, W-19, 20
Shell stone, S-38, 58; S-65, 65
Shingles, wood painted, W-106, 40
Ship-lap joints, W-138, 48
Shorea negrosensis. See Red lauan.
Shot-sawn finish
    granite, S-45, 60
    stone, S-97, 73
Shutter, W-90, 35
    louvered, W-149, 50
    pine, W-104, 39
Siding and shingles, wood, 40–43
Siding, steel, ME-52, 207
Sidewalk. *See* Walkways.
Siena marble, MA-72, 105
    carved staircase detail, MA-77, 106
    veneer, MA-62, 103
Silicon bronze, ME-8, 198
Silver Travertine, Italy, marble, MA-29
Silverado granite, S-13, 54
Simulated tumbled brick, B-29, 129
Single-bead board siding, W-148, 50
Single-bead diagonal boarding, W-88, 35
Single-leaf veneers, W-47, 24; W-50, 24
Sitka spruce, W-33, 22
Skip-trowel finish, stucco, P-33, 164; P-46, 167
Skyros Greek marble, MA-81, 107
Skyscraper windows, G-68, 246
Slate, S-6, 53; S-27, 57; S-28, 57; S-29, 57; S-30, 57; S-31, 57; S-49, 61; S-95, 73
Smooth texture brick, B-16, 127; B-35, 129; B-54, 133; B-83, 138; B-84, 138
Southern yellow pine, W-31, 22
Spalling, in brick, B-145, 152; B-152, 153; B-153, 154
Spalted maple, W-40, 22
Spanish cedar, W-30, 21
Spanish Coralito random-matched veneer, MA-60
Spiral column, MA-111, 114; MA-112, 114
Split-faced
    ashlar, marble layout, MA-79, 104
    beach pebbles, S-71, 67
    concrete block, P-72, 173; P-75, 174; P-88, 177; P-90, 177
    retaining wall block, P-73, 173
Split finish
    brownstone, S-145, 84

granite, S-2, 52; S-94, 72
    partially honed split finish, S-51, 61
    stone in coursed rubble, S-94, 72
Spray enamel, painted brick, B-133, 150; B-134, 150
Stacked bond, brick, B-59, 134; B-62, 135; B-63, 135; B-111, 144
Stained glass, G-38, 241; G-39, 241; G-40, 241; G-41, 241
    tinted roundels, G-42, 242
Stainless steel
    architectural mesh, ME-27, 202
    brake-formed mirror, ME-20, 201
    bronze lettering on, ME-100, 219
    buffed lettering, ME-99, 219
    canopy, ME-47, 207
    cast, ME-18, 200
    clock, spun bronze, ME-125, 224
    fluted, ME-25, 202; ME-26, 202
        with mirror finish, ME-32, 203
    grate, ME-80, 215
    hand-brushed finish, ME-11, 198; ME-25, 202; ME-31, 203; ME-34, 203
    mirror, ME-20, 201; ME-26, 202
    mirror-finish, ME-49, 207
    muntins, ME-38, 204
    nondirectional finish, ME-34, 203
    perforated design, door, ME-54, 208
    sculpture, ME-42, 206; ME-102, 220
    window, ME-43, 206
Staircase, MA-77, 106
Starburst parquet pattern, W-80, 33
Statuary finish
    bronze, ME-73, 213; ME-77, 214
    lettering, ME-94, 218
Steel
    beam, painted, with cast fastener, ME-5, 197
    cast and welded grate, ME-78, 215
    corrugated, ME-157, 232
    exterior enamel on, ME-111, 222; ME-112, 222; ME-113, 222; ME-142, 228; ME-147, 230
    hardware, ME-135, 226
    metallic paint, ME-143, 228
    oxidizing paint, ME-148, 230
    rust, ME-153, 232
    siding, ME-52, 207; ME-151, 231
    stainless, ME-11, 198
    unpainted, weathered, ME-136, 227
    weathering, ME-8, 198
    welded lettering, ME-219
    zinc galvanized, ME-12, 198
Steel street plate, ME-87, 216
Stipple-textured stucco, P-8, 160
Stone, 52-88
    architectural stonework, 76–82
    artificial, S-14, 54; P-70, 172
    dimension stone, 68–73
    fieldstone, 63–67
    manufactured, P-96, 178
    in masonry wall, P-107, 181
    ornamental stonework, 83–85
    paving stone, 74–75
    rusticated and honed, S-128, 81

tiles in mosaic, T-6, 255
types and finishes, 60–62
worn and weathered stone, 86–88
    stucco painted, P-106, 180
Structural steel, ME-115, 222
Stucco, W-99, 38; S-4, 53; S-8, 53; P-109, 181; P-117, 183
    adobe, P-163, 193
    colored, P-3, 158; P-115, 183
        with mildew and mold, P-168, 194
    combed inserts, P-116, 183
    combed texture, P-11, 160
    decorative uses, 187–88
    brick, P-150, 190
        with scratch coat visible, P-118, 183
    brownstone, P-102, 179
    exposed timber framing, W-99, 38; P-100, 179
    over precast concrete, P-56, 169
    finishes, P-104, 180
        coat over brick and stone, P-2, 158; P-99, 179
        combed, P-47, 167
        directional skip-trowel, P-10, 160
        fine sand skip-trowel, P-10, 160
        floated sand, P-38, 165
        knocked down, P-11, 160; P-37, 165
        patterned directional skip-trowel, P-46, 167
        sand float, P-10, 160
        painted, P-5, 159; P-115, 183
            smooth, P-42, 166; P-43, 166
            textured, P-40, 166
            trowel textured, P-113, 182
        pigment textured, P-33, 164
        random troweled texture, P-34, 164
        scored pattern, P-45, 167
            over brick or stone, P-108, 181
        scratch coat, P-31, 164; P-146, 189
        skip-trowel, P-33, 164; P-46, 167
        smooth
            over brick, P-162, 193
            with natural patina, P-152, 191
            painted and colored, P-148, 190; P-149, 190; P-151, 191; P-155, 191
        stipple-textured, P-8, 160
        trowel-sweep finish, P-33, 164; P-33, 164
        whitewashed, P-167, 194
    incised coarse aggregate, P-114, 183
    with limestone, S-150, 86
Stump figure veneer, W-50, 24
Sugar pine, W-25, 21
Supren, marble, MA-50, 100
Supren Pink, Turkey, marble, MA-21
Swell bellies, brick, B-47, 132
Swietenia macrophylla, W-24, 20
Swirly grain, veneer, W-48, 24

Taiwan Dark Green, Taiwan, marble, MA-19, 93
Tan mortar, B-91, 140
Tar-paper shingle, W-5, 17
Taxodium distichum. See Cypress.

Teak, W-20, 20; W-77, 32
    flooring, W-80, 33; W-82, 33
Tectona grandis. See Teak.
Terra-cotta
    architectural
        cornice, B-109, 144; T-87, 272; T-94, 273; T-102, 275
        crazing, T-92, 273; T-103, 275
        figure, with sprayed spatter glaze, T-91, 273
        imitation stone, T-93, 273
        matte-glazed, T-84, 272; T-86, 272; T-89, 272
        spattered glaze, T-83, 271; T-91, 273; T-95, 273
        speckled glaze, T-81, 271
    bands, architectural brickwork, B-130, 149
    building top, T-95, 273
    glazed tiles, T-70, 268; T-76, 270
    natural clay, T-77, 270; T-79, 270
    painted, glazed, T-105, 276
    roof tile, T-1, 254; T-68, 268
    tile floor, T-104, 276
    tiles, T-47, 262; T-48, 264; T-72, 268
        flat and shaped, T-73, 269; T-75, 269
    weathered, T-78, 270; T-101, 275; T-102, 275; T-103, 275; T-104, 276; T-107, 276; T-108, 276; T-109, 276
    tiles, T-71, 268
Terrazzo, P-7, 159; P-120, 184; P-132, 186; P-133, 186; P-134, 186
    with metal strip dividers, P-17, 161
Tight-grained wood, W-72, 31; W-73, 31
Tigre, Greece, marble, MA-32
Tile, 254-76
    Cuenca decorated tile, T-19, 258
    exterior, glazed, T-10, 256; T-11, 256; T-12, 256; T-13, 256; T-96, 274; T-97, 274; T-98, 274; T-99, 274
    glazed and sculptured, T-3, 254; T-8, 255
        with efflorescence, T-96, 274
    Guastavino ceiling tiles, T-5, 255
    hand-cut, painted, T-25, 259; T-26, 259; T-27; 259; T-28, 259
    inlay, in concrete, P-54, 169
    limestone and black stone, T-32, 260
    Majolica painted, T-20, 258; T-21, 258
    marble, MA-5, 91; T-6, 225; T-29, 260; T-30, 260; T-31, 260; T-33, 261; T-34, 261; T-35, 261; T-36, 261; T-37, 261; T-38, 261
    mosaic, T-4, 255; T-100, 274
    opalescent glass, G-37, 240; G-41, 241
    stenciled, T-24, 259
    weathered, 274-76
        handpainted, T-22, 258; T-23, 259
Timber, exposed, W-99, 38
Tin, weathered, ME-138, 227
Tinted glass window, G-70, 247
    See also Stained glass.
Tombstone, S-141, 83
    marble, MA-134, 121
Tower, rust, ME-158, 232

Trap rock, in fine aggregate concrete, P-27, 163
Travertine, S-26, 56; S-102, 74; S-114, 77
    blocks with serpentine bands, MA-57, 102
    capital, S-115, 77; MA-94, 110; MA-96, 110
    carving, S-147, 85
    cornice, MA-110, 114
    Desert Gold marble, MA-52, 100
    flagstone in red mortar, S-108, 75
    laid in running bond, S-103, 75
    marble, MA-54, 101
    Roman column, MA-103, 112
    stone tile, T-36, 261
    on volcanic stone base, S-125, 80
Trowel smooth stucco, P-45, 167; P-47, 167
Trowel-sweep finish, stucco, P-32, 164
Tuckahoe marble capital, MA-105, 112
Tumbled brick, B-12, 126
Tumbled marble, T-29, 260; T-36, 261
Two-leaf veneers, W-43, 23; W-44, 23; W-45, 23; W-46, 23; W-48, 24

Untooled joint, mortar, B-91, 140
Untooled mortar, interior wall, B-92, 140

Velour texture brick, B-9, 126; B-17, 127; B-30, 129
Veneer, marble, MA-47, 99
    cracked, MA-136, 121
    random-matched wall, MA-69, 104
    Rojo Alicante marble, MA-73, 105
Veneer, wood, 23–24
    cluster burl character, W-47, 24
    olive character, W-44, 23
    single leaf, W-47, 24; W-49, 24
    two-leaf, W-43, 23; W-44, 23; W-45, 23; W-46, 23; W-48, 24
Verde Alpi marble, MA-60, 103
Verde Antique marble, MA-48, 99; MA-71, 105
Verde Aosta, MA-71, 105
Verde Lavras granite, S-11, 54
Verde Meragozza granite, S-10, 54
Verde Rosa, Mexico, marble, MA-37, 96
Vermilion, W-35, 22
Vermont Crystal Stratus marble, MA-44, 98; MA-63, 103
Vermont Danby Imperial marble, MA-68, 104
Vermont Danby varieties, marble layouts, MA-61, 103; MA-70, 104
Vermont Verde Antique, USA, marble, MA-15, 93; MA-82, 107
V-grooved letters, S-138, 83

Vitrified, paving brick, B-100, 142
Volcanic stone, S-1, 52
    coursed broken-ashlar pattern, S-122, 79
    mosaic or cobweb pattern, S-60, 64
    with travertine, S-125, 80

Walkways
    broom finish, concrete, P-66, 171
    colored glass, G-44, 242
    floated swirl finish, concrete, P-65, 171
    tinted, texture concrete, P-59, 170
Walls
    concrete retaining wall, P-73, 173
    exposed plaster, interior, P-171, 194
    glazed ceramic tile, T-10, 256; T-16, 257; T-17, 257; T-18, 257
    glass window, G-27, 239
    mosaics, T-62, 267; T-63, 267; T-66, 267; T-67, 267
    structural concrete block, P-85, 176; P-89, 177; P-91, 177
Walnut, W-23, 20; W-57, 27; W-63, 28
    burl, W-62, 28; W-67, 29
    interior woodwork, W-76, 32
Water-struck brick, B-154, 154; B-156, 154
Weathered
    Botticino marble, MA-55, 101
    brick, 152–56
    carved marble, MA-2, 90
    column, MA-113, 114
    concrete, 189–94
    door, W-146, 50
    glass, 249-52
    louvered shutter, W-149, 50
    marble, 118–27
    metal, 227–37
    oak, W-51, 25
    picket fence, W-119, 44
    plaster, 189–94
    sculpture, MA-122, 117
    ship's hull, W-138, 48
    stone, 86–7
    tile, 274–6
    white marble, MA-95, 110
    wood, 46–50
Weatherproofing
    creosote, on wood, W-128, 46
    roof, gold-colored on anodized aluminum, ME-88, 217
Wenge, W-41, 22
White marble
    column with travertine capital, MA-96, 110
    dentil molding, MA-100, 111
    fountain, MA-118, 117
    inlay, MA-98, 111
        in serpentine, MA-114, 115

patina, MA-99, 111
rope molding, MA-98, 111
in serpentine facade, MA-109, 113
weathered, MA-95, 110; MA-125, 118
White oak frame, W-67, 29
White quartzite, S-44, 59
White wash, over red paint, W-127, 46
Whitewashed brick, B-5, 125
Windows, 244-47
    arches, S-146, 84
    beveled facets, G-48, 243
    brick and terra-cotta, T-80, 271
    broken, G-77, 249; G-82, 250; G-85, 250
    copper bay window, ME-53, 208
    cyanite glass, G-80, 249
    glass brick, G-86, 251
    partially painted, G-84, 250
    pineshutters and clapboard, W-104, 39
    replacement glass, G-82, 250
    sills, W-90, 35; S-129, 81; B-124, 148; B-125, 148
    stainless steel, ME-43, 206
    textured glass, G-6, 234
    weathered stucco, P-148, 190; P-149, 190; P-150, 190
Wire-cut brick, B-13, 127; B-15, 127; B-17, 127; B-25, 129; B-26, 129; B-28, 129; B-30, 129; B-38, 131; B-39, 131; B-41, 131; B-42, 131; B-44, 132; B-45, 132; B-49, 133; B-52, 133; B-55, 134; B-59, 134; B-68, 136; B-80, 138; B-81, 138; B-84, 138
Wire glass, door grill, G-78, 249
Wood-molded brick, B-8, 126
Wood peg joint, W-89, 35; W-96, 37; W-102, 39
Wood rot, W-129, 46
Wood, 15–50
    border designs, W-76, 32
    exterior woodwork, 34–39
    interior woodwork, 27–33
    painted and weathered, 46–50
    tight-grained, W-72, 31; W-73, 31
Wormy chestnut, W-14, 19
Woven garden fence, W-120, 44
Woven split bamboo, W-114, 42
Wrought iron, ME-79, 215
    hardware, ME-135, 226
    painted and weathered, ME-144, 228

Yellow birch, W-10, 18

Zebrano, W-39, 22
Zebrawood, W-39, 22
Zinc, ME-17, 200
    galvanized steel, ME-12, 198

ABOUT THE CD-ROM

The accompanying CD-ROM contains screen resolution TIFF files for all of the images in the book with the exception of seven photographs in the Glass section (G-23, 24, 26, 35, 48, 49, and 51), rights to which do not belong to the author.

With the appropriate graphics software, on either Macintosh or Windows platform, the CD images can be used by artists and designers in developing concepts, preparing presentations for clients, and communicating visual information to others. Although the images are primarily intended for on-screen display, they can also be printed on either a black and white or color printer.

Further information about the image formats can be found on the readme.txt file on the CD.

Original images can be obtained from the author. Write to P. O. Box 7206, Wilton CT 06897.